DIRECTIONS
IN NEW ERA ASTROLOGY

Directions
in New Era Astrology

by

S. Rajagopala Iyer, BA, BL

PRINTWORLD
Publishers of Indian Traditions

Cataloging in Publication Data — DK

[Courtesy: D.K. Agencies (P) Ltd. <docinfo@dkagencies.com>]

Rajagopala Iyer, S., 1895- **author.**
Directions in new era astrology / by S. Rajagopala Iyer.
pages cm
Reprint.
ISBN 9788124612095

1. Astrology. I. Title.

LCC BF1701.R35 2025 | DDC 133.5 23

ISBN 978-81-246-1209-5
First Published by The Newman Trading Company, Madras [1941?]
Reprinted in 2025
Author: S. Rajagopala Iyer (b.1895)

Printed and published by:
D.K. Printworld (P) Ltd.
Regd. Office: "Vedaśrī", F-395, Sudarshan Park
ESI Hospital Metro Station, New Delhi - 110015
Phones: (011) 4172 2626, 98713 94815
e-mail: indology@dkprintworld.com
Website: www.dkprintworld.com

DIRECTIONS
IN
NEW ERA ASTROLOGY

BY

S. RAJAGOPALA IYER, B.A., B.L.,

AUTHOR OF

Lessons in Elementary Astrology
Essays in Fourth Dimension

Printed at

THE NEWMAN TRADING CO.,

222, Thambu Chetty St., Madras.

Price { Rs. 12/14/.
27 sh. 6 d.
$ 6.50.

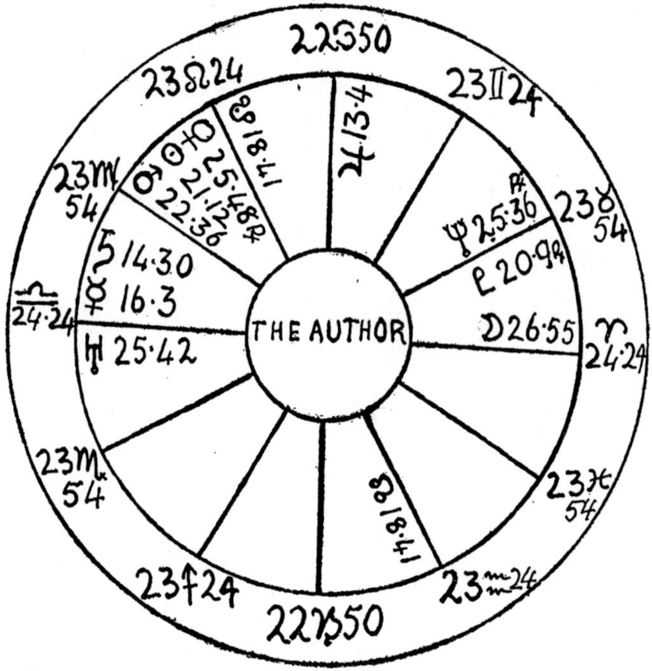

Born at Mannargudi, Tanjore Dt., Madras State, on 7th October, 1895

CONTENTS

EXAMPLE HOROSCOPES

SYMBOLS

Signs		
Aries	—	♈
Taurus	—	☿
Gemini	—	♊
Cancer	—	♋
Leo	—	♃
Virgo	—	♍
Libra	—	♎
Scorpio	—	♏
Sagittarius	—	♐
Capricornus	—	♑
Aquarius	—	♒
Pisces	—	♓

Planets		
Sun	—	☉
Moon	—	☽
Mercury	—	☿
Venus	—	♀
Mars	—	♂
Jupiter	—	♃
Saturn	—	♄
Uranus	—	♅
Neptune	—	♆
Pluto	—	♇
Rahu	—	☊
Ketu	—	☋

ASPECTS

Conjunction	—	☌	—	0°
Sextile	—	✶	—	60°
Square	—	□	—	90°
Trine	—	△	—	120°
Quincunx	—	⚻	—	150°
Opposition	—	☍	—	180°

———

FOREWORD

In so far as it relates to genitures prognostic astrology can be divided into two main divisions (1) Natural and (2) Symbolical. The former assumes that the Sun, Moon and planets permanently impress their individual influences on that portion of the circle of the Zodiac that they each happened to occupy at the moment of birth and that the subsequent transits (crossings) of the planets over these natal positions modify these influences. As the dates of such transits can easily be determined from astronomical almanacs or ephemerides– computed many years in advance,—or by the direct observation of the night skies, the astrologer has at hand a direct means of making and timing a prediction. Suppose by way of illustration, a person was born at 0^h 39^m a. m. G. M. T. on July 25, 1920. On this date and time, the planet Venus was in exact ecliptical conjunction with the fixed star **Asellus Australis** ("The Southern Ass".) Catalogued as Delta Canceri and situated in 13° 54′ of the constellation Cancer. Tradition affirms and empiricism confirms that the amatory impulses are in some inexplicable way bound up with this planet. Tradition and empiricism also attest that Jupiter is the bringer of joy and Saturn of sorrow. Had an astrologer consulted the 'Nautical Almanac' for 1943 he would have found that Jupiter in its course transitted "The Southern Ass." on August 7, 1943 (This transit could not be seen in the night skies, as Jupiter was then a day—star being close to the Sun) that is over the place in the ecliptic occupied by Venus at birth, and he would have been safe in predicting that the native would be successful in his love affairs at this time, and Cupid would have brought him great joy? On the other hand had he scanned the night skies immediately after sunset of July 1st 1947 he would have seen that Saturn was close to "The Southern Ass." and he would know that the native was then meeting with disappointment and reverses in his love affairs and all was not too happy in his domestic circle.

The Varshapraves (Solar Return) and the Masapraves (Lunar Return) come within the field of prognostic astrology. The former is a chart of the heavens for the precise moment that the Sun transits the ecliptical position it occupied among a fixed stars at birth, which happens annually about the birthday anniversary; and the latter, the moment when the Moon transits its own natal place, which happens about every 27 days. The Varshapraves indicates the main events for the ensuing year, while the Masapraves denotes the particular happenings for the ensuing 27 days. Many occidental astrologers are convinced that the Masapraves is the most reliable predictive instrument extant. The popular birthday predictions of news-paper astrology, based on the transits of the planets to the Sun's position at birth; and the monthly Janma—Rasi method deservingly popular in India and based on the transits of the planets in relation to the Moon's position at birth also come within the scope of natural prognostic astrology. The glory of natural prognostic astrology is that it directly relates the birth horoscope to the natural phenomena taking place in the ambient, and it is not beset by the complications and variables met with in prognostic symbolical astrology.

But astrologers employ other methods of making predictions which come under the heading of symbolical Prognostication. These include Directions (Primary and Secondary), Arabic Progressions, the Indian Dasa Systems, and Symbolics proper. Primary directions are related to the **Mundane sphere** and not to the ecliptic circle. Claudius Ptolemy, the disputed author of the Tetrabiblos in which the theory is first expounded, believed that the planets at birth left a permanent impress of their influences on the positions they occupied in the mundane sphere (i.e. in the Bhavas or "Houses"). Suppose birth occurred at sunrise about the time of the Vernal Equinox (March 21st) when Mars was precisely on the upper meridian (Midheaven) the Sun being on the ascending degree. According to this theory the influence of Mars — irrespective of its zodiacal position — is indelibly impressed on the midheaven, as that of the Sun is impressed on the eastern horizon. Six hours after birth would be noon, when the Sun would have come to the upper meridian (culminated) and hence it would be **mundanely** in conjunction with Mars; and as Ptolemy believed one hour of equinoctial time to be astrologically equivalent to I5 years of life, then the effects of this direction would operate in the native's 90th year. The secondary method is on 'all fours' with the primary except that directions "In Zodiaco" are made to the ecliptic degrees occupied by the natal planets. Assuming a life span of 120 years all possible directions would occur within some eight hours of birth, Ptolemy's method of effecting these directions by proportion of semi - arcs is open to serious mathematical objections. R. C. Smith (the first "Raphael") very logically suggested that such directions should be made under the Poles of the significators but Sepharial's formulæ for computing these Poles is trigonometrically inaccurate. Incidentally these systems were never popular since they called for at least a working knowledge of trigonometrical functions, apart from the fact that they were laborious, tedious and time-consuming. The system most popular in the West, and still in vogue, is the Arabic method of progressions which is based on the assumption that every day after birth is equivalent to one year of life. According to this theory if the Sun and Jupiter come into mutual conjunction 30 days after birth, then the wonderful effect of this configuration would be experienced in the native's 30th year. In India the Dasa system of predicting by planetary periods is in popular use. As the method is explained with much detail by our author in this book it is not necessary to enlarge on it here.

But notwithstanding all that was claimed for these systems, astrologers were far from satisfied. Directions and Progressions obviously did not account for all events that befell one, while many of them appeared to 'miss fire'; and so in modern times several new symbolical systems have been invented. Symbolical prognostic astrology to no small extent owes its origin to the fact that the circle of the Zodiac from the most ancient times was divided into 360 equal parts called degrees, each degree being further subdivided into minutes and seconds of arc. As the equatorial circle ("dial") of 24 hours is equivalent to 360 equatorial degrees (termed hours and degrees of Right Ascension respectively) it follows that one hour is equal to 15° and 4 minutes to 1 degree, hence in the so called Ptolemaic system, one degree of Right Ascension is prognostically equal to one year of life. Some astrologers have extended this idea to the ecliptical circle itself, making one degree of the zodiac equivalent to a year of life. Suppose the Moon at birth was in Aries 1° and Venus in Aries 27° the difference between them is 26° and hence the symbolist would say that the Moon and Venus would be in conjunction in the native's 26th year when he would probably get married.

Having ventured so far the symbolist is tempted to devise several other measures of time based on the splitting of the degree, as for example the making $\frac{1}{2}^{\circ}$ or $\frac{1}{4}^{\circ}$ equivalent to one year of life, according to the particular geometrical system envisaged. Suppose he equates $\frac{1}{4}^{\circ}$ to one year then perforce he feels obliged to postulate the existence of other Zodiacal configurations not previously recognised, for these two bodies are separated by 25° then their "conjunction" would not in this case, maturate until the native's 100th year; so in order to get them into some mutual relationship within the span of one's lifetime configurations and their supplements much smaller than unctile (30°) must be assumed. To encompass all possible events that may fall to one's lot some symbolists accept as valid several different measures of time, for it is assumed by them that all events, be they 'incidents' or 'accidents' must be shown in the geniture and its directions.

As an exceptionally brilliant exponent of natural prognostic astrology Sri S. Rajagopala Iyer has for many years been contributing to the astrological press, under a nom-de-plume, which professional etiquette unfortunately does not permit him to reveal. His articles and other contributions have been read with avidity by all sections of the astrological public and have won unstinted praise for the depth of their erudition and their broad encyclopædic contents. He is no less '*au fait*' with Western as he is with Indian astrology and I personally have derived much profit from his copious dissertations.

In this book the author reveals that he has an equal mastery of Western Astrology with all its virtues and defects. By a process of compromise with Indian Astrology he attempts to remove most of the more glaring defects, and incidentally makes public for the first time his own novel system of symbolical directing. To the Western astrologer this book should prove a boon for therein he will find a complete exposition of the Indian method of directing and so clearly and simply expressed that he will have no difficulty in applying the method to his own or his friends' horoscopes; and the Indian astrologer will find in it all that is needed to be known of Western methods. As a competent book for study and reference it should be on the bookshelves of astrologers the world over but none should relish it more than the Schools of Frankland and Carter.

Cyril Fagan

PREFACE

In this period of world-wide Renaissance in Astrology when intensive research is being directed towards the predictive side, a new book on Directional Astrology is no strange thing. Various new systems of direction have come into vogue, the symbolic systems holding the front of the stage. The Radix system of Sepharial developed by Robson, Frankland's measures, and Carter's comprehensive directional system are among the most prominent. Among other new systems based on transits, we have that of Tucker based on transits of fixed stars by planets, the Solunars rationalised and popularized by Cyril Fagan etc. These added to the many that are already in existence, make a good number and one may be tempted to think, as humorously suggested by Alan Leo that probably all are wrong since they cannot all be right. Yet it is the claim of the exponent of each system that his method gives better results according to his experience !

After making the above observation, Alan Leo says "It is quite clear however that the tests of two people with regard to any system of directions will not be of equal value, even though the investigators be of equal integrity and ability. For, one will look for his results in one direction, for financial losses, say, while the other looks for death, perhaps, or personal suffering ;—this is only given as a crude illustration of the difference in mental bias between the two experimenters (which differance of out-look will inevitably have its effect upon all aspects coming under their notice) and it is not, of course, to be taken too literally: Nevertheless, the mere fact that careful individual investigators swear by many different systems, is strong presumptive evidence of a good measure of truth in each; and it immediately suggests itself to the mind that this common measure of truth is a fundamental principle, the operation of which through different media (so to speak) is observed and recorded by different witnesses".

The principal reason for difference in opinion is as stated by the above author the personal factor which interprets the same set of directions, relating them to different spheres of human activity. It is this source of difference that is sought to be eliminated as far as possible in the system that is outlined in the following pages where the sphere of operation of the influence of directions based on a particular measure is limited to that which is characteristic of that measure itself. Each directional measure operates in a field of its own. Thus the task of prediction is greatly simplified.

The events that led to the discovery of this fact make quite a story. Ever since the study of astrology was taken up about forty years ago, I had continual conflict with tradition which is only what is to be expected of one having Herschel within the first two degrees of the ascendant. Beginning with the study of Indian Astrology, I went over to the Western system and back again to the Indian system and back and forth several times until I came to realize that a correlation of the two systems is necessary to achieve the best results, and materials were slowly accumulating for a book embodying my views on the subject. For more than twenty years the unsatisfactory nature of the directional systems of East and West bothered me not a little and it was about that time that I came in contact with the symbolic systems that were being developed in the West. It struck me then that perhaps a solution can be found here and while investigating the directions for the death of King Edward VII according to symbolic measures, the germ of an idea developed which virtually is the origin of the system outlined here. But this work I had intended should succeed the one on "Basic Concepts of New Era Astrology" (**in preparation**) but latterly I decided that this should be brought out first because of the great interest that is now being evinced in directional systems and the increasing popularity of the symbolic methods. Still this book contains all the relevant ideas and has been made an independent and self-contained work. As some of the ideas contained herein will be necessarily new to the student of Western Astrology, he may well skip over all such portions, and even so, he will have a complete system of directions at his service which he can employ to the exclusion of all others and which for ease of working and certainty of results will outrival every other system that is being practised in the East or West.

But here and now let me not fail to acknowledge the great debt I owe to Frankland and Carter who have blazed the path before me in many respects and what all is contained here are only further discoveries along that path. While some credit for such of these discoveries may be due to me, it is quite obvious that without their work and their examples before me this task would never have been done not even thought of! It is inevitable therefore that their names recur continually throughout this work.

Because of some additions and extensions in dealing with the main theme in the course of preparing the matter for the press not originally thought of, it has not been found possible to include the chapter 'Transits in New Era Astrology' in this book itself. This has to be brought out separately as a booklet.

In the preparation of this work I have derived much help from K. Sivasubramanya Iyer, a scholar in both systems of astrology and also an expert proof-reader. T. R. Pattabhiraman a young engineering student checked a part of the mathematical work without whose collaboration, the book would have contained many glaring mistakes and to both my sincere thanks are due.

Being entirely new to the task of writing a book and bringing it out before the public, I had to surmount a great many difficulties not visualised by me before. I tried to interest a large number of printers of Madras to print my book. While most of the prominent firms did not condescend to reply, some stated they had their own work to do and so could not take up mine. One or two quoted rates that I considered too much. My thanks are due therefore to the Newman Trading Co., for having courageously undertaken this task and for bringing out this book in nice print and good get-up and also incorporating all my suggestions without sparing neither time nor labour.

In spite of the best care that has been taken I am conscious that still many mistakes may be found. I would request the indulgent reader to correct the self-evident errors himself and communicate to me the more serious ones which would be gratefully acknowledged and corrected in the future editions.

The Author.

CHAPTER I

INTRODUCTION

Astrology has a great antiquity behind it. Its origin is unknown. It dates back to the Vedic times and is considered to be a part of the Vedas. The astrologers who evolved the science are not known to history. Any author whose works are now available says he compiles them with the aid of already existing sources. The name that stands as a Colossus in Astrology to this day is Parashara, the author of the encyclopædic work 'Parasara Hora'. He has written other works also. All authors that follow him have but reproduced parts of this work in their own style and language. It is Parashara who has explained the Asterism System of Directions which is widely prevalent in all parts of India to-day. The same author has expounded numerous other systems of direction some of which are found described in other works also. But just as, much later in the history of astrology in the West, the secondary system of direction has practically supplanted the Primary System, the asterism system of planetary periods and sub-periods has survived all others for the same reasons—simplicity of calculations coupled with tolerably good results.

Next to that of Parasara, the name that frequently comes up is "Varaha Mihira". The title of 'Varaha' which means a boar was conferred on the astrologer by king Vikramaditya for the correctness of his prediction that the Royal Prince would be killed by a boar at a particular time and date. The Boar was the Royal Emblem and was the highest honour that could be conferred on a person at the time. Varaha Mihira gives a compendious presentation of Parasara astrology to the world in his work 'Brihat Jataka' which is still a standard treatise on the subject of Nirayana astrology—the astrology of the Fixed Zodiac as distinguished from the Sayana Zodiac that is in use in the West. 'Ayana' means the arc that represents the increasing gap between the starting points of the two Zodiacs. "Nir" in Sanskrit means "without", So, "Nir-Ayana means 'without Ayana,' 'Sa' means 'with' and so Sayana means 'with Ayana'. Therefore it is perfectly clear that the retrogression of the Vernal Equinox was recognised very early in the history of astrology and the rate of annual retrogression was fixed to a nicety and compares very favourably with the rate as calculated by modern astronomers. That both systems of astrology flourished once in India there is no doubt as I have- come across 'Nadis' according to both systems. "Nadis" are gigantic works containing delineations of individual horoscopes to be born centuries thereafter and are found to exhibit a surprising degree of accuracy and wealth of details.

The names of Mantreswara, author of 'Phala deepika', Vydyanatha, author of 'Sarvartha Chintamani,' Kalyanavarma, author of 'Saravali,' Kalidasa,* author

---

* Not the Sanskrit dramatist and poet of that name.

of 'Uttarakalamritha', Mahadeva, author of 'Jathaka Tattva' must be familiar to all students of the Indian System. But none of the above authors have contributed anything new or original to the system of directions and have only described the older methods. To this date Astrology in the East has not progressed further. It may on the other hand be said to have deteriorated as the 'Science' is not now being practised in the manner envisaged by the earlier writers, after estimation of planetary strength, house strength, bhavasputa etc, by the majority of Indian Astrologers, with regard to which Heinrich Daath says "the conception is of too colossal proportions for our Western ideas." †

Directional Astrology in the West has definite beginning from the time of Ptolemy who appears to have flourished in the first century A. D. and who perhaps gave the first scientific exposition of the science of Astrology itself to the West. Yet the name of Ptolemy is associated with the Geocentric System of cosmogony and this belief persisted till the time of Copernicus who expounded the Heliocentric basis of Astronomy for the first time in the 16th century A. D. This system even during the time of Copernicus was known by the name "System of Pythagoras" (6th century B. C.) who taught that "the Sun is a movable sphere in the centre of the Universe and the other planets revolved around it", as we see from a decree of the Holy congregation of the Index "Whereas it has come to the knowledge of the Holy Congregation that false Pythagorean doctrine

† Medical Astrology p. 66.

altogether opposed to the Holy Scriptures on the mobility of the earth and the immobility of the Sun" quoted in an article in the Nineteenth Century Magazine of May 1816 under the title "Case of Galileo". All this is Ancient History no doubt, but cited here to show that Astrology has had a much more ancient origin in India.

Ptolemy explained the Primary System of Directions. He dealt only with Direct Mundane and Zodiacal directions, but as Sepharial points out, to him must be accorded the honour of setting astrologers on the right track with regard to the correct measure of time by reference to the Equatorial degrees, separating one planetary body from another or one body from the longitude or aspect of another as seen from the place of birth and to Placidius 'the credit of having elaborated that part of directional astrology which has regard to directions in Mundo. The procedure was of course to work by the Semi-arc method of taking one third of a Semi-arc as equal to one house space. But from the beginning, this method was recognised to be astronomically unsound and various methods have been suggested by various authors to rectify this defect. Sepharial himself in his Directional Astrology propounds a new Method of working 'Primary' Directions. Harwood has published a small book on Primary Directions by the Polar Angle Method providing the necessary tables and other requisites for working them according to his System. Owen in his Primary Progressed Horoscope also suggests a new method for which he claims excellent results. From time to time, attempts have been made and devices put forward to render the mathematical part of working Primary Directions easier ; but with all these modifications, it is a fact that Primary Directions have not become popular and have not flourished and are no longer worked with the same zeal as before, if worked at all. The Secondary System of directions is no doubt comparatively easy of manipulation, but this too has not been found up to the mark.

The unsatisfactory condition of these systems of directions has been voiced by more than one Western author, Raphael in his Preface to the "Guide to Astrology" says that the most unsatisfactory part of astrology is that dealing with directions or the calculation of future events and that at present* there is no system that will give reliable results. He claims of course greater accuracy than any other systems, for the one taught by him, namely the Secondary System. But he is forced to admit that even here there appears to be 'Something lacking, some missing link which would explain was some directions fall out exactly like a thunderclap the others pass by without any appreciable event. Why this is, no one can tell ! Mr Carter Says** "From the point of view of practical astrology the most valuable part of our investigation will perhaps be that *which deals with the Zodiac as a basis of directing* (the italics are mine). Without a reliable and complete system of directing, all natal astrology tends to remain vague and abstract, yet all candid astrologers will admit that none of our present

* Xmas 1905

** Zodiac and the Soul September 1928, P. 64.

systems give entirely satisfactory results. Some are reliable so for as they go, at least in most cases, but while their positive side is accurate within certain limits, their negative aspects are uncertain. Thus, a given direction may as a rule operate, but events of importance occur without any corresponding direction. On the other hand some systems simply do not appear to work on occasion and a serious direction that may have caused much concern to the native, passes without any ruffle in the smooth surface of existence, or, more frequently a good direction is inoperative." The reason he conceives to be that nearly all the systems are astronomical and suggests that a symbolic system should do better. Mr. E. H. Bailey in stressing the importance of the Epoch Map as the basis for directing observes thus,* The value of directions computed from the Epoch cannot be too highly estimated. They fill in many of the gaps found in directions from the horoscope and supply the solution to the many anamolies which are found in judging the effects of Directions. They show why directions from the horoscope are held over or accentuated and why some do not appear to act at all. It has also been found that events occur in life and no directions in accord with the nature of the event can be traced from the horoscope." The conclusion of the writer is that all these deficiencies disappear if the Epoch horoscope is taken up for directions. Yet this quotation is made here only to show that this writer also points out the unsatisfactory nature of the existing systems of directions along with others,

* The Pre-Natal Epoch by E. H. Bailey P. 170.

but not for the efficacy of the solution offered. Of this more later.

The position of affairs with regard to this matter is summed up by Robson*. "Primary methods had practically fallen into disuse and the great majority of writers were relying solely upon the Secondary System with its facile method of working and its incomplete and inferior results. General dissatisfaction was growing, however, and new ideas were beginning to find their way into astrological literature. What was wanted was a method of combining the wealth of directions and the definiteness of predictions of the Primary System with the ease of working of the Secondary. The solution of this problem as of so many others was put forward by Sepharial when in 1918 he introduced the fundamental principles of a new System which he called the Radix System"†. This is mainly a symbolic system of directing and heralded the springing up of other systems of Symbolic directing.

From that time onwards Symbolic Systems as distinct from the astronomical systems of direction came into vogue and became popular because of the simplicity with which they can be calculated and the results were in no way less satisfactory than the already recognised methods. In fact, they appeared to give better results even. The systems though comparatively new to the Western school are not at all so to the Indian student. For he is accustomed to only Symbolic Systems of

---

* Introduction to Radix System P. 3. Oct. 1930.

† Introduction to Radix System P. 3. Oct. 1930.

progression and he has been using them for hundreds of centuries. Though I have been informed by scholars learned in Parasara astrology that there is basis for the kind of measures now employed in this work in Symbolic Direction in Parasara Hora, I have not been able to verify it owing to the scarcity of that work and so far I have not been able to find any references thereto. The idea which originated the method of directions outlined here struck me only when studying the Western systems. and I am indebted wholly to Farnkland and Carter whose treatment of this matter in "Keys to Symbolic Directing" and 'Symbolic Directions in Modern Astrology' respectively, provided the basis for the subsequent developments and research, the results of which I have sought to outline in these pages and it would be ungracious were I not to acknowledge the help I have derived from these authors. In fact, I am prepared to make the statement that without these two books, this book would not have been written.

It was more the remark of Carter in his 'Zodiac and the Soul' in the chapter 'Zodiac and the Art of Directing' that led me into this line of investigation. The value of Symbolic Systems in general has been referred to in that chapter and need not be repeated here, but I believe that his words, that it is highly probable that a great deal more may yet have to be discovered about the system, for instance, it my be found that each fraction has its own character, have indeed proved prophetic. For, that is precisely what I may be said to have discovered and this discovery I have sought to demonstrate by means of copious illustrations which have been chosen, not as isolated instances selected for the occasion in which case they can have only a secondary value as probable coincidences only, but only from authentic and published sources. I have taken horoscopes group by group and in a series to demonstrate the fact that the measures advocated here form part of a coherent and consistent system, and the public have had already the benefit of this through select channels for the past two decades and during which period, their confirmation by actual realisation of predictions made in hundreds of cases have left no doubt in my mind as regards their validity or efficacy.

CHAPTER II

BASIC CONCEPTS OF NEW ERA ASTROLOGY

§ 1. THE TWO SYSTEMS

The system of directions propounded here can be applied to any horoscope of either system and the results will be found to be satisfactory. But as already referred to in the Preface, a correlation between the two systems of astrology - Eastern and Western is attempted by me as that appears to give the best results. It is only in astrology there are two systems. In no other science it is so— in mathematics, physics, chemistry, botany or astronomy. There may be more than one method of approach but the system and the basic conceptions thereof are the same. Mr. Vijayaragavalu* voices the same opinion. "Astrology is an interplanetary or cosmic science that deals with the play of cosmic energy, be what it may, interacting between the planets of the solar system and their satellites. So it may also be termed Supra - Mundane science or the 'Science of sciences.' As a science it cannot but have one and only one aspect; so there can be no two systems of it. When the science is recomposed it would be found to present only one single face being an eclectic of all truths, wherever they may lie embedded and enmeshed."

* Essential Judgment of Hindu Horoscope Preface P. iv (30-12-33)

If Astrology is a science there can be but one system.

Also no science that is static can survive. Truth they say is dynamic and as any science is a revelation however partially or imperfectly of Truth, it too must be dynamic. The present time is a period of Renaissance in Astrology, and in the West at any rate, this is evident. Considerable activities are going on there in regard to this science and a large number of books are being published or reprinted on various aspects of astrology and in such a small isle as England I believe there are half a dozen astrological journals published each month. There is a Faculty of Astrology with Mr. Carter as President,* regular meetings held and subjects discussed. I have no accurate idea of the conditions on the continent and in America, but it is evident even greater activities are going on there also. Necessarily some of the theories advanced and conclusions drawn are hesitant, tentative and exploratory but that is only what can be expected when a science is advancing to new horizons. In India too a large number of books are being published but with very few exceptions the spirit of original research does not animate them. A crabbed policy of meaningless devotion to the Texts with all their anamolies, contradictions, and inconsistencies is pursued generally which bars all avenues of research and development abreast with the other sciences in which also India excelled in the past. Mr. Vijiaraghavalu says** "All books on Hindu Astrology published till now are of no scientific value, being translations of ill-arranged verses which are mostly

---

* Now Mr. R. C. Davison

** Essential Judgment of Hindu Horoscope P. 72.

medleys containing a few grains of truth copiously adulterated with spurious statements. The indiscriminating mind is led to believe that the greater the number of the detailed statements or so called principles in a book, the more valuable it is. The few grains of truth to be found in published books have to be very carefully sifted out, guided by common sense and experience from the overwhelming dross with which they are often mixed up." Of course not all publications can be characterised thus but it is a fact that as yet I have not come across any book in Hindu Astrology that embodies all the factors that are available to us with the advance of Astrology and allied sciences and even in books dealing with both systems of Astrology they are sought to be kept separate as if they are irreconcilable with each other.

In this work an attempt has been made at a correlation of the two systems at least so far as the directional or predictive side of astrology is concerned. But as this part cannot be completely isolated from the other parts of judicial astrology, such portions as are necessary are also embodied herein. To reconcile all the elements of the two systems as they exist at present is a much bigger task and must wait, though a work along these lines entitled "Basic concepts of New Era Astrology" is in course of preparation.

§ 2. EASTERN SYSTEM

This system with the Nirayana Zodiac as the basis is being practised with great success in India by innumerable astrologers. Perhaps it was unfortunate that whenever I studied this system, though it gave me great pleasure and also much knowledge, the smell of stale air and cobwebs never left me and in due course of time I realised that the chief defect of this system was that it has ceased to be progressive. It had become stagnant and I thought that the fresh breeze from the West could not but feel that what was felt as a breeze here was a storm there in which Western astrology was being tossed about helplessly and that the rusty trusty anchor available here would enable it to weather the storm and reach port safely.

§ 3. WESTERN SYSTEM

I could also visualise the Western system as a goodly pile of buildings but too rapidly sprung up to be free from structural flaws and resting on a somewhat insecure foundation. The Indian system though a magnificent edifice once is dilapidated and in most places overgrown with moss, briars, and brambles but with foundations still strong and enduring. If these overgrowths, the accretions of ages are cleared and the Western construction be made to more Daedalus fashion and be accommodated within the vast spaces here, we can have a system which with some further adjustments be made to endure for all time. In the former system, the clinging to tradition is too tenacious and in the latter the gaps are too wide.

Mr. Carter is impelled to exclaim* "Truly Scientific astrology is as yet but a babe; we are at the beginning

---

* Principles of Horoscopic Delineation P. 42.

of things. Tradition has been a faithful beast and has carried us for many centuries, but she is unequal to modern requirements." But my vision of scientific astrology is rather as an old man with nothing wrong about him except the weakness of age for which a blood transfusion is recommended which would give a further indefinite lease of life and I conceive of tradition rather as two beasts that were once yoked together to pull the weight but for unknown reasons parted company long ago each with its own share of load unequally partitioned between them. One of them wandered far west and even forgotten its mate and with its share of burden continually added on, is feeling itself unequal to the task and has become very near a breakdown while the other one feeling its load too heavy laid itself down and is contentedly chewing the cud and would not pull any further. The solution to my mind is obvious—Dump all suspicious loads off both, Yoke them together again and they will merrily jog on their way. But this is no easy task and certainly beyond the powers of any single individual.

§ 4. NEW ERA ASTROLOGY

Various methods of solving the problem were tried by me during several years of ardent research and after severe tests the following system has been evolved which I have dared to name 'New Era Astrology' and this is brought forward not as a triumphant achievement that solves all existing problems, but as an humble attempt that deserves to be experimented with. I am aware of its shortcomings and it is far from complete or perfect and I know I cannot make it perfect even if I work at it ceaselessly for all time so long as I live. Others may succeed where I have failed and make it perfect if it is brought to the light of day and it is brought out now after 25 years have passed since its first discovery. Tradition is adhered to as far as possible and the latest developments have been sought to be incorporated therein in a manner that would make it into an organic whole.

§ 5. CHOICE OF ZODIAC

There are two Zodiacs, Sayana (sa+Ayana) i.e., with Ayana employed in the west better known in recent times as the sign Zodiac or the Tropical Zodiac, and Niryana (Nir+Ayaṇa) i.e., without Ayana which is the basis of Hindu Astrology. 'Ayana' represents the distance or arc that separates the two Zodiacs. No Western Astrologer seems to have made a serious study of the Indian system with but very few exceptions. Sepharial has dealt with Hindu Atsrology in Book IV of his Manual of Astrology, and though it is apparent he has only imperfectly understood the system, he has praise for it. But a large number of Indian students of astrology have studied the astrology of the West and have even completely gone over to it, rejecting the Fixed Zodiac as unreal. As regards such, Sepharial observes thus* "A good deal of controversy has been raised in regard to this system by Hindus who have received a European education and who consequently wish to

* Sepharial's Manual of Astrology, Revised and Enlarged Edition P. 228.

appear in all matters 'up to date;' such persons claiming for the East a common use of the Tables of Houses, the computation of horoscopes by oblique ascension under the latitude of birth and a full knowledge of the Zodiac which begins with the equinoctal point. Despite the efforts of these gentlemen to improve their credit for intelligence at the expense of their Jyotish Shastra, we maintain that, although Mihira knew of the precession of the equinoxes and quoted Parasara and Garga to the same effect in his Brihat Samhita, he nevertheless used the Equinox beginning from Revati and referred all his rules and horoscopes to a Fixed Zodiac which is now (1898) 19° 34′26″ east of the Vernal Equinox. In proof of this, and to silence the contention that the system of Parasara was confined to the south of India, where it is yet in vogue, we refer critics to the Brigu Samhita, which is in the possession of Pandit Nandhikishor of Meerut, N. W. Province. We have in our possession over a hundred horoscopes from that colossal work and in none of them is there any observance of oblique ascension while the planets' places are referred to the Fixed Zodiac and not to the vernal equinox. Can any further, more reliable or more ancient authority be adduced to the contrary." I have made the above quotation not merely for the purpose of showing what Sepharial has pointed out in defence of the Fixed Zodiac. It also contains a fallacy that oblique ascension as per Latitude is not necessary for astrology based on the Fixed Zodiac. Brigu Samhita is a Nadi and Nadi astrology is peculiar; and nobody has hitherto succeeded in unravelling its mysteries though their existence containing delineations of thousands and thousands of horoscopes with minute details of uncanny accuracy is a fact. Nadis proceed on a system of their own and it cannot be inferred from the absence of mention of oblique ascension this should be ignored in the ordinary methods of hoıoscopical computation. But the conclusion is obvious that where an able and unprejudiced writer like Sepharial acknowledges the validity of Hindu Zodiac, it is futile for us to question its reality.

The increase of the interval between the two Zodiacs is only a **'Cosmic progression'** and the Fixed Zodiac is no more unreal than any Radical Horoscope from which the progressed places of the angles and planets are derived for the progressed horoscope. The Radical imprint is vital to the interpretation of the progressed planets and angles. Similarly the Fixed Zodiac beginning with the end point of Revati can be conceived to have validity for a stated period say **Kali Yuga.** So, any system of Astrology which completely ignores the "other" Zodiac must needs necessarily be imperfect and cannot be expected to yield the best results. Yet no astrologer has as yet thought seriously of applying his mind to the problem of integrating the two Zodiacs in a common system. Such an attempt is made by the present author in the forthcoming publication of 'Basic concepts of New Era Astrology'. Yet in this work for our purposes in so far as the Directional part of astrology is concerned, it is not so necessary; it is even immaterial that this matter should be finally settled as we are concerned here more with the relative distance between planetary bodies and between planets and angles of the horoscope which always remain the same according to both Zodiacs.

The measures for direction given in this book were tested and developed only with the planetary longitudes and houses as cast by the Western school, as a large number of horoscopes cast according to that system were readily available to me for reference in the text books as also in the Notable Nativities and saved me the trouble of casting them. Their reduction to the Fixed Zodiac was only a later development after the directions from the Zodiacal points according to both were worked and compared and the results, as per Fixed Zodiac appeared to give better results. The directions according to the Tropical Zodiac also were found to give fairly good results. Therefore the Fixed Zodiac has been uniformly employed here and the horoscopical data also furnished on that basis in the Appendix. But if any student does not want to try this Zodiac and wants to work only with the Tropical Zodiac, the conversion is quite easy. He has only to add the Ayanamsa to the longitudes of the planets and the ascendant and M. C.

§ 6. AYANAMSA

This is a controversial matter and the controversy continues; nor is it known when it will be satisfactorily settled, each astrologer has his own Ayanamsa which apparently satisfies his requirements. The Ayanamsa propounded by L. N. Rao in the

Astrological Magazine of Bangalore* is that which is adopted here and this is very close to Chitra Ayanamsa. The Ayanamsa for January, 1953 is 23° 10′ 40″ whereas according to Hypsomatic Zodiac of Cyril Fagan it is 24° 11′ 16″. Corrected to minutes they are 23° 11′ and 24° 11′. The Hypsomatic Zodiac is exactly 1° ahead of the Chitra Zodiac and may be so taken for all practical purposes.

§ 7. APPEAL

To the Western reader I would make this strong appeal. You have tried the Tropical Zodiac for very many years. The Fixed Zodiac is well authenticated and we have used them for centuries and no change has been found necessary. Sepharial in the past considered it valid enough to devote Book IV in his Manual of Astrology. Cyril Fagan of the present time is a redoubtable advocate of this Zodiac. Maurice Weymiss considers both Zodiacs valid, his view being that the position of the planets at the moment when the Zodiacs coincided would be of importance for the next Great Cycle of world history and this he calls the World Horoscope. In 'Astrology' (Sept 1952) I find the following observation. "Dr Rosenthal pointed out that the Fixed Zodiac was successfully used by the Hindus and symbolised a universal cosmic Archetype of which our movable Zodiac was the reflection but the President (Mr. Carter) suggested that this concept might need to be modified since viewed from any other part of

* Ayanamsa, no longer a Speculation Jan. 1947

cosmos, the constellations would present a different appearance". But his objection can be met as it is a fact that we are concerned as in all the rest of the astrological data only as viewed from our planet and the whole of the structure of Astrological science rests on a geocentric basis. Mr. Carter appears to think that if we depart from the sign Zodiac and adopt that of the stars it would involve declaring that all the astrology of the last few centuries was rubbish. No such inference necessarily follows if the view is taken that both Zodiacs should be taken up for judgment in all matters, in which case the anamolies entailed by the adoption of either exclusively will disappear or will become greatly reduced.

There is at present a tendency in the West to search for the 'other horoscope'; some want the Epoch horoscope also and others the Tropcial Epoch*. These may be excellent in their own way and I do not doubt that the advocates of either horoscope have good cause for doing so. But my suggestion is simpler namely the adoption of the 'Sayana horoscope' by the Indian astrologer and of the 'Chitra Zodiac' by the Western astrologer as the 'other' horoscope. Both have apparently yielded satisfactory results for their respective votaries over a long period of time and have got valid indisputable claims as cosmic configurations. In spite of contradictory maps which may be got with such

* A horoscope cast for the moment when Sun occupied the same longitude as at birth in the previous year is advocated by Sampson.

other data, you have here two horoscopes in which many things will have to be common. The house positions of the planets are the same in both and in a small percentage of cases, even the planets may be in the same signs.

Therefore I would beseech you to follow the illustrations here, especially with regard to the directions to and from the Zodiacal point of O° Aries; and compare the results with those obtained with the Tropical Zodiac in the matter of longevity, accidents, etc. The rules as regards the ascertainment of longevity have been collected from various texts and are presented in an orderly manner to facilitate easy application even by those who are not already familiar with such rules. These rules are given here as applicable to the Chitra Zodiac only. But I do not go to the extent of saying that they are totally inapplicable to the Tropical Zodiac as it will be against the position that has been taken by me all along. In fact I am prepared to go so far as to say that the results may be nearly as good. But it is better to place them where they belong. The study of astrology with the Fixed Zodiac will amply repay one's efforts.

§ 8. HOUSE DIVISION

This problem immediately follows upon the other. If the Fixed Zodiac is to be adopted, which system of House-divison is to be followed? In the Eastern school there is only one method-the method of trisecting the are of the ecliptic between the M. C. and the ascendant.

In the Western school there are very many methods of house division and the name of at least one celebrated astrologer is associated with each one of them. The Placedian system of domification is that which is most widely prevalent but the reasons for such a use are suggested to be not its inherent validity but because tables according to that system are easily available for all Latitudes; Margaret E. Hone* says "The use of any one system is a matter of choice and *the student should not think this is better than any other because it has been the only one for which tables have been widely printed*" (the italics are not mine). The earliest method was that of Ptolemy and the simplest, in which you have only to find the ascendant and mark off therefrom at the rate of 30 degrees for each house for all the twelve houses. Harwood of our time lends his support to this method and says that its correctness was brought home to him independently by the force of deduction and analogy when writing the book on "A theory of the Solar system†". I have not come across the method of house division adopted by Mr. Tucker but Mr. Lyndoe says‡ that he recommends the use of a Table of Houses in which the Midheaven is always at 90° from the Ascendant. Leon Sasson, a French astronomer and astrologer says that method of erecting horoscopes according to the system of Regumantanus is the only rational one §. But Maurice

* Modern Text Book of Astrology P. 119

† Easy Lessons in Astrology P. 37

‡ Practical Astrology by Edward Lyndoe P. 253

§ Practical Astronomy P. 7

Weymiss apparently finds very good reasons to prefer the method of Campanus*. This system of house division is also sponsored by the advocates of Solunars†. Mr. Carter has introduced a new scheme of house division‡ which he suggests may be called Poli Equatorial System in which the houses are demarcated by circles passing through the celestial poles and dividing the Equator into twelve arcs, the cusp of the first house passing through the ascendant and cites some examples where this method yields better results in the Judgment of a horoscope. This has the added advantage of one set of tables serving for all places in the world. This to me appears simplest and best and I have procured a copy of the table but have not had sufficient time to experiment with it in judgment as well as directions to be able to pronounce any opinion. Perhaps it is akin to that recommended by the Australian astrologer Zariel, or the same as the Babylonian method††.

The Hindu Method of House Division has got its votaries in the West also. It is the same as that recommended by Poryphyry much later and also adopted by Mr. Bailey the editor of Astrological Critic and Review. O.H.W. Owen adopts this method with a modification of his own. He trisects the equator instead of the ecliptic into three equal divisions and the ecliptical equivalents of the points so arrived at are the cusps of 11th & 12th

---

* Wheel of Life Vol. I Appendix I P. 128-130

† Bradleys' Solar & Lunar Returns P. 21

‡ Essays on the Foundations of Astrology P. 158

†† American Astrology, October 1953 P. 34

houses according to him. Mr. Carter criticises the trisection of the ecliptic from the M. C. to the ascendant and asks,* "If the horizon and the meridian divide the ecliptic unequally why should the succedent and cadent houses be obtained by equal division?" and adds that this method is used in India because near the Equator all systems produce very similar results. Without an attempt to defend this method on either mathematical or philosophical grounds, I can say that this system of house division laid down in the texts is *designed* for all latitudes. Charakandas (periods of oblique ascension) for each sign from 0° to 60° Latitude have been calculated and tabulated in the Ancient Texts*. In this book the horoscopes as cast by the Trisection method alone have been given. The results as demonstrated here may be compared with those obtained by other methods of domification by investigators and the results may be published to the world.

§ 9. ORBS

The question of orbs is closely bound up with the problem of house division, though this matter is not so vital for directions, as only Ascendant and M. C. are principally utilised for this purpose and these are common to nearly all methods. Still it is very important for *judgment* where interpretation of directions turns on house position of planets, rulership of houses by planets and where cusps of houses like

---

* Vide Manual of Hindu Astrology by B. V. Raman, Table I, P. 93, Third Edition.

that of the 8th and 6th are directed. In this work, tradition is strictly adhered to in regarding the cusp as the centre of the house as there are weighty authorities in support of this position. This I am confident will find ultimate and unanimous acceptance in the West also. Mr. Carter* in his Foreword to Some Principles of Horoscopic Delineation says (March 1934). "For almost twenty five years I have regarded the cusps as boundaries of the houses and I believe that ninety-nine out of every hundred astrologers have done the same. Nor do I consider that cusps have any orbs but as planets undoubtedly have them, a body within about seven degrees of a cusp will naturally shed a certain influence into the house beyond it." Further on he admits the plausibility of the case for the cusp which is the strongest part of a house being the centre with areas of gradually decreasing power on each side of it. The same subject is again dealt with by the learned author in Chap. VIII of his "Essays on the Foundations of Astrology P. 163". "The question of house orbs is a difficult one. Since we allow no orbs to signs and since we attribute meanings to the houses in correspondence with the signs and in every way treat them as the mundane analogues of these it appears prima facie unreasonable to ascribe any orbs to houses. But practical experience has always postulated something of the kind. Judged solely by this criterion, the author would attribute some 10° of orb to the ascendant and perhaps as

---

* P. 9.

much to the other angles whilst the succedent houses might be allowed somewhat less and the cadent houses perhaps 5°. These may be increased slightly for the Sun & Moon........ as for the contention of some (but not all) advocates of Campanus that the cusp is the centre of the house this squares neither with reason nor experience." In the Table of House Division published by Mr. Carter, it is suggested that a cuspal orb of 10° should be used and that planets falling within this orb should be regarded as influencing both the houses without regard to the cusp being an angle or otherwise or to the planets being Sun and Moon or otherwise.*

But since the influence of a planet beyond the cusp is believed to be a factor influencing the house position of a planet, the question of orbs in respect of the planets assumes added importance and considerations as to whether the cusp is an angle or otherwise becomes purely secondary. Mr. Lyndoe observes*, "there has always been wide divergence of opinion about orbs. Some astrologers insist on 10° for all bodies; some use only the orb of application, while yet others have devised a more complicated system of their own. According to the ancients (who can by no means be disregarded in these matters) the orbs were after this fashion........ most but not all modern authorities reject this scale."

---

* Towards the end of the discussion Mr. Carter observes that it is quite possible that there is some basis for more methods of domification than one. (P. 165)

The following comparative table embodies the various views :—

No.	Planet	Simmonite	Suggested by Lyndoe for research	Tajak (Sanskrit)
1	Sun	15°	15° to 17°	15
2	Moon	12°	10° to 12°	12
3	Mercury	7°	6° to 8°	7
4	Venus	7°	6° to 8°	7
5	Mars	7°	6° to 8°	8
6	Jupiter	9°	9° to 12°	9
7	Saturn	9°	8° to 10°	9
8	Uranus	7°	10°	—
9	Neptune	5°	10°	—
10	Pluto	—	—	—

In the matter of orbs Mr. Lyndoe is the most liberal of modern authors as he recommends for the ordinary student a general rule to allow 12° for Sun and Moon and 10° for the remainder of the planets.

As can be readily seen from the above table there is a remarkable conformity in this matter between ancient and modern authorities.

For the view that the cusp should be regarded as the centre of the house, I shall cite three verses from Sripatipaddhati and one from Phaladeepika.

Sripatipaddhati Chap. I.

Verse 8

वदन्ति भावैक्यदलं हि सन्धिं तत्र स्थितः स्यादफलो ग्रहेन्द्रः ।
ऊनस्तु सन्धेर्गत भाव जातमागामिजं चाभ्यधिकः करोति ॥

Verse 9

भावांशतुल्यः खलु वर्तमान भावोद्भवं पूर्णफलं विधत्ते ।
भावोनके चाभ्यधिके च खेटे त्रैराशिकेनात्र फलं प्रकल्प्यम् ॥

Verse 10

भावप्रवृत्तौ हि.फलप्रवृत्तिः पूर्णफलं भावसमांशकेषु ।
ह्रासक्रमाद्भाव विरामकाले फलस्य नाशः कथितो मुनीन्द्रैः ॥

Translation

Verse 8

A half of the sum of two contiguous bhavas is called their Sandhi (Junction). A planet that is in a Bhava Sandhi produces no effect. But the planet that is short of a Sandhi produces the effect of the preceding bhava. If it should be in excess of a Sandhi, it produces the effect of a bhava to come.

Verse 9

A planet that occupies the same longitude as the cusp of a house produces the full effect of that house. When the planet is away from this, its effect should be ascertained by rule of three process.

Verse 10

Sages have declared that when a bhava begins, its effect also begins. The effect becomes full in the middle i.e., cusp of that house. When a planet approaches the end more and more, the effects get less and less till the end of the bhava is reached when they become completely nil.

The same idea is expressed in a single verse in Phaladeepika Chapter XV.

Verse 14

भावेषु भावस्फुट तुल्य भागस्तद्भावजं पूर्णफलं विधत्ते ।
सन्धौ फलं नास्ति तदन्तराले चिन्त्योऽनुपातः खलु खेचराणाम् ॥

Translation

In the several houses, the planets that are occupying the exact degrees signified by any particular house (cusps) produces the full effect of that house. When a planet is in a bhavasandhi (Junction of two houses), it produces no effect. In the case of planets occupying intermediate positions, the effect should be ascertained by rule of three.

The only Western authors to my knowledge who have fully and unreservedly subscribed to the above view of the sages are E. H. Bailey and Alan Leo. In his Astrological Critic and Review, official organ of the British Astrological Society Vol. IV No. 2 (June 1952) E. H. Bailey says " Most of my readers are probably aware that I do not use the Tables of Houses given in the Ephemeris, the Placidean method...... The method is dealt with by Sripati, a Hindu astrologer who lived about the 10th century A. D. and is found in Sripathipaddhati. But Sripati was not the original propounder of this method of house division that is now known after his name........ Sripati merely explained the method of Parasara...... Sripati's method is therefore at least five thousand years old, since it was first used in India. Students will to make use of this method which is now used by several of our leading Astrologers, it being stated by one, that it solves many if not all of the anomalies to be met with in Astrology. It may also be pointed out that it also solves the problem of house division in high Latitudes".

The still older writer Alan Leo expresses himself thus*, "The sign and more especially the particular degree of the Zodiac rising upon the Eastern horizon at birth is known as the Ascendant. This term embraces the whole of first house and in the author's opinion about 15° above the first house may be considered as included in the ascendant". In a footnote appended to this statement, the position is made clearer that the 15° here spoken of is strictly speaking 15° of oblique ascension and not of the Zodiac but in a great many cases half a sign will be near enough. Though the other houses have not been expressly mentioned, it is obvious that the same inference follows by necessary implication.

§ 10. Aspects

Any student who has followed me thus far is apt to think that I am an irredeemable advocate of all that is old and ancient in astrological lore. But he will be rapidly disillusioned in this section. The system of aspects applied and uniformly illustrated in this book is according to the Western school. Yet this system had its origin in the East.

* How to Judge a Nativity, Chap. VI. P. 90.

There are three separate systems of aspects dealt with in the ancient works (1) Jaimini (2) Taijak (3) Parasara. Of these Jaimini system of aspects is peculiar and not generally known. In this system **all fixed signs** aspect **all cardinal signs** except the one adjacent and vice versa and **all common signs** aspect **all other common signs.** The planets in the respective signs follow suit. The system of aspects generally followed in the West is substantially the Taijak method with some modifications. The aspects generally followed in Hindu Astrology at present is the one most widely known-Parasara. But in the manner in which it is generally applied there is great divergence from what was originally laid down by Parasara in his Parasara Hora*.

As in all other matters, in the matter of aspects also Western astrology is not settled. The principal aspects are conjunction, Parallel of Declination, sextile square, trine and opposition. Other aspects considered weaker than these such as Semi Sextile, Semi Square, Sesqui quadrate, and Quincunx have also been in use for a long time. To this already formidable list, other aspects are also sought to be added on such as Semi Quintile (36°), nonagen (40°), Quintile (72°), Sesqui quintile (108°) and Bi-quintile (144°). Even now the list is not complete, Mr. Carter says† "It is the view of the author (Carter) that all multiples of 15° produce valid aspects, even though a narrow

---

* Vide article by K. Sivasubramaniam in January 1953 issue of Astrological Magazine.

† Essays on the Foundations of Astrology Chap. III. p. 50.

orb must be applied to such distances as 15°, 75° and 105°. In his personal experiences important results have coincided with the formation, by the progressed Sun, of aspects of these denominations. Indeed he would rate them as more potent than the quintile series. It seems reasonable too, to expect the division of the circle by 7 and 9 to yield valid contacts i.e., of 51° 26′ and 40°, with their principal derivatives. As to which of these aspects would be classed as "good" and which as "bad" only experience can show". The scheme of aspects according to the earlier text writers is much more limited.

This matter of aspects has received some "attention" at the hands of investigators on Radio and Electronic Research in connection with Radio disturbances and black outs. An article has appeared in Vol. XII March 1951 of R. C. A. Review, a technical Journal dealing with Radio and Electronic Research and Engineering. The author of the above article is Mr. J. H. Nelson of the Engineering Department R. C. A. Communications Inc. New York and the article is entitled " Short Wave Propagation and correlation with planetary configurations and the following is an extract therefrom :— P. 261 "The encouraging correlation found between ionospheric disturbances over North Atlantic and configurations (particularly of the multiple type for 1942, 1944, 1947, 1948 & 1949 suggest the following deductions :—

(1) That the most disturbed twelve month periods will be those preceding and following configurations

of the 0°, 90°, 180°, and 270° between Saturn and Jupiter.

(2) That the most disturbed twelve month periods in (1) will be those in which Mars is close to a configuration of the 0°, 90°, 180°, 270°, type either with Saturn or Jupiter.

(3) That the most disturbed part of the periods in (2) will be when the Earth, Venus or Mercury has a configuration of 0°, 90°, 180°, 270°, type either with Saturn or Jupiter or Mars.

(4) That the most severe disturbances of all will come when the combined influence of Mars, the Earth, Venus, Mercury are such that all four will be arranged in positions where there will be a great concentration of planetary influences near the 0°, 90°, 180°, 270°, part of Saturn-Jupiter teams during the configuration mentioned in (1).

(5) That the least disturbed periods of all will be those when Saturn, Jupiter, and Mars are equally spaced by 120°, the principal disturbances during these periods coming from configurations of the 0°, 90°, 180°, 270°, type that the inner planets Mars, Earth, Venus, or Mercury make among themselves or as a multiple with Earth, Saturn or Jupiter.

(6) That the least disturbed periods of all will be when Saturn, Jupiter, and Mars are equally spaced by 120°, the principal disturbances during these periods coming from configurations that Earth, Mercury, Venus make among themselves or as multiples with

Saturn, Jupiter and Mars configurations of the multiple type are less frequent during an arrangement of 120° among these three slow outer planets.

(7) That 60° relationship between planets will also tend to produce least disturbed periods since 60° is one-half of 120°.

These deductions were made after a close examination of short wave radio propagation conditions for a five year period and were found to accord generally as with the period of the greatest magnetic storms that occurred in 1946 and the least disturbed period in 1934 ".

The article from which the above extract is made gives further detailed figures, graphs, and other materials on which the above conclusions were based. This is support indeed for the traditional 'good' and 'bad' aspects from an unexpected quarter though the longitudes that have furnished the data for the above observations are helio-centric! The very same aspects having the very same kind of results have been noticed by the earliest astrological sources for geocentric longitudes. Some thinkers have compared the effects of planets in human affairs to the effects of planets on radio propagation and reception, and some authors doubt the analogy. Enoch Penn* observes thus " the changes and processes in the lives of men are impelled by the various and varying influences received from the heavenly bodies which

* Planetary Influences, Introduction P. iii.

influences play on man's body some what as electric impulses play upon the radio receiving set". If this analogy is a proper one this explains not only the significance of noting the planetary aspects in judging their effects on the affairs of man but also their classification into 'good' and 'bad' just at the time when a controversy regarding such a division has come to the forefront in the astrological forums of the Western school.

A direction is but an aspect. An aspect is formed when the planets and angles or cusps in a horoscope are at specified distances from each other. A direction is nothing but the formation of such aspects between the radical and the progressed horoscopes. It is the system of aspects above mentioned that is employed in this work throughout but the number of aspects that are utilised is limited to half a dozen of the principal aspects, conjunction, sextile, square, trine, Quincunx and opposition. The inclusion of Quincunx may need some explanation. That this aspect has greater relative value than is commonly supposed has been pointed out by Mr. Carter*. Henrich Daath is of the same view. Even the Parallel of Declination is omitted here, not because this writer is of the view that it has no place in symbolic directions nor because that it has no value but only to simplify the system of directions suggested here.

One positive reason for adoption of the westernised version of Taijak system of aspects has been

* Symbolic Directions in Modern Astrology. P. 49

given. There is another negative reason for avoiding the Parasara system. In the Parasara, all planets do not have the same aspects for exerting their influence. Mars, Jupiter and Saturn have got special places where their influence is believed to be exerted most and it is not known on what principle these special aspects were designed, nor can it be conjectured what special aspects are to be ascribed to the other superior planets Uranus, Neptune and Pluto. But where the scheme of aspects adopted is uniform for all the planets, it is obvious that this can be applied to all planets alike, new and old.

§ 11. PLANETS

It can be expected that at least this section should be free from controversy. Unfortunately it is not so. Hindu Astrology recognises only 9 planets including Rahu and Kethu (Caput and Cauda) The Trans-Saturnine planets do not find a place in the scheme. Indian astrologers are divided into groups on this issue. The majority, I believe, are for the inclusion of Uranus, Neptune and Pluto and the names given to them respectively are Indra, Varuna and Yama—appropriate names. Indra is said to preside over ether, Varuna over water, and Yama is the God of Death in Hindu Mythology. Some others are fanatically opposed to their inclusion. That these three planets do affect human affairs, I have no doubts whatever in my mind and hence their inclusion here. True, some difficulties will present themselves if they are to be incorporated bodily into the Hindu system and the following problems will arise (1) which are benefics and which are malefics (2) what signs they rule (3) do they have special aspects like the other superior planets, if so, what are their special aspects (4) How are they to be accommodated in the Dasa System and what is the number of years for each planet. These and other problems will have to be faced. But they will not be solved by their being simply ignored as at present. It is the argument of those who are against their inclusion that Hindu astrology as laid down in the texts is self-sufficient for all time, which I question. Varaha Mihira does not mention Rahu and Kethu and yet they are part and parcel of Hindu Astrology to-day. Some method of bringing the Trans-Saturnine planets within the scope of the Hindu system should be found out but it is also clear that all at once a method cannot be devised. I think it would be unwise to ignore them altogether.

But in the method of directing outlined here no such difficulties confront me. These planetary bodies also are directed just like others and interpreted according to the character of the measures employed and the aspects formed. There is sufficient literature in Western astrology to define* their inherent nature and characteristics.

§ 12. CHANGING NATURE

This is avowedly a controversial matter but it cannot be avoided here. This controversy seems to have existed even before the time of Plotinus. Plotinus charged the astrologers of his time for averring that

* Vide the brilliant articles by Mr. Van Ingersoll Allen in American Astrology.

planets changed their nature, the contention of Plotinus being that planets cannot change their nature. Two of our modern astrologers think that no astrologer ever made such a statement and that Plotinus was biassed or mistaken in making such an assumption.

The present writer has no knowledge of Greek and his acquaintance with Plotinus is purely secondhand through English translations of his works. I gather that Plotinus was no astrologer himself and even scorned the mathematical part of it†, 'but he more accurately investigated the doctrine of astrologers about the influences of the stars and not finding their prediction to be certain he frequently confuted them in his writings.' I am indebted to Heinrich Daath for the translation of a part of his criticism of astrologers given in his Medical Astrology P. 67‡. In the third book of the Second Ennead he (Plotinus) observes that they (the planets) are adjudged to change their signification by their change of course, and as they are located in angles or cadent therefrom. But the most important thing that they (the astrologers) **say that some among them are benefic, others evil, yet nevertheless the latter often perform as though endowed with the virtue of the former no less than the former acting as the latter.** They add that when the planets are in reciprocal aspect they act in one way and when they do not aspect each other they produce effects in another ....lastly a planet aspected by a certain favourable

† Select works of Plotinus (William Rider & Co.,) Introduction LXI.

‡ Alan Leo Astrological Manual Series No. 9, P. 67-8.

one bestows good only to be suddenly changed when it transfers its aspect to another. *They affirm likewise that they are changed in a certain manner according as the figure of aspectin is changed and that from the body or mutual conjunction still another form of influence is generated*", (The italics are mine). On this statement H. Daath comments as follows:— "In reality the stars do not change their nature by change of position and configuration as asserted; nor are some good and others evil. In themselves they are neither, what happens is a fresh polarisation, a rearrangement of the energic rays. Mars is always Mars, it never exhibits the qualities of Saturn nor presents itself in the form of the latter-coldness, gravity, concretion. But it cannot be gainsaid that the human organism is adversely affected when receiving rays through the medium of any of the evil aspects, even when the planetary bodies involved are otherwise beneficial; much more so when the combined forces are malefic. It thus becomes imperative to accept a division of the stars into benefic and malefic and to assume that there is an inherent capability among them for mutual mingling and transference of influence. Mr. Carter* comments thus, "It is the misfortune of astrology if truth in any form can be unfortunate—that even when it has been examined by brilliant intellects it has usually been studied only superficially and minds normally free from prejudice have apparently forgotten this virtue when engaged upon the subject. Even Plotinus misunderstood when

---

* Essays on the Foundations of Astrology P. 11

he condemned astrologers for speaking as if the planets, which the philosopher doubtless regarded as divine and therefore immutable, changed their natures. No astrologer has made any such assertion; but it is true that planets are said to be well or badly placed according to their own mutual relations or aspects and the signs through which their values are translated to us. In essence they remain unchanged ".

Both commentators grant the impartiality and the intellectual stature of the philosopher as one who is not likely to make a mis-statement yet both critics agree that no astrologers have ever asserted what according to them Plotinus says regarding change of nature by planets. But I doubt whether either of the learned authors appreciated what it was that Plotinus was criticising. I have purposely given the quotations in full length so that my view point may be understood and properly adjudged. The translation appearing in Mr. Daath's book reads to my biassed mind (because of familiarity with Hindu Astrology) suspiciously like references to the doctrines of the Nirayana school. The statement that when planets are in reciprocal aspect, they act in one way and when they do not aspect each other **they produce effects in another** is open to two possible interpretations. In Western astrology planets always aspect each other. That is how it is treated in this book also; that is, there is no instance of aspect in which it is not reciprocal and the above statement may be confined to this view of the matter and as postulating nothing more. But what is it that Plotinus means when he says, "When planets do not aspect each other **they produce effects in another way.**"! This statement would have some meaning if it is held to refer to cases of 'non-mutual' aspects as distinct from 'mutual aspects' which is possible only according to Hindu astrology where two planets may aspect each other or one planet alone may aspect another planet without its being aspected by the other planet. For example if Saturn is in 15° Capricornus and Mars in 15° Libra they aspect each other, as Mars has got special aspect in the 4th sign (90°) and Saturn has got a special aspect in 10th sign (270°). But if Saturn is in 15° Capricornus and Mars in Pisces 15° Saturn will aspect Mars by his special aspect in 60° degrees (third sign) but Mars has no aspect to Saturn. If Mars is in 15° Pisces and Saturn in 15° Libra, Mars will aspect Saturn by his quincunx aspect of 210° degrees, but Saturn will not aspect Mars; and in all the ancient texts a distinction is made between planets aspecting each other and one planet simply aspecting another. Such a distinction is necessarily absent in Western astrology. In this respect, my view may or may not be correct and this is mentioned for purposes of analogy only.

But in the matter of planets 'changing nature' I believe I am on firmer ground as it is an axiom in Hindu astrology that planets change their nature not in the sense that one planet assumes the nature of another planet, but the natural malefics behave as though they are benefics and vice versa where they happen to own angles and I presume that the reference of Plotinus to benefic planets being endowed with the virtue of the former no less than the former sometimes acting as latter is to this Hindu doctrine. No doubt "By owning angles" is not there; we have to import the condition there according to which astrologers of the time said planets changed their nature. Otherwise the statement has no meaning. This is a basic notion of Hindu astrology. But this would be also a notion that is likely to be criticized if it was seeking to make entry into the astrology of the West at that time and certainly on philosophical grounds by Plotinus with which aspect alone he was concerned. I believe all students when meeting with the statement that benefics become malefics by owning angles get a mild shock at the first instance. I mean even Hindus studying Hindu astrology. But as this is a necessary part of every item of interpretation, he soon gets over this and this maxim is relegated to the category of an axiom. Thus, one need not be surprised if this is what is criticised by Plotinus. All this is only an introduction to the doctrine of the change of nature by planets which is practically foreign to Western astrology and is conceived by this writer to be a necessary part of New Era Astrology.

Jataka Chandrika an elementary but authoritative work in Sanskrit gives the necessary information briefly and to the point. But there is no treatise on Hindu Astrology which does not embody this principle*

---

* Vide Chapters XVI and XVII, B. V. Raman's Hindu Predictive Astrology.

Stanza 5. Lords of konas (trines) give good while lords of 3rd, 6th and 11th houses produce evil.

Stanza 6. When benefics own quadrants they produce evil, when malefics own quadrants they produce good ; the good and bad planets become more and more powerful as they are lords of 1st, 4th, 7th and 10th houses, 5th and 9th houses respectively.

Stanza 7. The lords of 2nd and 12th houses give good or bad results according as they are in conjunction with the lords of other houses and the nature of the houses they occupy.

Stanza 8. Lord of 8th house produces evil because he owns the 12th house from the 9th (Bhagya). If he chances to be lord of 1st or combines with a benefic he becomes good.

Stanza 9. Jupiter and Venus owning quadrants become very malefic. When they occupy 2nd and 7th houses with such ownership, they become powerful in inflicting certain death on the native.

Stanza 10. Mercury is less malicious than Jupiter and Venus when owning quadrants. Sun and Moon do not give evil even if they rule the 8th house.

Stanza 11. Mars does not become benefic when he owns the tenth house only. He must also own the 5th house to become thoroughly good.

Stanza 12. Rahu and Kethu give the same results as those indicated for the houses they occupy and the planets they are in conjunction with, when they are powerful.

All text books on Hindu Astrology devote a chapter to the indication of good and bad planets for each ascendant Vide chap. XVII in B. V. Raman's Hindu Predictive Astrology entitled Key Planets for each sign which is only an elaboration of the above principles worked out in the case of each ascendant. The Western astrologer who keeps this change of nature in mind even with regard to the Tropical Zodiac will secure greater results and will have less anomalies staring him in the face. This modification of nature by rulership is not a trick to arrive at conclusions as has been characterized by some in the West. Such a table is subjoined here also. In it only the sign containing the ascendant is given on the assumption that the other eleven house cusps fall in the successive eleven signs. Where they fall in different signs according to the Latitude of birth place, the rulership of houses has to be taken accordingly and this fact will have to be taken note of in adjusting the nature of each planet individually in such cases.

Asc.	Benefics	Malefics	Neutrals
♈	☉, ♂, ♃, ♄	☽, ☿, ♀	Nil.
♉	☉, ♄, ♀	☽, ♃	♂
♊	♀, ♄	☉, ♃, ♂	☽, ☿
♋	♂, ♃	☿, ♀	☉, ♄, ☽
♌	☉, ♂, ♃	☿, ♀	☽, ♄
♍	♀, ♄	☽, ♂, ♃	☉, ☿
♎	☿, ♂, ♄	☉, ☽, ♃	♀
♏	☉, ☽, ♃, ♄	☿, ♀	♂

Asc.	Benefics	Malefics	Neutrals
♐	☉, ♂	☽, ☿, ♀, ♄	♃
♑	☿, ♀, ♂	☉, ☽, ♃	♄
♒	☉, ☿, ♀, ♂	☽, ♃	♄
♓	☽, ♂	☿, ♀, ☉, ♄	♃

With this table as the key to horoscopical judgment and interpretation of directions, many a vexed problem will find easy solution either in the Western or Eastern School of astrology.

CHAPTER III

DIRECTIONAL SYSTEM OF THE HINDUS

§ 1. GENERAL

"While the general outline of the horoscope is unalterable, the primary, secondary, and other systems (of direction) stand for rhythmical changes taking place within the limits imposed at birth; and because these rhythms must necessarily be co-ordinated with each other and with the whole, so all systems of directing must equally. be capable of co-ordination." Thus wrote Alan Leo in his Foreword to "Directions and Directing".* This is a far sighted statement as no system of Directions has as yet been formulated that can by itself solve the problem of mapping out the events of life with regard to a nativity. Yet the modern tendency in directional astrology at present is separative and there are very many more "systems" now in vogue than at any time previously in the history of astrology. Co-ordination is not even sought to be attempted.

The principal difficulty with regard to any system of directing that is practised in the West is that facilities are wanting to enable one to have a survey of the whole life and events at a glance without working

* Alan Leo Astrological Manual Series No. 5, (P. II)

endless calculations. No doubt the calculations are much less in the symbolic systems, still, the same directions between any two planets may recur more than once in the course of a normal span of life, and some directions more so than others and transits most of all; and these have to be differently interpreted in the different stages of life. This limitation is recognised by all. For example a direction that is usually considered almost infallible in bringing about wedlock will be apparently inoperative in this respect when the age is too tender for marriage or when the native is too old. It may not be operative at all to produce marriage at any age if the radix is against such an event, but have effects in other ways.

Therefore the two principal factors that govern the interpretation of directions, whatever the system of direction may be, astronomical or symbolical, Primary or Secondary, are :—(1) the limitation of the radix (2) the limitations arising from the stage of life in which the directions occur. Thus even after working all the directions that are formed in 'a life' of 100 years according to any system, the delineation of events is no easy task. Yet a third difficulty arises when a number of directions that are characteristic of an event are to be found within the range of probability as to age. Suppose there are powerful directions for marriage at 22, 25, 27, and 30 years of age. Of these which age is to be selected as the one in which marriage will surely take place? Say a powerful direction or set of directions such as will ordinarily cause death occurs in the 32nd year of life. Will the native die then or live beyond that age? No doubt these are problems for which the ultimate solution lies in the radix but it will require a certain maturity of judgment. Till that is fully developed there must be something available in the directions themselves, some clue which should point to either probability in such cases for guidance. This clue is provided in this system of directing.

§ 2. DIRECTIONAL SYSTEMS OF THE HINDUS

We shall first deal with the directional systems of the East. All these systems are purely symbolical. I have not come across any directional scheme based on astronomical methods here. Of these there are a great many variety however. One feature that is common to all these systems is that the life span is divided into several sections, each section being considered to be ruled by a planet which gives the clue to the main characteristics and events of that period. These are called Dasa systems.* It is not claimed for these systems that the three limitations pointed out above do not obtain here. Yet it is boldly stated that the Dasa systems of the Hindus are the best so far available to the modern student to enable him to map out a whole life in advance with the least possible trouble. In any one of these systems, it will be possible within a few minutes of the casting of a horoscope to divide the entire life into several broad sections, fix the

* They are not Alfridares as will be seen later.

principal landmarks and judge the major events probable in each at a glance with practically very little work done in the matter of actual calculations. The one most prevalent in India at present is the Asterism System of Dasa—Vimsottari and that is explained here.

§ 3. VIMSOTTARI DASA SYSTEM

This will be referred to here simply as the Dasa system as no other system is treated here. In this system the Zodiac is divided into three equal parts of 120° each and each part contains nine equal sections of 13° 20′ each of which is ruled in turn by the nine planets in the following order, Kethu, Venus, Sun, Moon, Mars, Rahu, Jupiter, Saturn and Mercury beginning from 0° Aries round the entire circle. The following table explains the scheme.

No.	1	2	3	4	5
1	♈ 0° 0′–13°20′	♌ 0° 0′–13°20′	♐ 0° 0′–13°20′	☋	years 7
2	13°20′–26°40′	13°20′–26°40′	13°20′–26°40′	♀	20
3	♈ ♉ 26°40′–10° 0′	♌ ♍ 26°40′–10° 0′	♐ ♑ 26°40′–10° 0′	☉	6
4	♉ 10° 0′–23°20′	♍ 10° 0′–23°20′	♑ 10° 0′–23°20′	☽	10
5	♉ ♊ 23°20′– 6°40′	♍ ♎ 23°20′– 6°40′	♑ ♒ 23°20′– 6°40′	♂	7
6	♊ 6°40′–20° 0′	♎ 6°40′–20° 0′	♒ 6°40′–20° 0′	☊	18

	♊ ♋	♎ ♏	♒ ♓		
7	20° 0′– 3°20′	20° 0′– 3°20′	20° 0′– 3°20′	♃	16
	♋	♏	♓		
8	3°20′–16°40′	3°20′–16°40′	3°20′–16°40′	♄	19
9	16°40′–30° 0′	16°40′–30° 0′	16°40′–30° 0′	☿	17

The native begins his life with the period of the planet who rules the division occupied by the Moon (Fixed Zodiac) at birth, and the portion that has elapsed at birth is calculated by proportion from the longitude of the Moon. Suppose Moon occupies 8° 10′ of Gemini at birth. Reference to the above table shows (item 6) Rahu dasa rules at birth (Col 4.) The excess of the longitude of Moon over the longitude that begins in item 6 (6° 40′) is 1° 30′. The proportion represented by this quantity to the total is to be calculated in respect of 18 years (the total period of Rahu (☊) and this is the portion that has elapsed at birth. Thus 11° 30′ to 13° 20′ is the proportion in 18 years that has to run after birth in Rahu (☊) dasa (period).

13° 20′ : 11° 50′ : : 18 : No. of years to be passed

= 810′ : 710′ : : 18 : No. of years to be passed

$=\frac{710}{800}\times 18$ years=15 years 11 months 21 days

of Rahu's period remains to be passed.

N. B.— The reader is however saved the trouble of this calculation as Appendix G. gives the balance to be passed in any period for any degree and minute of the Zodiac.

§ 4. FURTHER PROCEDURE

The period of Rahu (☊) lasts for 15 years 11 months and 21 days after birth, then 16 years of Jupiter have to be passed, and then 19 years of Saturn and so on : Thus,

		y	m	d
Rahu	(☊)	15	11	21
Jupiter	(♃)	16	0	0
Saturn	(♄)	19	0	0
Mercury	(☿)	17	0	0
Ketu	(☋)	7	0	0
Venus	(♀)	20	0	0
Sun	(☉)	6	0	0
		100	11	21

Rahu's position in the horoscope by sign and house and the aspects he receives combined with his own inherent nature are to be taken into account in interpreting the results of the first 15 and odd years ruled by him. Rahu has no sign rulership. The next 16 years ruled by Jupiter are to be judged with reference to his location, rulership of houses and his aspects. Similarly the next 19 years with regard to Saturn, the ruler of the succeeding period, and so on till the end.

These are no doubt big divisions in a life and are none the less useful because they are big, since they give a general idea as to the nature of those periods in life, the dominant note of each will be that struck by the planet who is the overlord. Greater exactitude however can always be secured by a further sub-division into nine effected in the case of each major period. Each such sub-division is called a 'bukti' or sub-period and is ruled by the same nine planets in the same order, beginning from the major lord or overlord. The period of time contributed by each sub-lord is in the same proportion. (Vide. Appendix F.)

The nature of results to be expected in each Sub-division will be according (1) to the inherent nature of each sub-lord, (2) his location in the horoscope by sign and house, (3) his rulership, (4) his location as from his major lord, but all these effects will be wholly subordinate to the influence of the major lord. This judgment of results has to be made with respect to each individual horoscope and the effects in no two horoscopes may prove to be the same. Still the intrinsic nature of each such combination of sub-lord with the overlord has been studied and found to have certain attributes and the results of such observation have been recorded in the texts. An adaptation from one of such texts, Kalamrita, has been given by Sepharial in his Book IV of his Manual of Astrology. Rules for interpretation of these effects with such modifications as to suit them to individual cases have also been given there which anybody possessing a copy of that book may peruse with advantage. But that book I believe is out of print or not easily obtainable. Some rules of interpretation are given here so as to enable any student to judge the results of any sub-period in any major period.

GENERAL RULES

1. The intrinsic nature of each planet is of primary importance.
2. The modification of this nature by rulership of house is of no less importance.
3. Further modification by location in sign and house comes next along with the influence exerted by aspects.
4. Subject to above considerations, the periods and Sub-periods of planets occupying 1, 3, 4, 5, 7, 9, 10 and 11th houses will be generally favourable and their occupation of 6, 8, and 12th houses will generally prove unfavourable. The occupation of second house is neutral except in matters concerning longevity. (There are some notable exceptions however).
5. The occupation by a sub-lord, of a house or sign that is 1, 3, 4, 5, 7, 9, 10 or 11th from that occupied by the major lord enhances the favourable significations of the sub-lord and reduces the evil if any. The occupation of other signs and houses acts unfavourably.

N. B.— Rules 2, 4 and 5 have not been noticed by Sepharial.

§ 5. EFFECTS OF PERIODS AND SUB-PERIODS

In the following sketch of results of planetary Sub-periods in major periods which is a collection from such standard works as Parasara Samhita, Phala Deepika, Saravali etc., the inherent effects of such combinations alone have been given. If the combination is a good and harmonious one, the probable good results alone are given. If evil and inharmonious, the probable evil effects are given. It is not likely however that either the good or the bad results alone described here will be experienced throughout the sub-period because the effects are subject to various modifications by ownership of houses, location, aspects etc. Hence in the application of these results to actual cases individual judgment is indispensable. Otherwise much that is promised may not happen and other events not mentioned as likely to flow from the combination may present themselves. It will not be possible to deal with all such possible combinations in this small book nor for the matter of that in any book. But readers desiring to obtain more information are referred to Parasara Samhita, a summary of which is given by Rele in his Directional Astrology of the Hindus.

MAJOR PERIOD OF SUN (6 YEARS)

Sub-lord	y	m	d
☉ (Sun)	0	3	18

Health troubles, dyspepsia, dental troubles, Fevers and colds, ailments in right ear, illness to wife, abortion, domestic troubles and misunderstandings, enmity of highly placed persons, changes in environment.

N. B.— These troubles are due only if Sun is in 6th, 8th or 12th houses. Favourable results such as good health, favour of highly placed persons etc. are to be expected, if Sun is in 1, 4, 7, 10th houses.

Sub-lord	y	m	d
☽ (Moon)	0	6	0

If well placed: Happiness, gains, vehicles, marriage etc.

If badly placed: Enmity of females, troubles in left eye, diarrhoea, accidents in water or watery diseases.

	y	m	d
♂ (Mars)	0	4	6

If well placed: gains of land, good health, auspicious celebrations.

If badly placed: Health troubles due to heat and bile, quarrels, loss of money damage to property, reduced income from lands.

	y	m	d
☊ (Rahu)	0	10	24

Health troubles incidental to intake of unwholesome food, ill health to children; accidents.

Partition in joint family or dissolution of partnership.

A son goes abroad.

Sub-lord	y	m	d
♃ (Jupiter)	0	9	18

Gains through bullion, trade etc. Success in litigation.

Purchase of real property, acquisition of cattle.

Happiness, good friends, spread of name and fame.

Birth of issue.

If badly placed : Illness to members in the family circle.

Loss of a near relative.

Heavy expenditure.

	y	m	d
♄ (Saturn)	0	11	12

Gains through black grains, objects or articles.

Auspicious celebrations.

If badly placed : Domestic troubles and estrangement, loss of cattle, grains.

Troubles through enemies; even friends become enemies.

Losses in business and decrease in affluence.

Health troubles, rheumatism, fever, diarrhoea, ulcers, strangury.

	y	m	d
☿ (Mercury)	0	10	6

Gains through trade, business, from abroad.

Increase in affluence, luxuries.

Sub-lord (Mercury contd.) y m d

Access of dignity, spread of name and fame.

Expenditure, charitable works, litigation, good health.

If badly placed: Enmity of relations, even friends turn into enemies.

Illness-eczema, boils, jaundice, abortion.

Troubles and anxieties through children. Irregular habits, short journeys.

☋ (Ketu) 0 4 6

Sorrows through relations, quarrels inside domestic circle.

Litigation, losses-money, land, vehicles, friends.

Recovery of lost property only to be lost again.

Illness-head or feet, ear or eye troubles.

Serious illness of wife or husband.

Reduction of income from real property, investments.

Long distance journeys.

Change of residence.

♀ (Venus) 1 0 0

Gain of gold and silver ornaments.

Pilgrimages to holy places.

Good food, luxuries.

Marriage, auspicious celebrations.

Cure of previous illness; but if Venus is afflicted-causes sickness.

Total 6 0 0

PERIOD OF MOON (10 YEARS)

Sub-lord	y	m	d
☽ (Moon)	0	10	0

Marriage or auspicious celebrations.

Birth of issue, Pilgrimages.

Progress in business, successful termination of projects started earlier.

Gains in bullion, cattle, grains, dealings, vehicles.

Benefits through mother or maternal relations.

Public activities, heroic actions.

Changes in residence.

♂ (Mars)	0	7	0

Health troubles, Headache, fever (malarial) or eruptive fevers.

Disorders of bile, stomach, diarrhoea etc. Quarrels and litigation between brothers and women in domestic circles.

Losses or damage through fire, theft, enemies.

Receipt of unwelcome intelligence.

Obstructions.

If well placed: Improvements to land, renovation of house etc.

☊ (Rahu)	1	6	0

Hysterical troubles, sickness to children.

Sub-lord (Rahu contd.)	y	m	d
Disorders in health through infection of food and drink, fevers, cutaneous disorders, urinary difficulties.			
Dangers through wind and fire.			
Separation and estrangements.			
Losses in trade or business, investments.			
Heavy expenditure.			
Delays and hindrances in all matters.			
Enmity of superiors.			
Birth of issue.			
♃ (Jupiter)	1	4	0
Charitable works and enterprise, help through persons of position and power.			
Increase in name and fame.			
Gains through cattle, real property investments, bullion.			
Success in litigation.			
Expansion in business, increased returns.			
Birth of son, auspicious, celebrations, luxuries.			
♄ (Saturn)	1	7	0
Break up of routine, failures.			
Taste for forbidden things.			
Debility and ill health, surgical operations.			
Losses in cattle.			

Sub-lord (Saturn contd.)	y	m	d
Enmities with relations and friends; Mischief through dark-skinned persons.			
Death of a relation.			
If well placed: Good for starting new enterprises.			
☿ (Mercury)	1	5	0
Gains through trade, dealings.			
Enjoyments, Sartorial acquisitions.			
Increase in knowledge, wealth.			
Purchase of land, construction of new buildings or outhouse.			
Dignity, appreciation, praise.			
Birth of issue.			
Long journey or going abroad.			
☋ (Ketu)	0	7	0
Public odium; dishonour.			
Swelling sickness, troubles to left eye, hurt by fire.			
Decrease in affluence.			
Inveterate enmities and misunderstandings.			
♀ (Venus)	1	8	0
Change of place to more favourable environments.			
Release from debts, increase in affluence, credit, standing, popularity with friends and relations.			

Sub-lord (Venus contd.)	y	m	d
Dealings in bullion; cultivation, gardening, additions to family circle.			
☉ (Sun)	0	6	0
Dyspepsia, gastric troubles, urinary disorders, bodily pains. Serious illness to wife. Litigation with paternal relations. Loss or alienation of property. Change of place, change of residence.			
Total	10	0	0

MAJOR PERIOD OF MARS (7 YEARS)

Sub-lord	y	m	d
♂ (Mars)	0	4	27
Enmity of close relations. Separation from brethren, family members. Business failure, winding up of business. Injuries to person, dog-bite, small-pox, skin troubles, fever, hysterical troubles. Death.			
☊ (Rahu)	1	0	18
Hysterical manifestations, cutaneous diseases, injuries to person, ailments of head and eyes. Victim of deceipt, foul play.			

Sub-lord (Rahu contd.)	y	m	d
Forced to part with usufruct of land. Decline in profits of trade, business etc., change of business or venue. Enmities and misunderstandings. Loss of relations. Death.			
♃ (Jupiter)	0	11	6
Gains of lands, wealth. Success in litigation, general success. Help of highly placed persons. Release from worries. **If badly placed:** Ear troubles, beginning of chronic respiratory troubles.			
♄ (Saturn)	1	1	9
Losses through confiscation, theft etc dissipation. Grief and wailings. Abortion, skin eruptions, gastric troubles. Fulfilment of vows, pilgrimages. Morbid cravings. Quarrels and litigation. Loss of near relations by death. Loss of position.			
☿ (Mercury)	0	11	27
Success, access of dignity, esteem. Increase in wealth. Good food, luxuries, enjoyments, vehicles.			

Sub-lord (Mercury contd.)	y	m	d
Marriage celebration.			
Academical distinctions			
Change to better surroundings.			
☋ (Ketu)	0	4	27
Mind does not function normally.			
Heavy drains on purse.			
Increase of enemies.			
Obstacles in business routine.			
Troubles due to poison, illness, of stomach and eye, Danger from electric installations.			
Family quarrels and dissensions.			
Compulsory and unwelcome journeys.			
Danger to life of wife or husband.			
♀ (Venus)	1	2	0
Popularity, name and fame.			
Happiness, luxuries in food, drink, dress, perfumes, vehicles.			
Winning over of even enemies to your cause.			
Increase in cattle wealth.			
Property through wife, or wife's people.			
Pilgrimages, holidaying, picnics.			
Business success.			
Birth of issue.			

Sub-lord	y	m	d
☉ (Sun)	0	4	6

Ill health to self and members of the family, fever, inflammatory disorders Heavy expenditure with lack of ready cash.

Failure in studies, business.

Interviews with highly placed persons.

Enemies increase.

Danger from fire.

	y	m	d
☽ (Moon)	0	7	0

Philosophical and metaphysical studies.

Rheumatic troubles, debility.

Enmities with near relations.

Losses in cattle.

Obstacles.

Improvements and repairs to house etc.

Moderate gains.

Changes in business or environment.

	y	m	d
Total	7	0	0

MAJOR PERIOD OF RAHU (18 YEARS)

Sub-lord	y	m	d
☊ (Rahu)	2	8	12

Quarrels and dispute with defeat.

Domestic unpleasantness.

Injuries to person through animals.

Poisonous ailments and danger of septic poisoning.

Sub-lord (Rahu contd.)	y	m	d
Servant or agent betrays your interests and causes undue losses, expenditure or danger. Distrust all black individuals in such a position.			
Obstacles to all projects.			
Journeys to foreign parts.			
♃ (Jupiter)	2	4	27
Gain of wealth and increase in affluence.			
Vehicles, increase in dependents, cattle wealth.			
Acquisition of real property.			
General success.			
Profits through banking or in other ways monetary deals and investments.			
Advance in metaphysical and philosophical studies.			
Marriage or re-union.			
Birth of issue.			
♄ (Saturn)	2	10	6
Falls from trees, accidents to thighs.			
Rheumatism and bilious troubles.			
Mind suffers through bad company.			
Heavy expenditure, losses, capital depreciation.			
Litigation, disputes with brothers and brethren.			
Falls from position.			
Dangerous sickness to wife.			

5

Sub-lord	y	m	d
☿ (Mercury)	2	6	18

Gains money, bullion, ornaments.

Gains through trade, capital appreciation.

Termination of litigation, strife, success.

Enjoyments, auspicious celebrations.

Marriage, birth of issue.

Good results generally, proportionate to endeavour.

	y	m	d
☋ (Ketu)	1	0	18

Piety.

Ill-health-Swellings and inflammations.

Ailments pertaining to head.

Thefts in house.

Untimely meals.

Enmities with close friends.

Illness of children.

Serious illness or death to wife.

Receipt of sorrowful news from abroad.

Danger to position.

	y	m	d
♀ (Venus)	2	8	0

Pleasure trips, globe trotting, enjoyments.

Inveterate enmities end.

Academical distinctions.

Access of wealth, luxuries.

Gain of lands, real property, cattle.

Marriage.

Sub-lord	y	m	d
☉ (Sun)	0	10	24
Misunderstandings with one's own kith and kin. Obstacles. Holy pilgrimages. Serious illness, eye troubles, ailments pertaining to head. Illness to wife and children. Expenditure, failure in litigation. Changes to—position, residence.			
☽ (Moon)	1	6	0
Falls from vehicles, accidents in water. Diabetes, jaundice, unstable health. Gain of lands. Educational successes and academical triumphs. Change to better environment. Success, auspicious celebrations. Death.			
♂ (Mars)	1	0	18
Health troubles, bile, fever, stomach disorders-gastric ulcer, jaundice, heart troubles. Marriage. Gain of wealth. Visicisstudes in business or profession. Loss by theft. Quarrels and misunderstandings.			
Total	18	0	0

MAJOR PERIOD OF JUPITER (16 YEARS)

Sub-lord	y	m	d
♃ (Jupiter)	2	1	18

Gain in lands, grain, wealth servants, vehicles.

Gain through dealings.

Gain of objects and luxuries from abroad, good credit facilities, success and prosperity.

Friendship of wealthy lords.

Marriage or auspicious celebrations.

	y	m	d
♄ (Saturn)	2	6	12

Illness: Eye troubles, rheumatic pains.

Illness to wife.

Your relatives and friends act against your interests.

Losses in dealings: through wayward son.

Difficulties in business and profession, Failure of credit.

Failure, Heavy expenditure

Unworthy companions, surroundings, criminal proceedings etc.

Relief from all these conditions before end of sub-period.

	y	m	d
☿ (Mercury)	2	3	6

Auspicious celebrations, marriage, Pilgrimages.

Sub-lord (Mercury contd.) y m d

Enjoyments, music and picnic parties etc.

Profits through trade in luxury articles, perfumes and also in other ways.

Gain in knowledge, good name, fame.

Help from superiors.

☋ (Ketu) 0 11 6

Serious illness to self, children, fever, diarrhoea; injuries from sharp instruments.

Heavy expenditure, lack of ready cash.

Losses through theft.

Troubles and sorrows through brothers and brethren.

Enmity of highly placed persons, relations.

Wanderings: Engaging in unworthy actions.

Separation from relatives and friends.

Changes in environment.

Death of wife.

♀ (Venus) 2 8 0

Gains in gold, lands, wealth, ornaments, luxuries.

Gains through advice of friends.

Release from all worries, anxieties and perplexities and embarrassing situations with peace of mind.

Harmony at home; social activities.

Sub-lord (Venus contd.) y m d

Birth of issue or other auspicious celebrations.

Appointments, promotions.

Good success in business or profession.

☉ (Sun) 0 9 18

Gain of lost property, vehicles.

Illness-head, face, eyes.

General success, prosperity, but enmities abroad.

Family dissensions.

Losses through fire, hurricane etc.

☽ (Moon) 1 4 0

Purchase of costly luxuries, vehicles real property etc.

Recovery of lost property.

Gains through trade, business, general success with defeat of rivals.

Advance in knowledge, academical qualifications.

Auspicious celebrations, birth of issue.

♂ (Mars) 0 11 6

Injuries to person from animals.

Eye troubles, inflammatory affections.

Serious illness, mental depression, gloomy outlook.

Change of place, disappointments and wanderings.

Sub-lord (Mars contd.)	y	m	d
Irregular income, losses through business rivalry.			
Debts; losses through thefts.			
Loss of near relations.			
☊ (Rahu)	2	4	24
Death of elderly relations.			
Misunderstandings and quarrels through partners' affairs.			
Serious illness, Inflammation of extremities, dental troubles.			
Losses through dissipation, deceit.			
Gains through overseas trade.			
Long journeys or voyage.			
Death.			
Total	16	0	0

MAJOR PERIOD OF SATURN (19 YEARS)

♄ (Saturn)	3	0	3
Sufferings by voluntarily involving one's self in other peoples' affairs and shouldering their responsibilities, probably relatives.			
Losses through theft, suretyship.			
Dishonour.			
Sufferings from nervous disorders, lumbago.			
Danger through water.			
Emaciation; gastric ulcer.			

Sub-lord (Saturn contd.)	y	m	d
Troubles to children, loss of children.			
Inveterate enmities arise.			
Decrease in affluence.			
Necessity to remain away from home or native country.			
☿ (Mercury)	2	8	9
Additions to ancestral property by fresh acquisitions, prosperity.			
Happiness, Enjoyments, luxuries.			
Honour, credit, good name.			
Increase of knowledge, affluence.			
Birth of issue, auspicious celebrations.			
Illness to brother and child.			
Holy pilgrimages; religious and spiritual inclinations.			
Gains through trade, business, agriculture etc.			
Favour of superiors.			
☋ (Ketu)	1	1	9
Failures in business, loss of money.			
Enmity of wife's relations and separation from them.			
Quarrels at home.			
Cutaneous disorders and blood impurities, malaria, hemicrania, rheumatic troubles.			
Irregular meals, mental distress.			

Sub-lord	y m d
♀ (Venus)	3 2 0

Liability to venereal complaints.

Gains of money agricultural produce, luxury articles, vehicles.

Builds and enters a new home; auspicious celebrations.

Esteem and goodwill of relatives, friends.

Happiness and prosperity.

Gains over rivals and overthrows enemies.

Accession to wifes properties, wealth etc.

☉ (Sun)	0 11 12

Enmity of highly placed persons and of relations caused by your own actions.

Misunderstandings with members of the family circle.

Eviction from home and familiar environments.

Loss by theft.

Wanderings in distant places.

Cutaneous infections, burning eruptions, eye disease, gastric troubles.

Accidents.

Death of elderly relations.

Loss of wife and children.

Death.

Sub-lord	y	m	d
☽ (Moon)	1	7	0

Piety and devotion, charitable acts.

Minor illnesses to wife and children. with quick recovery.

Enmity of relations, family dissensions.

Mental afflictions, serious illness.

Increase in cattle wealth, affluence.

At times great need for money and even forced to borrow.

Change of place under distressing conditions.

Colds, urinary troubles, diabetes, jaundice.

	y	m	d
♂ (Mars)	1	1	9

Eye disease, danger of accidents, arthritis.

Distress to friends and brothers.

Loss by theft, fraud, expenditure through opposite sex.

Enmities that are lasting arise.

Wanderings and change of place.

	y	m	d
☊ (Rahu)	2	10	6

Heavy expenditure practically exhausting all available resources.

Danger of imprisonment.

Diarrhoea, choleraic diarrhoea, continued fevers.

Sub-lord (Rahu contd.)	y	m	d
Germ caused diseases, danger of poisonous bites. Mental distress. Inveterate enmities and continuous troubles. Travels abroad.			
♃ (Jupiter)	2	6	12
Gains of various kinds of precious stones, costly articles, wealth, luxuries. Charitable works, spread of name and fame. Expansion of business day by day. Overthrow of rivals and success over enemies. Auspicious celebrations, baths in holy waters. Birth of sons, grandsons, happiness. Realization of one's ambition through help of powerful friends. Attainment of rank.			
Total	19	0	0

MAJOR PERIOD OF MERCURY (17 YEARS)

Sub-lord	y	m	d
☿ (Mercury)	2	4	27
Association with learned Pandits. Metaphysical studies and increase of knowledge, original research.			

Sub-lord (Mercury contd.)	y m d
Gains through trade, dealings, grain, good yield.	
Marriage, birth of issue.	
Happiness and prosperity, success.	
Charitable works.	
Acquisition of house and luxuries.	
☋ (Ketu)	0 11 27
Friends turn enemies, mental apprehension, anxieties.	
Failure of business; losses through deceit, through governmental action, thefts.	
Alienation of properties, vehicles.	
Health troubles-hysterical, afflictions of right eye, debility, falls.	
Changes in environment.	
Troubles and harassment from superiors, aimless wanderings.	
♀ (Venus)	2 10 0
Wanderings cease, good health.	
Release from all worries and debts.	
Gains wealth, luxuries, vehicles.	
Trade or speculation in bullion with profits.	
Auspicious celebrations like marriage etc., enjoyments.	
Birth of issue.	
Acquisition of knowledge, lands, wealth.	

Sub-lord	y	m	d
⊙ (Sun)	0	10	6

Anaemia, brain fever, rheumatic fever, disorders in eye-sight.

Accidents through animals, vehicles.

Illness to wife, mental anxieties.

Alienation of movable properties, cattle etc.,

Capital depreciation, unexpected reverses in business and expenditure.

Obstacles and troubles through superiors.

Danger through fire.

Enmities.

	y	m	d
☽ (Moon)	1	5	0

Increase of affluence and gains through help of friends; success and prosperity.

Acquisition of real property.

Marriage.

Domestic harmony, happiness.

N.B.— This period can prove very bad if Moon is afflictcd and badly placed and produce such results as mental afflictions, quarrels, troubles through females, anaemia, dropsy of extremeties, risk from cattle.

Sub-lord	y m d
♂ (Mars)	0 11 27

Dissipation of wealth through opposite sex.

Misunderstandings, enmities and quarrels.

Business stops or undergoes a crisis.

Indigestion, jaundice, accidents, eye troubles.

Loss of paternal relations.

Wanderings.

☊ (Rahu)	2 6 18

Dissipation of wealth through opposite sex and bad company and associations.

Apprehensions, suspicions, jealousy.

Business failure, and enmities alround, adverse litigation.

Ailments of left eye, loss of appetite, headache, hemicrania.

Changes.

Sudden opposition from unexpected quarters.

Trouble to brothers.

Death.

♃ (Jupiter)	2 3 6

Success and prosperity; access to luxuries.

Sub-lord (Jupiter contd.)	y	m	d
Acquisition of lands and wealth. Income from real property, cultivation and agricultural pursuits. Gains by trade. Pilgrimages, residence in holy places and surroundings, initiations. Marriage birth of issue. Academical qualifications.			
♄ (Saturn)	2	8	9
Change in environment. Quarrels with relations. Losses through dealings in black commodities. Reversals and bad luck. Obtuse inclinations and risky enterprises. Illness to self and members of the family Fever, inflammatary and rheumatic diseases, right leg. Loss of children. Death			
Total	17	0	0

MAJOR PERIOD OF KETHU (7 YEARS)

Sub-lord	y	m	d
☋ (Ketu)	0	4	27
Troubles and ailments through poison or sepsis; skin ailments, wound ulcers, respiratory troubles.			

Sub-lord (Ketu contd.)	y	m	d
Loss of wealth, bad news.			
Obstacles and failure in all attempts; business failure.			
Hatred of near relations and friends.			
Danger to life between September 15 to October 15 if this month occurs in this period.			
Danger of restraint, detention imprisonment.			
♀ (Venus)	1	2	0
Dealings in bullion.			
Success, happiness, luxuries			
Freedom from worries and anxieties.			
Recovery of money or articles lost or considered lost.			
Unexpected gains.			
Acquisition of real property.			
Birth of daughter.			
☉ (Sun)	0	4	6
Enforced wanderings from home.			
Illness through excessive heat, encephalitis, debility.			
Enmities, mental distress, disappointment.			
Heavy expenditure through paternal relations.			
Confinement, detention, fines.			
Illness to wife.			

Sub-lord	y	m	d
☽ (Moon)	0	7	0

Good health and spirits.

Success in business, profits in business with which the watery element is connected in some way.

Acquisition of real property vehicles.

Loss of a valuable jewel or article Thoughts of going abroad.	If Moon is badly placed or in angles.

	y	m	d
♂ (Mars)	0	4	27

Changes and removals.

Accidents, injuries, wounds, poison, danger from fire.

Waste of money, litigation, loss of property.

Hatred, enmities, mental afflictions, trouble to wife.

Obstacles.

Travel to foreign countries.

Danger to life.

	y	m	d
☊ (Rahu)	1	0	18

Ill-feelings and misunderstandings with close relations.

Ill-repute.

Litigation, loss of property waste.

Ill-health and sufferings through impure blood, infections.

6

Sub-lord (Rahu contd.) y m d

Hysteria, Epileptic affections, malaria.

Obstacles to all progress, sufferings through machinatious.

Enemies.

Loss through fire or governmental action.

♃ (Jupiter) 0 11 6

Favours with Government, success, overthrow of rivals.

Release from worries, happiness.

Good gains in business and profession.

Honour and respect.

Good health, marriage, birth of issue.

Religious tendencies.

Favourable changes and travels.

♄ (Saturn) 1 1 9

Success.

Trade in black articles, overseas commodities etc.

Beginning of new business, enterprise and gains.

Dealings in money and profits.

Respect and honour from kinsmen.

Luxuries, happiness, increase of wealth.

Illness to wife, worries.

Change of residence, foreign travels.

Interviews with exalted persons, Favours.

Sub-lord	y	m	d
☿ (Mercury)	0	11	27

Release from worries.

Gains through trade.

Material advancement of knowledge, academical successes.

Increase in wealth, prosperity, luxuries and enjoyments outside.

Acquisition of real property.

Auspicious celebrations, birth of issue.

Loss of cattle, failure of crops.

	y	m	d
Total	7	0	0

MAJOR PERIOD OF VENUS (20 YEARS)

Sub-lord	y	m	d
♀ (Venus)	3	4	0

Alround success, respect and honours.

Good gains, gains through foreign. implements or articles. Government contract.

Elevation in status, grade or rank.

Good health, enjoyments at home, luxuries, vehicles, apparel.

Recovery of lost property.

Auspicious celebrations like marriage.

Building and entry into new house.

Travels to places in the west.

Sub-lord

	y	m	d
⊙ (Sun)	1	0	0

Obstacles,heavy expenditure.

Mental distress through maternal relations.

Enforced absence away from home surroundings.

Danger of typhoid fever (if in 6th from Moon) danger from water, undiagnosed ailments if moon is lord of 7th house.

Haemorrhage or other blood disorders prove serious.

Decline in afffuence, paucity of income from immovable properties.

Estrangements, enmities of near relations, quarrels and litigation.

	y	m	d
☽ (Moon)	1	8	0

Success, gains, release from worries, enjoyments.

Cooperation of brothers and partners.

Friendship of affluent persons.

Profits through dealings, money transactions, overseas trade, iron, steel, timber.

Gifts from abroad, vehicles.

Gain through maternal relations.

Death of a maternal relation.

Profits through foreign travels in connection with business.

Sub-lord (Moon contd.) y m d

Auspicious celebrations, birth of issue.

Responsible positions and avocations.

♂ (Mars) 1 2 0

Acquisition of real property.

Success over rivals and enemies.

Considerable increase in affluence.

Pilgrimages.

Birth of issue, auspicious celebrations.

Unless well placed: will prove a difficult period in many respects such as heavy expenditure, loss of money.

Bodily illness, eye troubles, bilious disorders.

☊ (Rahu) 3 0 0

Dissensions with low caste people.

Troubles and dissensions with grown-up sons.

Wanderings from home.

Ill health through overdose of medicines or poisonous substances.

Injuries through fire; accidents.

Rheumatic troubles, gastric ulcers etc.

Wife suffers from disease.

Losses through friends.

♃ (Jupiter) 2 8 0

Favours from highly placed individuals.

Settled income.

a

Sub-lord (Jupiter contd.) y m d

Increase in affluence, general success.

Luxuries, enjoyments, auspicious celebrations.

Marriage, happiness, fame.

Birth of issue.

Philosophical studies.

♄ (Saturn) 3 2 0

Gains in business, trade, profession, dealings etc.

Success over rivals.

General success, prosperity, luxuries, enjoyments.

Health troubles, piles, rheumatism, aversion to food.

Acquisition of real property.

Birth of issue.

♀ (Venus) 2 10 0

Gains through trade.

General advancement in all matters pertaining to business, profession.

Success in litigation.

Favours from people of high position or superiors in office.

Pilgrimages, study of sacred texts, philosophy.

Academical triumph, or literary achievements.

Sub-lord (Venus contd.)	y	m	d
Acquisition of vehicles, real property etc.			
Auspicious celebrations.			
☋ (Ketu)	1	2	0
Health troubles, swellings in the body, jaundice.			
Misunderstandings with wife and family members.			
Bad company, heavy expenditure.			
Poisonous bites, infections, injuries through cattle.			
Loss of near relations, sorrows.			
Failure in undertakings.			
Total	20	0	0

CHAPTER IV

DIRECTIONAL SYSTEMS IN WESTERN ASTROLOGY

§ 1. GENERAL

Both astronomical and symbolic systems are in vogue in the West and the latter are of comparatively recent origin. In both systems, the horoscope of birth is the basis and the planets and angles are progressed in a particular manner to form aspects with radical positions and the nature and timing of events are judged from these aspects according to well recognised rules of interpretation. The system of periods and sub-periods to judge events is absent in Western astrology and Alfridares is only a poor substitute for it and has never functioned as a system of direction.

The only difference between the two systems lies in the fact that in the former, the position of planets and angles as they move along the Zodiac at their respective rates of motion along the equator or the ecliptic are considered. The symbolic systems are different only in the sense that all the angles and the bodies are progressed at a uniform rate in the Zodiac. Yet the astronomical systems so called cannot be said to be wholly free from **Symbolism** in any shape or form because in the Primary system the movement of planetary bodies and angles during 4 minutes and in the secondary system during 24 hours are held to symbolise the events of one year and this is nothing but a symbolic expansion of the time scale. An aspect which is formed say 20 days after birth is said to take effect twenty years after birth.

The basis of the symbolic systems of the West is the same as the basis in the Dasa system of the Hindus where the Moon is symbolically moved through equal divisions of the Zodiac to represent the effects of different planets for different periods of time.

A brief sketch of the evolution of symbolic systems in general in the West has already been given in Chap I. It is now necessary only to describe the extant symbolic systems of directing before we can proceed to the **New Era Measures** which are themselves an evolution from the existing systems.

§ 2. RADIX SYSTEM

This system of direction was propounded by Sepharial in 1918. The measure suggested by Sepharial is 59′ 8″ to one year based on the average motion of Sun per day-similarly Moon's average motion per day 13° 10′ 35″ is also utilised for the lunar directions. Ever since its introduction this system became popular and in 1930 Robson published "The Radix System" with extensions and additions of his own. The extensions made by Robson are (1) the application of the measures to the cusps of the radical horoscope in addition to the longitudes of the planetary bodies

(2) working converse directions with the same measures (3) the introduction of mundane parallels, rapt parallels, quadrate parallels (4) midpoints. The claims of the author as to the merits of this system so worked are best given in his own words*. " It will be found that a conscientious and methodical study of the different classes of directions described will enable the student to time the event to the day and if he cares to take the trouble to the very hour and minute " and the **procedure** laid down by the author to attain this result is given in that book as follows :—

(1) Erect the directional chart and calculate the major directions, parallels, and cuspal directions.

(2) Erect the converse chart and calculate the converse directions.

(3) Tabulate all major directions and note signs and houses involved.

(4) Calculate the lunar minor directions both direct and converse and the minor directions of the bodies involved in the major arcs. Note the stimulation of the latter and look to transits and diurnal passages of the angles to define the day and time of the operation.

(5) For general monthly influences, pay chief attention to the Moon etc. etc.

Not being familiar with the current astrological literature of the West, I am not in a position to state whether the system as outlined above is being practised

---

* Robson's Astrological Series No. 1. P. 60.

for purposes of prediction and if so by what proportion of Astrologers and with what results.

The adoption of the astronomical mean motion of Sun and Moon as standard measures in this scheme does not make this system "purely" symbolical however and I would call purely symbolical the systems expounded by Frankland and Carter where the measure of one degree = one year of life is the **basis** of almost all measures suggested by them.

§ 3. FRANKLAND'S MEASURES

Frankland seems to have at first conceived of symbolic measures only as furnishing a basis for estimating the strength or weakness of the native's position to react to the directional influences in force by Primary, Secondary methods rather than as an independent system by itself. In his earlier work* he suggests two measures only and these are applied to the Zodiac beginning with V. E. (1) **Point of Life.** This point is deemed to move from 0° ♈ at the rate of $4\frac{2}{7}°$ to one year and the position of the planets in the horoscope are compared with the areas thus marked off and related to corresponding events or experience. This is illustrated by some examples. (2) **Age along the Zodiac :** This is moved at the rate of one degree per year from V. E. and aspects formed by this method are similarly related to the other points of the nativity. In his later book † a more

* Frankland's Astrological Investigations.

† Keys to symbolic Directing (Feb. 9, 1930.)

comprehensive system is evolved which is summed up with the following words "The system here laid down lays no claim to perfection. It is given in the belief that by these methods valuable results can be obtained with a minimum of labour and a maximum percentage of success".

Briefly stated, the methods of this system are :—

(1) Examine the point of life for any partieular year.

(2) Apply $\frac{4}{7}^{\circ}$ per year to the Nativity.

(3) Apply this measure of $\frac{4}{7}^{\circ}+70$ as well as $\frac{3}{7}^{\circ}+70$. Having formed an estimate of the influences overshadowing the year as a whole.

(4) Multiply the age in years by 20, call the result degrees, and use the measure for ascertaining the particular parts of the year affected.

These methods comprise a system that will amply repay the student". For a wealth of other details and examples furnished in proof thereof, I must needs refer the reader to the abovementioned work. But I can say here and now that directions as per item (3) in the above scheme applied to the event of assasination of Mahatma Gandhi are very characteristic and be speaks the validity of the method employed.

§ 4 CARTER'S MEASURES.

Carter evolved his system of symbolic directions out of the existing materials, and not only enriched and enlarged their scope by adding some measures of his own but also suggested the possible future lines of development. As the New Era System of Symbolic Directions is developed further along these lines, it is necessary for a proper understanding and apprecia-tion of the principles contained herein that Carter's system has to be noticed in greater detail than the others that preceded his. I am not aware of any further developments in the West beyond the limits fixed by Carter in the matter of Symbolic Directions.

Three stages are discernible in the evolution of Carter's system. His earliest exposition of the system I find in Chap VI of his Zodiac and the Soul* where he suggests that the use of the one degree method and lunar secondaries and transits would constitute a pretty complete guide to the life. He also visualises the possibilities of a Fractional system of Directing and gives illustrations of $\frac{1}{7}°$=one year and concludes thus, "I trust the above examples will tell the reader all there is at present to know about this system. Some inklings of which I have had in my mind for a year or two but which I have only recently investigated sufficiently to embolden me to lay it before the astrological world as a contribution towards the symbolical aspect of the science. **I hope that it will arouse some interest and may even achieve something towards the permanent**

* Chap. VI. The Zodiac and the Art of Directing P. 64. (September 1928)

elucidation of our directional difficulties which have generated a weltering *melee* of Conflicting practices. I would warn students not to judge fractional directions too separatively; it is necessary to calculate all the important arcs for a period and to judge them collectively. It is very often impossible, or at any rate very misleading to try to take life to pieces; it is an organic whole, and so too in a true directional system all the parts are interlocked. Subject to this, the system is very simple and easily tested **but it is highly probable that a great deal may yet be discovered about it. For instance it may well be found that each fraction has its own character.** I hope I will be pardoned for the full quotation of the text as I found it could not be 'taken to pieces'. The portions italicised are my own and it is my modest claim that the ideas and the hope contained in them have been fulfilled in the **New Era Measures of Directing** and to that extent I would state that they have proved prophetic indeed. As a supplementary following the above quotation by me Carter has pointed out the value of the duodenary measure in directions and given some illustrations also.

Further investigation along the same lines led to the publication of "Symbolic Directions in Modern Astrology" by Carter and the final conclusions arrived at by the author are best given in the summary at the end of the book and a workable plan for calculating the Directions is also superadded:—

(1) The Calculation of the directions of all bodies by $\frac{8}{7}^\circ$ measure or by $\frac{4}{7}^\circ$ measure, whichever the student finds more exact *

(2) The same with the one - degree and duodenary progression ($2\frac{1}{2}^\circ$ to one Year) bearing in mind the fact that the results of the former (in particular) may be spread over several years after exactitude.

(3) The Sub duodenaries ($12\frac{1}{2}'$ to one Year) are few in Number, the measure being very slow but they appear valuable acting over prolonged periods.

(4) The point of life should be included.

(5) Important lunar and interplanetary secondaries should be calculated especially conjunctions and oppositions.

(6) Major aspects by the Sun and Moon according to the R. A. method........though never very different from the corresponding one-degree directions are valuable because of their frequent closeness in time especially for one who for any reason desires this feature.

(7) Eclipses, lunations, and transits should all be observed and noted if they fall near any important radical place.

For the plan of working these directions I must necessarily refer the reader to the above-mentioned

---

* Note that the $\frac{4}{7}^\circ$ Measure is for bad and $\frac{8}{7}^\circ$ Measure is for good events as suggested by Frankland the originator of the measure.

work as it will occupy too much space if given here. Finally the learned author observes that novenaries and septenaries are probably less important than the methods tabled above and may be left for enthusiasts. Numerous examples illustrate the above measures. For purposes of exactitude, the measure of 59′ 8″×12 to the year is suggested.

This subject is again touched upon by the author in his Principles of Horoscopic Delineation. He says therein* " In my own work on the subject numerous symbolic measures are adduced to show their efficacy. It is however not intended that in practice all these increments should be employed but they should be tested and that each student should adopt those that he finds most effective. The above four progressions are my selection." These four are " I have found the most reliable to be $2\frac{1}{2}$° to a year as a quick measure, 1° to a year as a medium measure and $\frac{1}{4}$° and $\frac{1}{8}$° to a year as slow measures which occur comparatively rarely. All these can be employed as supplements to the transits and secondaries and angular progressions........If I abandoned all others I would at least retain the 1° to a year measure." The aspects recommended are limited to conjunction, opposition, square, trine and sextile along with Parallel of Declination.

Before proceeding to describe the New Era Measures in directing I wish to refer to another measure suggested by an Indian Astrologer.

* Chap. X. Directional Delineation P. 126 at 135

F. C. Dutt* who divides the Zodiac of 360° by 100 the normal span of human life in years) and derives his measure of 3° 36′ to one year. This is very close to the novenary measure of 3° 20′ to one year suggested by Carter but the difference in arc will be considerable as years advance. I have not tested these measures sufficiently to pronounce an opinion on either or upon their comparative merits.

---

* Predictive Astrology P. 54

CHAPTER V

NEW ERA DIRECTIONS

§. 1 ORIGIN

"In certain circles there is a strong dislike of the symbolic methods and the question of the place that they will occupy after another twenty-five years or so can be only a matter of conjecture." Thus wrote Mr. Carter in March 1934 and nearly twenty years have gone by. It is about 26 years since these measures called New Era Measures were conceived and begun to be tested. They have stood the tests in the author's experience and some predictions made for this distance of time are being fulfilled now. Mere dislike of any system in certain quarters has never destroyed any system if it contained even a germ of truth. The derivation of the measures from the divisions of the Zodiac and assigning each measure its character accordingly was the first idea and this idea has not suffered any modifications up to now. But other changes from the original conception were made from time to time while they were being tested and it is the final form that is presented here.

The first change that was made was from the Sayana Zodiac (Tropical Zodiac) to the Chitra Zodiac. In the beginning it was the Tropical Zodiac that was started with and worked. The second change was from the Placidean method of domification to the trisection method of house division. The third was to limit the number of aspects as well as the range of orbs; and the fourth was the principle of averaging the directions for purposes of exactitude. None of the changes are new in conception. The first two mean only closer adherence to tradition and the other two have already been suggested by Carter. But their combination as parts of a single system of directing which is self-sufficient without other adventitious aids from other modes of directing is what may be said to be unique and my final conclusion at present is that all these changes are amply justified. But it is not claimed that this is the last word in symbolic directions. Other changes may be deemed necessary by the author or by others who are more proficient in the science.

Ample proofs will be furnished in the following pages by means of illustrations with nativities well-authenticated as to time and place of birth and already published. In fact the very cases dealt with by the learned authors above referred to are taken up as examples so that a comparison of results can be made without difficulty and an independent verdict can be given by any student who cares to apply his mind to the task. It is not claimed that the ideal system has been found. For, as M. Blavatsky says such a system may not be within the reach of the uninitiated. The aim has been to make a near approach to the ideal which in the definition of Carter† would provide an event or at least some appropriate unfoldment for each direction, and a direction for each event each appropriate to each and also synchronous within a reasonable limit."

To the mind of a Hindu there is nothing objectionable in pursuing symbolic methods of directing. To him it is more natural than the astronomical methods. To the Hindu symbolism is his lifebreath. He sees the symbol of the Universal Spirit in the little idol he worships at home or in the temples. To him the Sun-God is a visible representation of the one Almighty. He addresses him "You are Brahma, you are Vishnu, you are Siva." "You create beings. You are also their destroyer only to create them anew etc." Coming to Astrology, as Harwood asks, what is not symbolical? "The whole of Astrology, indeed may be termed the symbology the language, the human message, which astronomical factors convey to mankind.‡ It is believed here that astronomy was developed to serve the ends of astrology. In very ancient times a certain position or a configuration of the Heavenly bodies was observed to tally with certain terrestrial phenomena. This observation was astrology. To find only when such a configuration would take place next is astronomy. Astronomy was the handmaid of astrology in the past at any rate in India.

† Principles of horoscopical delineation P. 136

‡ Primary Directions by The Polar Angle Method P 24

Symbolism is the link between the seen and unseen spheres. The ancient seers who were more familiar with the unseen spheres and were able to correlate the two in better fashion have handed down to us only symbolic systems of direction and plenty of them. They were aware of the Precession of the Equinoxes and calculated the rate of its annual retrogression to a nicety that has excited the admiration of modern astronomers only to deduct it from the longitudes of the planets and cusps of houses when the matter of judgment and prediction was taken up. Therefore it seems only logical to apply symbolic measures to the Sidereal Zodiac. Here no suggestion is made that the Tropical Zodiac of the West is not valid nor that it has produced no results whatever. Which is better, or both better is the only question that arises.

When the position thus far reached is assumed or granted, the trisection method of house division being the only one handed to us (Hindus) seemed a logical sequence. But it was not any considerations of theory that induced the adoption of either the Fixed Zodiac or the trisection method of house-division. These are only as stated above, latter day developments in the New Era system of Directing forced on the writer by the results in hundreds of cases that came under his notice or were submitted to him. Nor is it his wish that anybody should grant or concede this position but follow this argument to the finish and go through all the examples given here before pronouncing a verdict.

But what was conceived in theory very early and rigidly adhered to all these years was the derivation of the measures from the twelvefold division of the Zodiac. In the extant systems of symbolic directing hitherto noticed, the principles of Kabala were applied to the Zodiac to derive the symbolic measures. The utterance of the Psalmist David that the days of our years are three-score years and ten has led Frankland to utilise number 70 to derive his measures.* He divides 360° (circle) by 70 to derive $5\frac{1}{7}°$ which again divided by 9 (number of Mars) yields the measure 4/7- Dividing $5\frac{1}{7}°$ by 12 (the number of signs) the measure of $\frac{3}{7}$ is derived and these two measures are treated as being complementary to each,—"They are the Divisions of the mystic 7 that are symbolic, of the four elements and three qualities. They are the symbol of the Cross and the Trinity of Acuteness and Harmony." From these two, the other measures of $\frac{4}{7}°+70°$ $\frac{3}{7}+70°$ are evolved. Again for purposes of an exactitude measure this number 70 is deducted from 90 (quadrant of circle) and the measure 20° to one year is recommended for this purpose. Referring to this $\frac{4}{7}°$ measure Sepharial suggests it would be more accurate if $\frac{3}{5}°$ measure is adopted instead. This also is stated to be derived through Kabala by dividing the circle of 360° by the Naronic period of 600 years which yields the required fraction. We have seen that F. C. Dutt has recommended a division of the circle of 360° by 100 the normal span

---

* Keys to Symbolic Directions P. 52, 55-57,

of human life. The difference between $\frac{4}{7}°$ measure and $\frac{3}{5}°$ measure is not much and amounts to only $\frac{1}{35}°$ but will increase by one degree in every 35 years. But it is to be borne in mind that Sepharial never recommends the adoption of the Naronic measure as an independent system of direction but says that the astronomical directions are found to gain additional significance when the two sets of indications agree. Mr. Carter derives his measure of death from the number 4. "the number of manifestation; under its influence we assume and discard our physical frames".*

My own idea is that when the principles of Kabala were applied to the Zodiac to derive directional measures, the course of Symbolic Directing in the West was shunted on to a devious route. This procedure cannot possibly be wrong as the results show. The writer was also carried along that route before he could arrive at his present conclusions; and now that a shorter way is found I consider the other measures as no longer necessary and the measures here described are quite self-sufficient; at any rate these may be viewed as an alternative or an additional system.

The argument advanced here is that the twelvefold division of the Zodiac is a self-sufficient basis for the derivation of directional measures. The Zodiac is divided into twelve equal parts for all purposes in

---

Symbolic Directions in Modern Astrology P. 70.

Astrology and each division stands for a certain type of activity human or mundane:— the first for body and general characteristics, the second for wealth, the third for brethren, short journeys, the fourth for mother, conveyances etc; the fifth for issue, speculation etc, the sixth for illness, accidents and enemies, the seventh for partnership but principally for marriage and married life, the eighth for legacies, death etc; the ninth for long journeys, voyages, the tenth for profession, business, credit etc, the eleventh for gains, friends etc and twelfth for losses, confinement, duress etc. The scheme of twelvefold division is peculiar to the Zodiac whereas I fancy it is not so in Kabala, where number 9 is the appropriate limit. There is no extension up to twelve. Either all numbers are reduced to nine or any lesser number or goes on in an unbroken series to more than one digit. The scheme of twelvefold division is a complete self-sufficient unit in astrology which is based on the Zodiac and comprises all activities. The two systems are separate and do not necessarily square or fit into each other though there are analogies, It is not to be thought for a moment that the system of directions based on measures derived Kabalistically is disparaged here though it is claimed that the present system appears to yield superior results, and self-sufficient for all practical purposes without recourse to any astronomical methods or even transits as an adjunct. The writer does not feel concerned about its future. If it is based on truth and also found to be useful it will take its proper place among other systems of direction in vogue and if found to be better than others, will survive all others; otherwise fade into oblivion in due course.

This idea of deriving measures from the natural divisions of the Zodiac arose when both $\frac{3}{5}°$ (Naronic) and $\frac{4}{7}°$ (measure of Frankland) were worked to produce directions for the death of King Edward VII and compared with each other. Then $\frac{7}{12}°$ measure was found to work apparently better and closer than either of the above measures. **The apple fell.** 7/12 was the fraction which the 8th sign bore to the circle of the Zodiac and Scorpio the eighth sign represents death. Because of this definite pointer, the idea was tested in numerous other cases and the measure stood the tests well. Then the application of this principle was extended to other signs and similar measures were derived such as $\frac{1}{2}°$ to one year for marriage and other events of the 7th house, $\frac{5}{12}°$ to one year for illness and accidents, $\frac{3}{4}°$ to a year for profession and these were put to test in a very large number of cases and were found to give a high degree of satisfaction in the results. Thus New Era directions were born. Carter's observation in "the Zodiac and the Art of Directing" that a great deal may yet be discovered about it (fractional directing) and that each fraction may have its own character has indeed proved prophetic. In laying claim to this original departure, I do not disclaim that all the materials provided by the above two authors (Frank-

and Carter) were necessary to give birth to these. Without such material before me, this discovery could not have been made and in presenting this work to the world, I fully acknowledge my indebtedness to these two great authors as I have availed myself fully of the suggestions thrown out by them in their writings and freely copied their methods though not their substance.

These measures were first tested with longitudes as per Tropical Zodiac. Then the Sidereal Zodiac forced itself upon the scene because of superior results. Similarly, these measures were only tested at first with Placedian tables, and cusps according to these tables. The cusps by the trisection method were also tried side by side and there was sufficient difference in their results in favour of the latter method to justify its adoption exclusively. That is why to facilitate the study of this work horoscopical data is furnished according to the above requirements, namely Nirayana longitudes with horoscopes constructed on the trisection method of house division. I do not doubt for a moment that in some cases the very same horoscopes converted to conform to the Western system may produce results that are even superior illustrating the validity of that Zodiac also. But I do not also doubt that in the majority of cases the system adopted here will give better results. After all, the difference is not much as in these directions we are concerned with the relative distances between planetary bodies and angles and this is the same for both horoscopes.

It is only in directions to the Zodiacal points and to cusps (5th, 8th and 9th) that differences are likely to arise and such directions form only a small minority of the total number of directions in any group.

§ 2. NEW ERA MEASURES

The twelve divisions of the Zodiac furnish the twelve measures of the scheme 1/12°, 1/6°,·1/4°, 1/3°, 5/12°, 1/2°, 7/12°, 2/3°, 3/4°, 5/6 11/12° and one degree. Of these twelve, some can be safely ignored for purposes of predicting events. e. g. 1/12, 1/6, 5/6 and 11/12. These were found to have not much of practical value. They are valid of course but do not represent important events in life, and come in only very rarely. **One degree measure is the all-important measure.** Carter says even if he would abandon all other measures he would still this one. In this book, the arcs formed by the application of the one degree are designated B. A. (Basic Arc). The arcs furnished by the other measures, as they indicate the specific nature of the event or events to be expected are termed C. A. (characteristic arcs). As there are several such measures the fraction of that C. A. has also to be indicated. Thus measure of death is 7/12. When directions are formed by this measure the appropriate designation would be C. A. (7/12). When the measure of marriage is worked it would be indicated as C. A. (1/2). The measure of accidents would be C. A. (5/12). The measure of the meridian would be C. A. (3/4). The reversed measure also is part of the scheme. The reversed measure for death would be 12/7°, for accidents 12/5°; for marriage 2/1°, for profession 4/3° and so on and they will be indicated by the symbol R.C.A. (12/7), R.C.A. (12/5), R.C.A. 2°, and so on.

Suppose the year of life for which directions are to be worked is 24th year. B. A. is 24°. If the seventh house matters such as chances for marriage have to be ascertained, C. A. of course is 24×1/2=12° and R.C.A. 24×2=48°. Directions have to be worked for all these three arcs to see whether such an event will happen. Suppose the professional aspect for that year has to be estimated. B. A. is 24°. C. A. is 24×3/4=18° and R.C.A. will be 24×4/3=32°. These three arcs have to be taken into consideration.

§ 3. ADVANTAGES

First, these measures are easy to work; secondly the measures themselves give a clue to the nature of the event and a lot of trouble is saved for ascertaining in what department of life a particular direction will precipitate its effects by a judgment from the location, rulership, intrinsic nature etc of the planets that form the directions. Thirdly the whole life can be planned out easily for any particular sphere of activity in advance quite easily by working out the directions formed by the appropriate C. A. and R. A. The beginner who does not want to have to work too much may quite well content himself by taking C. A. alone and judging directions formed by this measure. He will find matters to his entire satisfaction as this has

been found to demarcate all the principal events of a life with reasonable accuracy. No other aid from any of the astronomical systems of direction or even from transits has been found to be necessary though if transits are also to be taken into account according to a new system evolved by your author,* the very day can be easily ascertained.

One possible objection is here met. It may be said that there are twelve measures in this system and if both C. A. and R. A. are to be worked it will amount to 36 measures for each year and this is really too many for any system of directions. This difficulty is only in theory and will not be felt in actual practice as will be evident if the student follows the plan of working suggested. The measure 5′ to one year as also 10′ to a year will not occupy any time and may be even generally ignored. The measure 15′ to a year will come in for greater attention and will not in actual working necessitate examination for each year of life as one degree itself covers four years. Nor will the measure 20′ to the year bother the student very much. **The principal fractions that will lead all others in demarcating the life events are 5/12, 1/2, 7/12, 3/4, 2/3 and these are not too many.**

§ 4. TIMING EVENTS

The above plan of working B. A. and the appropriate C. A. (even leaving out R. A.) directions will suffice for the reading of any life and can be accomplished with far less trouble than is involved in

* Transits in the New Era (in preparation.)

any other system of directing. Life sketches prepared for a large number of clients on the basis above suggested have proved very satisfactory. Events predicted have happened even in the month and year foretold but in a large majority of cases within a few months of the time of prediction. Therefore further investigations were made to bring the event closer to the time indicated by the directions and a special technique has been developed which would enable any astrologer to time events within a month. It was found that an average of the various directions as per C. A. measures was good enough but the best solution was presented by an average of the time indications of directions as per B. A., C. A., and R.C.A. measures and it is this method that has been followed throughout in the examples cited to illustrate the working of New Era measures and those who want meticulous accuracy in their predictions can follow this method and secure the desired results. Suppose the chances for marriage in the 25th year of a native's life have got to be examined. The arcs for this year are 25° (B. A); 12°30′ (C. A.); 50° (R.C.A.). Directions are to be worked for each of these arcs and an average of the time indications struck for each. Then the grand average for all these three averages will point to the month of marriage. This method also serves as an excellent means of rectifications of birth time. Examples for all these will be given in the ensuing pages.

§ 5. FACTORS FOR DIRECTION

As already noticed, there are twelve planets that have to be taken into account. Asc and M. C. are necessary factors in any system of directions. In addition the relevant cusp has to be taken as a point for directing and the arcs have also to be applied to the points of the Zodiac and directions noted. No other points for direction enter into this scheme. The Part of Fortune is not included nor midpoints, not because their efficacy is denied but because they have been found unnecessary. At least there is some controversy as regards Part of Fortune; some go to the extent of denying for it any authority. One word as regards mid-points This writer considers them very useful, especially when two planets are close to each other. They also have the support of a number of first rate astrologers, such as Alan Leo, Sepharial, Robson, Carter and in the East F.C. Dutt. Robson says* "The importance of mid-points, has been realised only within the last few years and there is still much to be discovered concerning them. It is probable that aspects from the luminaries and planets to the mid-points will prove to be of considerable importance and the student is advised to make a list of all the mid-points in his horoscope and keep them under constant observation." Mid-points are very good material for research purposes but this author feels that in a well-defined system of directions they have no place. The number of points that are utilised for directions is already large and each planet has necessarily a mid-point with every other planet and if they are to be included the number of factors for direction will become unwieldy. Still in this system, the mid-points neces-

* Radix System P. 50 - 51

sarily play their part without adding to the number as their effects will be embodied in the average and grand average timings of events. Now-a-days there is a tendency to extend the factors for direction still further by including heliocentric longitudes, longitudes of hypothetical planets that have yet to be discovered, longitudes of fixed stars etc. The writer confesses to an 'invincible" dislike for such a procedure as there will be no end and the art of prediction would become extremely and needlessly complicated, whereas it is his object to simplify it still further. Nor has any necessity been felt to include progressed places of planetary bodies and angles for then the question will arise, progressed according to what system of progression and there are so many in the field. As this New Era System of directing is brought forward as a symbolic system complete and self-contained by itself, my own view is, it would be illogical to apply these symbolic measures to astronomically progressed positions of planets or angles.

§ 6. ASPECTS

These have been strictly limited as already observed :-only conjunction, opposition, sextile, square, trine and quincunox are taken into consideration. Not even parallel of declination. This greatly adds to ease of working the directions for, to do all the directing that has to be done under this system, no other thing than the horoscope of birth is necessary. If parallels are to be included constant reference to the Ephemeris will be necessary. Another parctical convenience that arises from the limitations of aspect to those above-named is that you do not have to add or subtract 15 degrees or any other quantity to the longitudes in the horoscope to see whether aspects are formed or not which will be certainly necessary when such aspects as semi-square, sesqui-quadrate, quintile, bi-quintile are included. All the aspects under this scheme will have the same longitude (degree and minute) as the planets, or other sensitive points of the radical horoscope because aspects based on subdivisions of signs have been omitted. They are not omitted because they can have no value whatever. They are certainly weaker and their inclusion adds greatly to the number of directions which is bound to make them unwieldy and they do not contribute materially towards the definition of the events or their timings and in averaging they more or less cancelled each other out.

§ 7. ORBS OR RANGE

It has been usual to allow one degree of orb to all directions in the symbolic directional systems in general irrespective of the fact whether the measure applied is a slow or rapid one. The result is that there is a great variation in their range from the point of view of the period allowed for their action. If the measure adopted is a slow one e. g. subduodenary ($12\frac{1}{2}'$ to a year) or 15′ to a year (Carter's measure of death) and if one degree range is allowed for each of one of these measures there will be a total range of $9\frac{3}{5}$ years in the one case and 8 years in the case of the other for their action to manifest as events. In my estimation it is too liberal, though these measures may have effects for such duration of time as a sort of background influence lasting so long for their formation and dissolution. I believe that any measure that is held to extend its influence beyond one year either way will not to be of much value as indicative of the timing of an event. This limitation is imposed solely for purposes of averaging the time indications of directions and does not mean that the directions have no influence at all beyond this range. Averaging is not new and has been done before, notably by Carter; but he averaged the directions, formed with any group of fractions without any time limits. In this system, averaging is confined to directions formed by a measure or a specified set of measures, and only to such directions as are formed within one year less before and after the time of happening of a particular event. It is not therefore to be inferred from this that the author is of opinion that aspects have no effect at all beyond these limits. Far from it. They are to be considered as back - ground influences potent to change with their influence, the operation of the directions formed within orbs as regards the nature of the event but they do not seem to affect the timing to any great extent and are not reckoned in this scheme for this reason only. This limit is intended only as a convenient method of timing the action of directions and if it is found to serve that purpose in a large majority of cases as will be amply demonstrated in these pages, there can be virtually no objection to its being adopted as an astrological technique in working directons, if nothing more. The measures themselves are rooted in the cosmic principles underlying the structure of the Zodiac and the limitation as to aspects and orbs are only a working rule of convenience.

§ 8. CHOICE OF EXAMPLES FOR ILLUSTRATION

Therefore it is that the examples given here to illustrate this rule have been taken only from already published and well authenticated sources, nay, the very cases selected by exponents of other methods of directing have been mostly employed. It is thus possible to compare the results given by each method without much difficulty or labour. Wherever possible, cases have been taken group by group, or in a series e. g. the crowned heads of England, the greatest men of India and so on so that there can be no room for any criticism that the cases have been selected for purposes of demonstration. Criticisms there should be and *constructive* criticism should always be welcomed as that is the only method by which existing flaws could be brought to light and will be gratefully acknowledged. For, in the history of astrology, or in the history of any science for the matter of that no perfect system came out from the mind of a single individual ready made however clever he may be or think he is.

CHAPTER VI

LONGEVITY

§ 1. GENERAL

The determination of the length of life is a difficult matter and success is attained only after years of experience in judgment. Still this is the first task that confronts the astrologer at the outset in the reading of a nativity and he has to arrive at some conclusion or other before proceeding to other matters.

The Text Says*

जाते कुमारे सति पूर्वमार्यैरायुर्विचिन्त्यं हि ततः फलानि।

"The first thing to be done by elders when a son is born is the determination of longevity or otherwise, and then only the others."

Sripatipaddathi Chapter V Verse 1.

आयुर्ज्ञानादेव होराफलानां कर्तुं यस्मान्निर्णयः शक्यतेऽत्र।

"Since the affirmation or proof of the events to be predicted by means of astrology at a person's nativity is possible only upon a correct knowledge of the extent of his life etc.

Ptolemy says the same thing in chap. XI of his Tetrabiblos " Duration of Life, "—" Of all the events

* Phaladeepika Chap. XIII Verse 1

whatsoever which take place after birth the most essential is the continuance of life and it is of course useless to consider in cases where the life of the child does not extend to the period of one year what other events contingent on its birth might otherwise have subsequently happened, the enquiry into the duration of life consequently takes precedence of all other questions, as to the events, subsequent to birth." Simmonite*' puts it more briefly thus,—" Of all events which take place immediately after birth, the chief is the duration of life; for it is useless to consider events contingent on the birth if the duration of life is very short and the discussion of the enquiry is by no means simple and easy of execution." Ptolemy, Simmonite and all other later writers, give certain rules by which this important matter could be judged. The works of Sepharial, Alan Leo, Robson, Carter etc contain a Chapter on Longevity. In the latest text books however, this feature is noticeably absent e. g., Hone's Modern Text Book of Astrology which and the entire work contains barely any reference to this important matter. Even with such rules as are given for guidance the determination of the actual length of life by the computation of all directions to find out when the strain of bad directions will be too severe to sustain life still remains a stupendous task.

The ancient writers abovenamed have given elaborate rules based on the 'Hyleg'. But later writers have not attached the same importance to this factor. The earliest rules for ascertaining the Hylegiacal

* Arcana of Astrology § 247.

a

place in a horoscope were given by Ptolemy. But so many alternative suggestions have been made since, that at present there is no general consensus of opinion as to which is the 'Hyleg'. Even if this is settled in some fashion, there is some difference as to what it signifies, health or length of life or both. There is also difference as to whether it is constant throughout life or shifts as the horoscope progresses. With all this, grave doubts have been entertained as regards its validity in authenticated quarters. Carter says* "The examination of a few dozen cases of early death or on the other hand of examples of marked longevity will probably cause the student to entertain grave doubts on the whole question of the hyleg for it is not hard to find cases where death seems certainly due to a violent affliction to a luminary in the 4th house or at least well removed from hylegiacal positions, and instances are also found where the native has attained great age with the hyleg violently afflicted". Therefore it is no wonder that 'hyleg' does not figure largely or at all in modern Text Books in connection with the longevity question.

§ 2. HINDU ASTROLOGY

In Hindu Astrology, there is much better guidance. From the radical horoscope a judgment is made as to which of the categories, the nativity belongs:- (1) Balarishta or period of infant mortality extending

* Principles of Astrology Chap. VII

up to 12 years of age (2) Alpayu or short life (12-33 years) (3) Madhyayu or medium life (34-70 years) and Poornayu or long life extending upto 100 years. The nearest approach to this conception in Western Astrology has been made by Alan Leo who had been to India and had discussions with celebrated Indian Astrologers. He says.* "Directions are always of secondary importance to radical indications; and it is highly probable that a fuller knowledge of the subject may enable us to judge not merely the events of the life **but also the time of their occurrence from the birth map alone, without needing to have recourse to any of the present day systems of directing.** In dealing with this question of probable length of life it is convenient to divide nativities, roughly speaking into three classes: those that die young, in infancy, or childhood; those that live to middle age; and those that endure to old age". But he is careful to add however that they are intended only as rough approximations for the convenience of the student and not as scientific divisions. But they are such in Hindu Astrology.

In spite of the importance of the subject, it cannot be said that either in the East or in the West the matter of determination of longevity has received the attention it deserves at the hands of modern text writers. Modern text-books in Hindu Astrology cite a number of combinations for each of the above classes of life and the matter is left at that. In some, the rules for ascertaining the maraka lords (death

---

* How to Judge a Nativity P. 145.

inflicting planets for a particular horoscope) are given and the student is left to judge the longevity therefrom. Even special treatises on longevity only give the principal methods-mathematical and otherwise. But I have to acknowledge the great help I have derived from "Span of Life" by G. Sri Ramamurthi.

According to either system of Astrology, the task of judging longevity is not easy. As regards the directions to determine the time of death Carter* says that the conventional systems of direction are of uncertain value and the general rules are quite inadequate and brings forward his 'Measure of Death' to remedy this defect. Compared with the Western methods the Hindu method of judging duration of life by a set of rules provided therefor and also the maraka lords and calculating when their periods fall due is much more definite and satisfactory.

With all the difficulties of this subject in full view an attempt is made here to present an orderly system synthesising various methods and practices collected from a variety of sources by which the longevity of a horoscope can be judged and the time of death determined with a fair degree of accuracy and without much trouble. This not being a special thesis on the subject, the matter cannot be exhaustively dealt with.

§ 3. CLASS OF LIFE

This has to be judged from the (1) general strength of the nativity, ascendant, third and eighth

* Symbolic Directions in Modern Astrology P. 67

houses and their lords, (2) Formulae (Set rules prescribed for this very purpose). Naturally these are to be related to the Nirayana Zodiac.

General strength : For long life, the ascendant lord should be strong and well placed as also lords of 3rd and 8th houses. They should be in conjunction with benefics or aspected by them. These should occupy angular houses. The strength of Sun as giver of vitality and Saturn as conservor of vitality is important for long life. If the testimony in above respects is unequivocal and no evil aspects bear upon lagna, 3rd and 8th houses the native would reach an age between 70-100 years. If mixed conditions prevail, some of the influences being strong, and others not so, judge life to belong to the medium group (34 to 70 years). In the case of adverse testimony in almost all the above respects, the nativity can be relegated to the short-lived category (up to 33 years only). No doubt, the above is a brief statement of the principles and should suffice here. These can be further elaborated to any extent but even so, guidance cannot be given for all manner of combinations. Each case must be tackled individually.

Formulae : The Hindu texts on astrology contain very many formulae. The one that has been found to give correct indications in a large majority of cases is described here. Some new suggestions of the author are also embodied to make the system complete. But in any event to rely on any formula alone exclusively without regard to the general strength of the horoscope will give misleading results.

Jaimini formula: This method is described in Jaimini Sutras (Aphorisms of Sage Jaimini). Three sets of factors are taken up for consideration.

(1) Lord of Ascendant and lord of 8th house.

(2) Sign containing Ascendant and sign containing Moon.

(3) Sign containing Ascendant and sign containing Hora Lagna.

If both the factors in each set are found to occupy cardinal signs or one is in a mutable sign and the other in a fixed sign—then the indication is for *long life.* If both such factors are found in mutable signs only or one in a cardinal sign and the other in a fixed sign—then the indication is for *medium life.* If both such influences are found in fixed signs or one is in a cardinal sign and the other in a mutable sign then life is *short.* In cases where the indications are not uniform in the case of all the three sets, the rule of majority applies. If all the three differ from each other, then the third set namely Lagna and Hora Lagna gives the correct indication except where Moon occupies the first or seventh house. In such a case, the indication of the second set namely Lagna and Moon is taken as final. There are very many other rules, exceptions, promotions, and reductions from one class to another etc. for which the reader is referred to the original sources. The Author has introduced two more sets into this scheme for one of which there is authority and for the other there is none except the observations of the writer. B. V. Raman observes.* "There is a suggestion in III Section 2 (of Jaimini's Aphorisms) that in determining longevity, the Lagna (Ascendant) and Atmakaraka should also be considered in the same manner as Lagna and Moon. The addition of this would make four sets for which the rule of majority cannot be applied. It has come within the observation of this writer during an examination of hundreds of horoscopes in this connection that the signs containing lord of Ascendant and lord of sign containing Moon should also be taken up to form five sets where the rule of majority can be applied in case of differences.

Atmaraka is the planet who has advanced most in any sign.

EXAMPLE

Horoscope of Mahatma Gandhi

I.	Lord of Asc Venus occupies Libra	-Cardinal Sign	Long Life
	,, 8th Venus ,, ,,	,,	
II	Ascendant falls in Libra	Cardinal Sign	Medium Life
	Moon occupies Leo	Fixed Sign	
III	Ascendant falls in Libra	Cardinal Sign	Long Life
	Hora Lagna§ ,, Libra	,,	
IV	Lord of Asc. Venus occupies Libra	-Cardinal	Long Life
	Lord of Moon's sign Moon ,, Cancer	do	
V	Lagna falls in Libra	- Cardinal	Long Life
	Atma Karaka Jupiter occupies Aries	do	

* Studies in Jaimini Astrology P. 107 § 112.

§ Vide Appendix H.

The traditional method of judging from the first three sets indicates long life. If the two other sets as suggested here are also taken into consideration, this is confirmed.

Now let us take the case of Queen Victoria which seems to be a difficult case according to ordinary standards. The Nirayana horoscope is No. 15 in Appendix I. She was born on 24—5—1819 at 4-15 a. m. London. She died before completion of 83rd year and so is a case of long life.

General : Venus, lord of ascendant is in twelfth with a trine aspect from Mars and Neptune from the eighth house. Both the luminaries are in Ascendant (1st house) and five in angles. Moon being Exalted Sextile Saturn. Jupiter lord of 8th is in angle 10th house). Even the tyro in Hindu Astrology will perceive there are two combinations for long life—all planets occupying 7th to 12th houses and Moon and Jupiter being in angles.

Jaimini Formula :

(1)	Lord of Lagna Venus in Aries, Cardinal sign ,, of 8th house Jupiter in Capricorn do	Long Life
(2)	Lagna falls in Taurus — a fixed sign Moon occupies ,, — ,,	Short life
(3)	Lagna falls in Taurus — a fixed sign Hora Lagna ,, — ,,	Short life

The majority indication is for short life which is obviously wrong.

(4)	Lord of Lagna Venus occupies Aries-Cardinal Sign Lord of Moon's sign Venus occupies Aries Cardinal sign	Long life

(5) Lagna falls in Taurus a fixed Sign
Atma Karaka Mars occupies a Common sign } Long life.

When those two additional items are taken into consideration as suggested here, there is a majority of three over two for long life.

§ 4. LENGTH OF LIFE

This is ascertained from the maraka lords of the horoscope and calculating when their periods are due. **Maraka Lords.** (Death inflicting planets):— The third and eigth houses are useful to determine the class of life to which a nativity belongs. Second and Seventh houses serve to indicate the Maraka lords. The powers to inflict death for the planets in a horoscope are ranged in the following order of preference.

Longevity Table I

(1) Malefic planet or planets in association with lord of 2nd house

(2) Malefic planet or planets in association with lord of 7th house

(3) Malefic planet or planets in occupation of 2nd house

(4) ,, ,, ,, ,, of 7th ,,

(5) Lord of second house

(6) ,, ,, Seventh house

(7) Benefic planet or planets in association with lord of 2nd house

(8) Benefic planet or planets in association with lord of 7th

(9) ,, ,, ,, in occupation of 2nd house

(10) Benefic planet or planets in occupation of 7th house

(11) Lord of the 8th house

(12) Lord of the 3rd house

(13) Saturn when connected in any way by association aspect or exchange with any of the above planets.

(14) Saturn even when unconnected in any way with any of the above planets, *but only if no one else is available.*

(15) If none of the above are available or appropriate a malefic in 12th house or twelfth lord or any planet connected with lord of 12th house.

(16) Saturn, Mars, Rahu or Kethu or waxing moon posited in a quadrant.*

Besides the above considerations which are common for all horoscopes, certain planets are declared to be the natural marakas for each of the Zodiacal signs rising at birth beginning from Aries. But this is no invariable rule and to rely on these alone will result in mistakes. But if any planet mentioned in the ensuing table as a natural maraka is also qualified according to the above rules of preference and if his period is due in the appropriate *class of life,* his powers to inflict death becomes all the more enhanced.

---

* The above have been composed from Standard Sanskrit Texts, B. V. Raman's How to Judge horoscope & G. Sriramamurti Span of life.

Longevity Table II

Ascending Sign	Maraka (Natural)
Aries	..Venus, Mercury, Saturn
Taurus	..Venus, Mercury, Moon, Jupiter
Gemini	..Sun, Mars, Mercury, Jupiter
Cancer	..Mercury, Venus, Saturn
Leo	..Mercury, Venus, Saturn
Virgo	..Mars, Jupiter, Venus, Moon
Libra	..Mars, Jupiter, Sun
Scorpio	..Mars, Saturn, Venus, Mercury
Sagittarius	..Saturn, Venus, Moon.
Capricornus	..Jupiter, Mars Moon.
Aquarius	..Jupiter, Moon, Sun.
Pisces	..Venus, Mercury, Sun, Saturn.

With the aid of the above rules, it would be possible to find the planet who during his period will most likely inflict death. But the duration of the periods of planets ranges from six years in the case of Sun to twenty years in the case of Venus. So it becomes necessary to find means for determining the sub-period of that planet in which death is probable. But the rules as regards this are scattered in very many places in various texts. The best set of rules in this respect is to be found in Bhavartha Ratnakara. Even here, they have to be classified and re-arranged before they could be put to practical use.

Longevity Table III

A. GENERAL

Major Lord	Appropriate sub-lord
I Malefic in second house	Malefic in association with lord of 12th house
II ,, in seventh house	(a) lord of 8th house in 8th or (b) lord of 8th house
III ,, in eighth house	(a) lord of 6th house or (b) Malefic 6th house
IV ,, in twelfth house	Malefic in association with lord of 2nd house
V Lord of 2nd house	(a) Planets in 12th house or (b) planets aspected by lord of 12th house
VI Lord of 6th house	(a) lord of 8th house or (b) planet in 8th house
VII Lord of 8th house	(a) Lord of 8th house (b) planets aspected by lord of 8th house or (c) planets associated with lord of 6th house
VIII (a) Lord of 8th house in 1st house	Lord of 8th house
VIII Lord of 12th house	(a) Lord of 2nd house (b) Planets in association with lord of 2nd house (c) planets aspected by lord of 2nd house or (d) malefics in 12th house.

B. Special

(a) PLANETS OCCUPYING FIFTH HOUSE*

(1) The sub-period of Mercury in the major period of Venus or the sub-period of Venus in the major period of Mercury if both occupy fifth house.

(2) Mars if he occupies fifth house owning evil houses.

(b) SATURN

Eventhough he may own favourable houses if he is in conjunction with maraka planets.

(c) RAHU AND KETU

These planets require special treatment as they are not said to "own" houses. They are malefics and become marakas *par excellence* under certain conditions. Their periods cover in all 25 years (Rahu 18 years and Ketu 7 years) in an aggregate of 120 years for all the nine planets, nearly one-fifth. Rahu and Ketu reflect more powerfully the effects of the planets in whose signs they are located and the planets by which they are aspected. Whether these planets derive maraka powers in this manner should receive first consideration. They derive maraka powers in other ways also but the rules regarding this are found scattered over in various texts and the principal rules will be found collected

---

* Bhavarta Ratnakara Chap. X. Stanzas 15-16

here. They are indispensable and many a death apparently unaccounted for has found an explanation in these. They are made mention of here in the hope that both the Western and Eastern students alike may study them and utilise them. So far as I am aware they are not found so collected anywhere else.

(1) If Rahu and Ketu occupy a Trikona (5th or 9th houses) and be conjoined with or aspected by the lord of 2nd or 7th houses, they are liable to cause death during their major periods.*

(2) If Rahu and Kethu occupy 2nd or 7th houses any malefic planet in conjunction with the planet owning the 2nd or 7th houses becomes most powerful in inflicting death.§

(3) If Rahu and Ketu be posited in 6th, 8th, or 12th houses and be conjoined with a maraka planet or with lords of these houses they bring about death.§

(4) If Rahu and Ketu are associated with lords of angular houses or trines and be posited in 6, 8, or 12th houses they can cause happiness at first to the native and then bring about death § (through violence?)

(5) If the lord of the ascending sign occupies 6th, 8th or 12th houses in conjunction with Rahu or

---

* Uttara Kalamritha Chap. VI. Verse 14-16.

§ Ibid Chap. VI. 17-19.

do.

do.

Ketu, the fatal dasa will be that of the planet associated with the lord of the rising sign or 8th house. If there be no planet so associated, the period of the planet owning the sign occupied by the lord of the rising sign or 8th house will prove fatal and death would take place in the Sub-period and antara period of Rahu in the fatal dasa when Rahu takes precedence of the other planets in ripening that portion of the fatal period.*

(6) When the lord of the 8th house occupies a Kendra (angles) his period will, if he should be eclipsed or conjoined with Rahu bring about of his native.§

(7) In the major period of Moon death is almost certain in the sub-period of Ketu if he occupies 2nd or 7th house.

(8) In the major period of Rahu, death is almost certain in the sub-period of Ketu if he occupies 2nd or 7th house.

(9) The sub-period of Rahu in the major period of Jupiter is one that is liable to cause death.

The application of these rules is not difficult though at first it may appear confusing to one not familiar with Hindu methods of direction. An application of these rules to ascertain the length of

---

* Jataka Parijata Chap. XIV verse 55.

§ Horasara Chap. XVI verse 9.

life in a dozen cases will familiarise the student with its technique and help far more than merely reading them over again or trying to memorize them as is done in India (where they are usually done with the original Sanskrit verses).

Let us continue with the example of Queen Victoria

Longitude of Moon Taurus 12°20′

	y	m	d
Balance of Moon's Major period at birth	8	3	9
Period of Mars	7	0	0
,, ,, Rahu	18	0	0
,, ,, Jupiter	16	0	0
,, ,, Saturn	19	0	0
	68	3	9
Period of Mercury	17	0	0
	85	3	9
,, ,, Kethu	7	0	0
	92	3	9
,, ,, Venus	20	0	0
	112	3	9

Because we have already settled that this nativity belongs to long life group death should take place in the major period of Mercury, Ketu or Venus. One can easily judge from the strength of Lagna, 3rd, and 8th houses life will not carry beyond 90th year. So Venus is ruled out though he has first class maraka powers being in conjunction with Mercury lord of 2nd house. (Rule (1) in L. T. I.) Ketu too has got maraka powers as he is in 5th house (Trikona) aspected by Mars lord of 7th house. (Rule I of L. T. III (c)) and the beginner may quite well conclude that death will happen in the major period of Ketu between 85th and 92nd years and will not be far wrong. But rule 5 of L. T. III (c) applies here as it is more general and involves the position of Venus ruler of the rising sign. It says that if the lord of the ascending Sign occupies 6th 8th or 12th houses in conjunction with Rahu or Ketu, the fatal dasa will be that of the planet associated with the lord of the rising sign or 8th house etc. Here Venus, lord of the rising sign is in twelfth house in conjunction with Rahu and Mercury. The period of Rahu or Mercury should therefore prove Maraka. The period of Rahu as it occurred in early years could not have operated to cause death in a long life horoscope. The period that is opportune is only that of Mercury.

The next question is in whose *Sub period* death should occur. Rule (3) in L. T III points to Mars as the planet in whose sub-period death may happen as the major lord is lord of 2nd and Mars is lord of the 12th house. But Mars is not listed as a natural maraka for Taurus Lagna but Jupiter is and he has additional powers under Rule (14) of L. T. I. He is lord of 8th & 11th houses both evil and he is in debility. His sub-period therefore caused the death of the Queen.

Not all cases would require so much discussion or scrutiny to arrive at the period and sub-period of death and this case was specially chosen as a difficult case to illustrate the method of approach in such cases.

The above is only a very brief exposition of the rules for ascertainment of Longevity according to Hindu astrology and is by no means exhaustive and can only serve for general guidance. There are in addition mathematical methods of ascertainment of longevity but the general consensus of opinion is that they are not very reliable. There are very many mathematical methods and it has to be inferred that a choice has to be made among them according to the individual peculiarities of each horoscope but as yet no one seems to have investigated this apect of the matter. And then there are any number of yogas or combinations which purport to state the longevity in each case where such combination is present. This again has not been found to be reliable as much depends on the strength of the planets entering into the combination and the number of years given can at best represent the maximum. Therefore these have been omitted here.

CHAPTER VII

NEW ERA DIRECTIONS

§ 1. GENERAL

The principles on which the New Measures are derived have already been explained. The method of computing directions as per these measures and their interpretation is somewhat different from the existing modes and comprises a combination of features from both schools of astrology—East and West. No part of this system is entirely new but the combination is unique and though in this form it is not difficult of application, its technique has to be thoroughly mastered to get the best results.

The first thing to be noted by the student of *western astrology* is that the Zodiac here used is the *Fixed Zodiac* of the Hindus and the Ayanamsa is Chitra and the house cusps of the horoscope are derived by the trisection principle, and the first thing that the student of *Indian astrology* has to accept for this system of direction is the *western system of aspects*. After all, it is but a modification of the Tajak system.

But in spite of a modern tendency in the West to avoid calling aspects and directions as good and bad and to describe them as harmonious and inharmonious, or as easy or difficult, the traditional nomenclature is adhered to. It is not to be inferred therefrom it is the author's view that 'good' directions cause only 'good' events and 'bad' directions only 'evil'. The radical configuration between the planets that form the aspects has also to be looked to.

The next is the doctrine of *change of nature* by planets according to rulership of houses. This is an integral part of Indian astrology and is familiar to all students of this science here but entirely foreign to the West

But the most important feature of this system of working directions and interpreting them which distinguishes it from all others is that it is the *measure that determines the nature of the effects* to be expected from a direction. The inherent nature of the planets their rulership of houses, their location, their modification by aspects are all here secondary. *It is the measure that rules all.* Thus an element of simplicity is introduced into the difficult and complex task of interpreting directions. There may be half a dozen or even a dozen directions yielded by an arc, say of $\frac{1}{2}°$= one year measure. In such a case it is the seventh house affairs alone that have to be looked to as the possible field for the 'expression' of the effects of these directions. If $\frac{3}{4}°$= one year is the measure that is responsible for these directions, it is the professional aspect alone that has to be looked to or the affairs of that house. If '$\frac{5}{12}$°=1 year' measure it is the sixth house matters and so on. For the event of death of courseit is '$\frac{7}{12}$°=1 year' measure that will be found to be responsible. Thus one particular aspect of the horoscope say the profession can be taken apart and judged and prediction made by working all the directions that would be yielded by the '$\frac{3}{4}$°=1' year measure throughout life. A considerable number of delineations furnished on the above basis have been found to presage events correctly over a period of 14 years and more.

§ 2. TECHNIQUE

I. The **factors** or sensitive points that enter into this scheme are

(1) Twelve planets including ☊ and ☋

(2) The first point of Aries always.

(3)a. Arc and M. C. always.

b. Relevant cusp and relevant point of the Zodiac. When 6th house measure (5/12°) is worked cusp of 6th house and 0° ♍ 0° If 8th house (7/12°) 8th house cusp and 0° ♏ 0°; for ninth house matters 9th house cusp and 0° ♐ 0″ and so on.

And no others.

N.B.–Zodiacal points are indicated by 'Zod' in the directions.

(4) Duplications are to be avoided when they yield the same directions between two sets of sensitive points.

II. The aspects are strictly limited to six, conjunction, opposition, sextile, trine, square, quincunx.

III. All directions formed are to be studied for purposes of estimating the effects of any year or a period of life in a nativity but when an event is judged as likely to happen at about a particular time, *the directions are to be averaged to time the event.*

§ 3. AVERAGING

Horoscopic delineation is not merely a matter of predicting life's events. Events are but the consummation of tendencies. The crest of a wave is preceded by a long course of upheavels and undulations and is dissolved soon after its formation. The proper study of a horoscope is a study of these formative tendencies. Otherwise the science of horoscopy itself can have but a limited value. But the prediction of events and timing them accurately is not an insignificant part of horoscopy and there should be a method by which this can be done within a narrow margin. So far there does not appear to be a satisfactory method for this as no limits are generally fixed to the time of operation of a direction and where it is a solar direction or in the case of a slow moving measure it is a question of years not even months. In this book it is suggested that the most practical method of effecting this is by averaging directions within well defined limits.

Obviously, this is the most rational method. It has been the uniform experience of all astrologers that a direction which we judge to be responsible for an event is not often found close to the event in point of time whereas some minor direction that is not even characteristic of the event is nearer to the date of that event. The reason is that no important event is brought about by any single direction alone. There are always a number of other directions that are not generally taken into account, apparently because of their nondescript or incongruous nature. e. g., who would think of taking such a direction such as, ♂ ⊼ ♄ along with ⊙ △ ♀ with regard to the event of marriage? No direction is wasted and has some effect or other and no directions can be ignored with impunity. A basis is provided here for correlating such directions. Mars forming quincux with Saturn May be lord of 7th house or Saturn may be lord of 7th. In the latter case Cancer or Leo will be on the ascendant and Mars will generally be lord of 4th and 9th houses or 5th and 10th houses, in which case he becomes auspicious, for the horoscope. His malefic nature undergoes on alteration and he becomes capable of doing good and can be the agent for bringing about auspicious events like marriage. This method of interpretation is along orthodox lines of Hindu astrology though the aspects that form the directions are not. **A further basis is provided in this scheme of New Era directing. If the characteric measure for marriage namely 1/2° to a year is the one that yields the two directions abovenamed an additional link is formed between the two directions that brings both to a common plane of human activity and these can be considered to-**

gether for purposes of judging the nature of the event and for timing it as well. This link is valid even if there is no other justification.

§ 4. LIMITS

The principle of averaging with a view to time the events of life, to be of any practical utility should have well defined limits. In symbolic directing it has been the practice to average directions without any limits either as to the measures, employed or as to time. Of course if an event if known to have happened on a particular date it would not be difficult to marshall some fractions so as to bring the average close to that time or even for the date in question, but this method will fail if predictions, are to be made as one does not know what fractions should be brought into play for a particular event. In this scheme, the measures to be employed are strictly relatable to the nature of the event and no other is to be considered. The limitations as to half a dozen aspects and no more have already been made clear. For purposes of averaging though not for interpretation the orbs of aspects for the working of directions are also strictly limited. The maximum orbs for any directional measure employed which is, itself less than a degree, the dimensions of the measure constitute its limits, e. g. for measure of death the maximum range is 35′, for measure of the meridian 45′, for partnership measure 30′, for accidents, sickness etc 25′ and so on. No directions formed beyond these limits on either side have to be taken into account for purposes of averaging.

Averaging directions under the limitations above imposed have been found to give quite satisfactory results separately for B.A. (one degree = one year) C. A. (characteristic Arc) and R. C. A. (Reversed C. A.) But the grand average of all these sets of directions has been found to be still more accurate and is recommended for all exact work; and this will be demonstrated in a large majority of cases dealt with as examples. Of course, it is necessary that house cusps and planets should be calculated correct to the minute. Otherwise the results will be proportionately affected adversely.

CHAPTER VIII

Measure of Death

Example 1

MAHATMA GANDHI

Since longevity is the first thing to be ascertained in a horoscope, we shall begin with this measure and give examples of its application. It is only proper that we take up the Nativity of Mahatma Gandhi as the first illustration. He was the Father of the Nation and the Architect of Indian liberty and was cruelly done to death by assassination. Gandhi was born at Porbunder, Lat. 21° 38′ N. Long 69° 36′ E on 2—10—1869. An elaborate article contributed by Cyril Fagan on "The Geniture of Mahatma Gandhi" has appeared in October 1950 of the Astrological Magazine, Bangalore and the planetary longitudes and house cusps have been calculated with meticulous accuracy. As a result of subsequent investigations however this horoscope has been slightly corrected in an article on 'Solunars' in January issue of the same Magazine for 1953. It is that which is adopted here. But the longitudes given by Cyril Fagan arc according to hypsomate Zodiac but the Zodiac adopted throughout this work is Chitra. The time of birth is 7-8-11. A.M.

Fig. 1

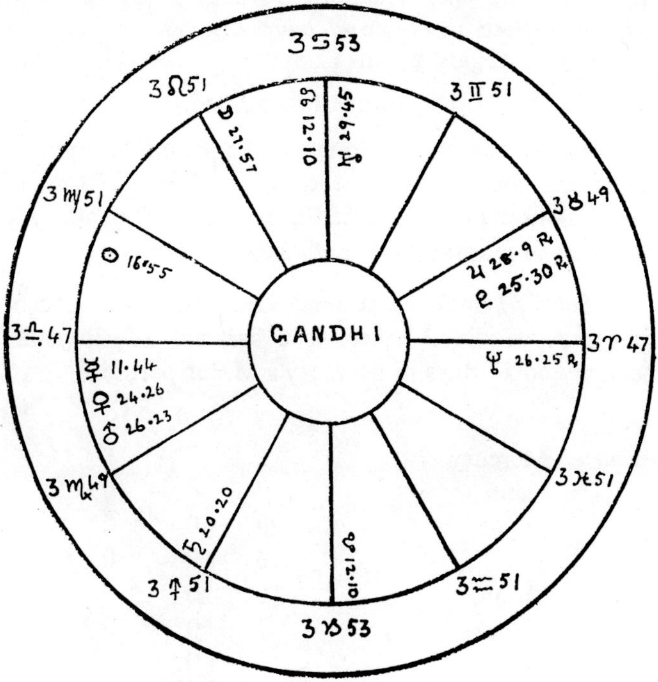

As is well known the assassination of Gandhi took place on January 30, 1948 for which the basic arc is 78° 20′. Astrologers all over the world would have examined the causes of his death according to the system of directions adopted by each. It will be our object here *to adopt throughout the special technique advocated for the New Era Measures for all other systems noticed already and have the results compared* at least with regard to this example.

I. HINDU ASTROLOGY

That this nativity belongs to the group of long life has already been shown according to Jaimini formula*, We shall now proceed to settle the time of death with reference to maraka lords and their periods.

Moon's Longitude at birth Cancer 27° 57′. According to Appendix G § there is a balance of 2 years 7 months and 11 days in Mercury's Major period.

	y	m	d
Mercury	2	7	11
Ketu	7	0	0
Venus	20	0	0
Sun	6	0	0
Moon	10	0	0
Mars	7	0	0
Rahu	18	0	0
	70	7	11
Jupiter	16	0	0
	86	7	11

PP. 124-5

Major period of death

With this calculation before us let us apply the rules. According to **L. T. I.** rules 3 to 14 are relevant and have to be examined.

According to rule	(3) —	Mars
	(5) —	do
	(7) —	Mercury & Venus
	(8) —	do
	(11) —	Venus
	(12) —	Jupiter
	(13) —	Nil
	(14) —	Saturn
	(15) —	Sun
	(16) —	Rahu Kethu

It will be seen at a glance that no planet except Rahu has got an opportunity. Jupiter though he does not figure as an important maraka in the above scheme is a natural maraka according to L. T. II for Libra ascendant and will have to be considered. He is also in 8th house which is another qualification. Jupiter's period from 70½ years to 86½ years is the only natural interval for death. in the long life group (70—100 years.)

Sub period for death

	y	m	d
Jupiter's major period begins	70	7	11
,, ,. Jupiter's sub-period	2	1	18
10			

Jupiter's major period Saturn's sub-period	2	6	12
,, ,, Mercury's sub-period	2	3	6
	77	6	17
Ketu's sub-period	0	11	6
	78	5	23

So death took place in the sub-period of Ketu in the major period of Jupiter. Independently of anything else Ketu has got maraka power when he is posited in a quadrant. (Rule 16 of L. T. I.) Phaladeepika attributes शस्त्रव्रणं and प्राणच्युति as effects flowing from their combination*, irrespective of location etc. Ketu has the square of Mercury lord of 12th house and the square is a very close one. He has also the distant squares of Venus, Mars, Jupiter and Pluto and the opposition of Moon. There are also sextiles from Saturn and Neptune and trine from Sun. The square of Mars betokens danger from enemy in war (or fight or hostilities).

II. NEW ERA MEASURE OF DEATH

Now we shall turn to the system cf directions recommended in this work for this case. The Basic Arc at one degree = one year is 78° 20′ and we shall work out the directions for this arc under the limitations suggested. This is the same as the O. D. or one degree measure of Carter but operated under the above limitations.

* For the combination of Jupiter as major lord and Kethu as sublord.

B. A. 78° 20′

(Maximum range for directions - one degree)

Directions	Difference from Exactitude in minutes	Total	Average	Equivalent in time
☿ □ Zod	+ 4			
♀ ☌ ☋	+ 36			
☋ ☌ Zod	+ 30	+ 89	+ $17\frac{4}{5}$	108 days after event
,, □ ♅	+ 45			
♃ ✱ ☉	— 26			

'Zod' means 0 degree of Aries (Nirayana) which is being directed or directed to in this system in the manner of Point of Life or Age along the Zodiac suggested by Frankland. The only difference is that all the directional arcs are applied to this point. The plus or minus represents the difference from exactitude. It will be noticed that all the directions except the last arc 'Evil' and the last though "Good" is as between planets that are marakas for the horoscope.

C. A. ($\frac{7}{12}$) 45° 42′

(Maximum range 35′)

♂ ⊼ ☊	— 5			
☋ ⊼ ☽	— 5			
☿ △ ☽	— 31			
♅ △ ☊	— 3	— 49	— $6\frac{1}{8}$	64 days before event
♇ △ ☿	— 32			
☋ ✱ ♃	— 17			
♆ ⊼ ☿	+ 23			
♂ ✱ ☿	+ 21			

Of above directions five are good and three are evil. The good directions are between marakas (planets powerful for inflicting death in a horoscope).

R. C. A. $(\frac{12'}{7})$ 134° 17′

(Maximum range one degree)

Directions	Difference from exactitude in minutes	Total	Average	Equivalent in time
♄ ☍ Asc.	+ 50			
♄ □ Mc.	+ 44			
☋ ⊼ ♂	+ 4			
☋ ✶ ♆	+ 2			
☽ ✶ ☊	+ 4	+ 159	+ $17\frac{2}{3}$	63 days
☿ ✶ ♇	+ 31			after event
☽ ✶ ☿	+ 30			
♃ △ ☋	+ 16			
☿ △ ♂	— 22			

In the nine directions furnished by this measure five are 'good' and four 'evil'. The same feature with regard to Marakas is to be observed.

Averaging the above directions or the three groups can be done in one of two ways, first by taking the average for these three groups and striking a grand average for all three. This method may be criticised as being not strictly mathematical though it will indicate how close the results are for each of these three groups. Secondly, a total of the arcs of all the directions formed or their time equivalents can be taken and divided by the total number of the directions formed and this will be the only scientific and accurate method of arriving at the correct result as this will indicate a point of time which registers the combined impact of all directional influences in operation. But it will be found after working a large number of cases that actually the difference in result is not much and practically negligible as will be demonstrated in some of the cases dealt with here.

Group Average

Average in the time equivalent for B.A. Group	+	108 days
C.A.	—	64 ,,
R.C.A.	+	63 ,,

Total + 107 days. Divided by three, Group average is 36 days after event.

True Average

If a uniform average of the directions formed in all the three groups are taken as indeed it ought to be done, the result will be to bring the timing even closer to the event.

B.A.

Directions	Difference from exactitude	Rate of conversion into time equivalent	Time in days
☿ □ Zod	+ 4		+ 24
♀ ☌ ☋	+ 36	60′ = 365 days	+ 219
☋ ☌ Zod	+ 30		+ 183
☊ □ ♅	+ 45		+ 274
♃ ⚹ ☉	— 26		— 158
a			

Direction	Difference	Rate of conversion	Time in days
		C.A. ($\frac{7}{12}$)	
♂ Ā ♑	— 5		— 52
☋ Ā ☽	— 5	35′ = 365 days	— 52
♆ Ā ☿	+ 23		+ 240
☿ △ ☽	= 31		— 323
☿ △ ☋	— 3		— 31
♇ △ ☿	— 32		— 334
♂ ✱ ☿	+ 21		+ 219
☋ ✱ ♃	— 17		— 177
		R.C.A. ($\frac{12}{7}$)	
♄ 8 Asc.	+ 50		+ 177
♄ □ Mc.	+ 44		+ 156
☋ ⊻ ♂	+ 4		+ 14
☋ ✱ ♆	+ 2	103′ = 365 days	+ 7
☽ ✱ ♆	+ 4		+ 14
☿ ✱ ♇	+ 31		+ 110
☽ ✱ ☿	+ 30		+ 106
♃ △ ☋	+ 16		+ 57
☿ △ ♂	— 22		— 78

The total will be + 595 days. Total number of directions 22. Therefore the average number of days beyond the event according to uniform average system is 27 days. Actually however no such elaborate calculations will be necessary as the same result can be arrived at by a much shorter method :—

Total of B.A. directions in minutes	+ 89′ × 1 = + 89′
C.A.	— 49′ × $\frac{12}{7}$ = — 84′
R.C.A.	159′ × $\frac{7}{12}$ = + 93′

Total 98′. Total number of directions 22.

∴ Average $\frac{98}{22}'$ converted into days at the rate of 60′ = 365 days = 26 days.

This method of working directions within the limits of a particular range of arcs and averaging the time equivalent of directions so formed need not necessarily be confined to the New Era measures only. This technique can be applied with success to all systems of direction and can be expected to produce quite adequate results, though in other systems the same facility for judging the nature of the events from the measures themselves is not available.

III

Sepharial's

Naronic Measure

36′ = one year

Arc for Gandhi's death 47°

Maximum range 36′ = one year

Directions	Difference in minutes	Total	Average	Time equivalent
Asc ☌ ♄	+ 27			
♀ ✱ ☿	— 18			
ℒ ⊼ ☋	+ 20	— 99	— 14$\frac{1}{7}$	143 days before event
☋ ⊼ 8 (Zod)				
8th C ☍♄	+ 29			
Mc □ ♄	+ 33			
⊙ ☍ 8th C	+ 6			
⊙ △ MC	+ 2			

These are characteristic directions for death though the element of violence contributing to the end is not patent.

IV

Robson's Radix System

59′ 8″ = one year

Arc for Gandhi's death (77° 23′)

(Maximum range 59′ 8″)

Directions	Difference in minutes	Total	Average	Time equivalent
♀ ☌ ☋	— 31			
♀ □ ☿	— 5			
☋ □ ♆	— 22			
☉ ⊼ MC	+ 15			
☿ ⊼ ♃	+ 48			
⊼ ♅	— 48			61 days
☽ ☌ ☋	+ 33	+ 132	+ $10\frac{2}{13}$	beyond
♅ ☌ ☉	+ 3			event
MC ✱ ♄	+ 46			
☋ ☌ Zod	— 37			
8thC △ ♄	+ 43			
☉ ✱ Asc.	+ 21			
⊼ 8thC	+ 18			

Thirteen directions and those that can be classed as good are not more than three.

V

Frankland's Measures

(i) Point of life 1° = one year from Zodiac ○ ♈ ○

Arc 78° 20′

18 ♊ 20 (Nirayana)—no directions
18 ♊ 20 (Sayana) Zod ⊼ ♂ ; Zod ✶ ♅

(i) Age along Zodiac

5 ♓ 43 (Nirayana) — nil
do (Sayana) — nil

(iii) $\frac{4}{7}'$ = one year

Arc 44° 46′

(Maximum range 34′)

Directions	Difference in minutes	Total	Average	Time equivalent
♂ ✶ ☿	— 35			
♅ ⊼ ☿	— 33			146 days
☿ △ ♆	+ 5	+ 69	$+\frac{69}{6}$	beyond event
☋ △ ♂	+ 33			
☽ ✶ ☊	+ 33			
☊ ⊼ ♆	+ 31			

Except first & last all others are 'good' directions so that it is not easy to deduce death. But the planets that figure in the directions are marakas doubtless.

N. B. Directions formed by aspects other than those specified in this work as well as directions beyond the range of the measures employed have been omitted to test the applicability of the technique recommended here in respect of other systems.

(iv) $\frac{4}{7}°+70°$

Arc 114° 46′

(Maximum range 34′)

Directions			Difference in minutes	Total	Average	Time equivalent
♅	☌	♀	+ 5			
☉	□	☿	— 3			
Asc.	□	♃	+ 24	+ 52′	+ 10$\frac{2}{5}$′	112 days
♇	□	♄	— 4			beyond event
MC.	☍	♃	+ 30			

To fix the range for this arc is not easy as the arc is 114° 46′ and is more than 1.46 times the Basic Arc of 78° 20′ and so according to the principle adopted here a maximum of one degree appears allowable in which case the following additional directions should also be taken into account.

Asc.	☍	♂	+ 36′			
♂	□	♄	+ 49′	+ 171′	+ 17$\frac{1}{10}$	103 days
♀	△	♄	— 51′			beyond event
♅	☍	♇	— 59′			
MC.	□	☽	+ 42′			

Four out of the five directions are distinctly evil and characteristic of the tragic event.

VI

Carter's Measures

(i) O. D. 78° 20′

This has already been dealt with under B.A. (New Era).

(ii) Duodenary 2¼° = one year)

Directions			Difference in minutes	Total	Average	Time equivalent
☿	□	☽	— 23			
♂	✱	☋	+ 3			
☊	✱	♃	— 9			
♅	□	☊	+ 5			
♆	☌	☿	+ 31			
☋	☌	☽	+ 3	— 132	— 12	29 days
L	△	☊	— 50			before event
8th	♇	♄	— 41			
Asc.	⊼	♄	— 43			
MC.	✱	♄	— 37			
♂	⊼	☾	+ 29			

Seven directions are evil

(iii) Subduodenary (12¼′ = one year)

Arc 16° 19′

(Maximum range 12¼′)

L	⊻	♀	— 5			
MC.	△	♄	— 8			
☿	☍	♃	— 6	— 15	— 2	88 days
☿	□	☽	+ 6			before event
8th	☍	♄	— 12			

The directions even within this short range are remarkable indeed and though the measure as such is **not relatable** to death, the directions 8th ☍ ♄, ☿ ☍ ♃ and L ⊼ ♄ are characteristic and significant.

Thus the New Era technique of restricting the orbs for directions to one degree or to the dimensions of the measure itself whichever is less and the aspects to half a dozen seem to apply to other systems of directions also with remarkable efficacy as illustrated in the above case of Mahatma Gandhi.

Example No. 2

RABINDRANATH TAGORE

(i) Preliminary

Tagore was born on 6–5–1861 at 3-52 A. M. 22° 40′ N. Long. 88° 30′ E. He died on 7-8-1941. Just after his death there was much discussion in the pages of the Astrological Magazine of Bangalore regarding the directional influences operating for the event.* Mr. Ghatak boldly stated that none of the systems of direction either Western or Eastern could account for his death. Mr. Motafaram † challenged this statement and in three articles contributed to the same magazine has tried to show how Radix System and Carter's measure of death sufficiently indicated the event. But the directions pointed out by him appear to me rather too wide. B. V. Raman, the talented Editor of the Astrological Magazine says ‡ that the horoscope of Tagore is an elusive one as regards the indications for his death and that planets supposed to be marakas did not kill the subject and the lord of the period in which he died, namely Jupiter gets his maraka powers in the Navamsa. E. R. Nayanar however in an article

* Astrological Magazine 1942.

† " " 1942 pp. 311, 351, & 398.

‡ How to Judge a horoscope P (7).

Fig. 2

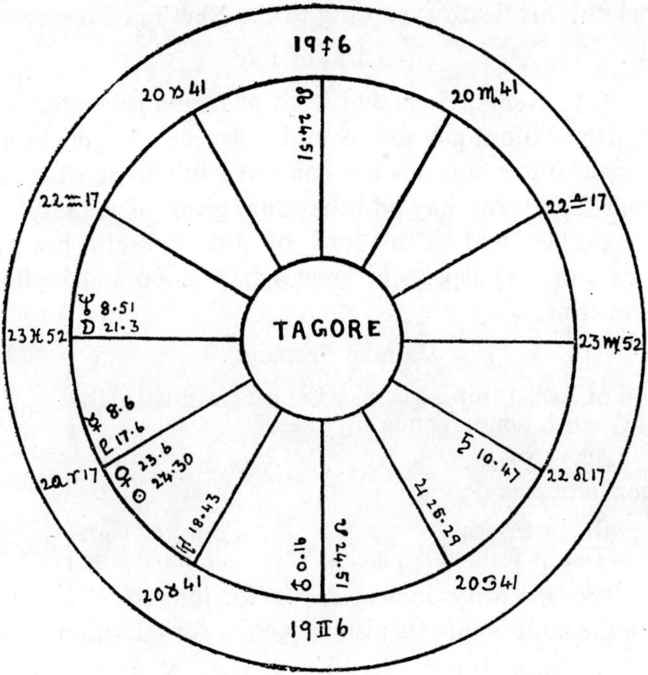
19 ♐ 6
20 ♑ 41
20 ♏ 41
22 ♒ 17
22 ♎ 17
23 ♓ 52
23 ♍ 52
22 ♈ 17
22 ♌ 17
20 ♉ 41
20 ♋ 41
19 ♊ 6
TAGORE
☊ 24.51
15.47
♆ 8.51
☽ 21.3
♃ 8.6
♇ 17.6
♀ 23.6
☉ 24.30
♅ 18.43
♄ 10.47
♃ 26.29
☋ 24.51
♄ 0.16

contributed to the same Magazine § shows that the longevity of Tagore according to Amsayurdaya method of computation is 80 years 2 months and 8 days. It is precisely because of this controversy, and also, as next to Gandhi he is one of India's greatest sons his horoscope has been taken as the second for illustrating the directions for his death according to the New Era Measures.

(ii) Class of Life

B. V. Raman Says that Lord of Lagna is exalted in the fifth without any unfavourable aspects, conjunctions or associations and this has conferred full term of Life (Long life). We may add that Sun, giver of vitality is also exalted and Venus lord of 3rd and 8th houses (houses of life) aspects his own sign. Moon and Jupiter are in trine.

Jaimini Formula

Lord of Asc. Jupiter occupies Cancer-Cardinal sign 8th house Venus ,, Aries do		Long
Asc falls in Pisces Moon occupies do	Common sign do	Medium
Asc falls in Pisces Hora Lagna falls in Aquarius	Common sign a fixed sign	Long

The majority indication is for long life. Let us take the additional sets also suggested for adoption.

Lord of Asc. Jupiter occupies Cancer - Movable Lord of Moon's sign Jupiter ,, ,, ,,		Long
Lagna falls in Pisces Atmakaraka Jupiter occupies Cancer-Movable	Common	Short

Still there is a majority of three in five for long life.

§ Astrological Magazine 1947 P. 497.

(iii) Maraka Lords

Longitude of Moon Pisces 20° 3′	y	m	d
Balance of Mercury's period at birth	11	4	28
Kethu's period	7	0	0
Venus	20	0	0
Sun	6	0	0
Moon	10	0	0
Mars	7	0	0
Rahu	18	0	0
	79	4	28
Jupiter's period Jupiter Sub-period	2	1	18
	81	6	16

Death took place in Jupiter's Major period and own Sub period. One should note the heavy afflictions* to which Jupiter is subjected to appreciate why he caused death at the onset of his period. He receives squares from Pluto, Venus and Sun and Jupiter squares the cusp of the 8th house.

(iv) New Era Directions

B. A. (80° 15′)

(Maximum range one degree)

Directions	Total	Average	Time equivalent
♇ □ ♀	— 45		
♃ ☍ ♇	— 52		
♂ ⊼ ☽	— 32		
Zod. □ ☽	— 48		

* According to the system of aspects advocated in this book.

Directions	Difference in minutes	Total	Average	Time equivalent
♄ ⚻ ♂	+ 46			
♅ ⚻ ♆	+ 7			
☽ ⚹ ♄	+ 31	— 65	— 6½	40 days
♅ △ ♀	+ 52			before event
♅ ⚻ 8th (Zod)	— 54			
MC. ☌ ♆	+ 30			

The majority of the directions eight out of ten are distinctly evil. Mercury and Saturn are natural marakas for persons born under Pisces (Vide L. T. II). Uranus is lord of 12th and hence also maraka. M. C. is quincunx Uranus (very close)

C. A. 46° 49′

(Maximum range 35′)

Asc. □ ♄	— 6			
♆ □ ♃	— 19			
♂ □ ℓ	— 1′			
8thC □ ♆	+ 15′	+ 25	+ 4⅙	43 days
☿ ⚻ ☊	+ 4′			after event
☉ ⚹ ♄	+ 32′			

Five out of six directions yielded by this measure of death are evil, notably that between Jupiter and Neptune supposed to be inevitable for death by Mr. Carter.

R. C. A. (137° 24′)

(Maximum range — one degree)

Directions			Difference in minutes	Total	Average	Time equivalent
Asc.	☌	♄	+ 39			
8th	☌	♆	+ 60			
♂	☍	L	+ 44			
♆	☌	♃	+ 26	+ 207	+ 23	81 days
☿	✱	☋	+ 49			before event
Zod	△	L	+ 28			
☽	△	♀	+ 31			
☽	⊼	♆	— 14			
8thC	⊼	♄	— 56			

Group Average

		Total	Average
B. A.	— 40 days		
C. A.	+ 43	+ 84	28 days after event
R. C. A.	+ 81		

But the correct system of averaging brings the equivalent in time even closer to the event.

Directions No.	Total	Equivalent in B.A. minutes	Total	Average
B.A. (10)	— 65 × 1′	— 65		
C.A. (6)	+ 25 × $\frac{12}{7}$′	+ 43	+ 99′	+ $\frac{99}{25}$′
R.C.A. (9)	+ 207 × $\frac{7}{12}$′	+ 121		

= 24 Days Beyond Event

(v) Comment on birth time of Tagore

F.C. Dutt gives the birth time of 4 A.M. on 7-5-1861 as that given by a very near relation of the poet though

11

as stated by some others it was between 2·30 A. M. and 3 A. M. Mr. Ghatak gives the time as 22 hours and 24 minutes after sunrise and this works to 3·48 A. M. E. R. Nayanar gives it as 4·2 A. M. Mr. Motafaram does not give the time but it works out to 4·52 A. M. and is the one adopted here. A slight shift of birth time by some seconds will give even closer results but as it is no part of our theory that directions should indicate the exact date of any event the birth time is left at that and not attempted to be 'rectified'. "Correct to the month" is close enough for any directional investigation.

(VI) Carter's measure of death

(15′ to one year) Arc 20° 4′

(Maximum range 15′)

The only direction within orbs is ♅ □ ♆ — 4′ which gives a time equivalent of 97 days before event which is remarkable in itself. But there are a number of other directions if the range is extended to the neighbourhood of one degree which the author of the measure would doubtless have allowed and they are :—

Directions	Difference in minutes	Total	Average	Time equivalent
☽ □ ♄	+ 20			
MC □ ☿	+ 64			
♄ □ ♂	+ 35			
♃ △ L	— 93			
♂ △ ☽	— 43	+ 39	+ $4\frac{7}{8}$	119 days after event
MC ✱ ♆	+ 19			
♅ ✱ ☿	+ 41			

It is remarkable that the directions work to nearly just as much beyond the event!

It would be interesting to work the directions as per other systems as well under the New Era restrictions as in the case of Mahatma Gandhi but considerations of space forbid and the diligent student may work out all that for himself.

Example No. 3

I. LONGEVITY

Jagadish Chandra Bhose

The horoscope of this world famous scientist is given in F. C. Dutt's Predictive Astrology page 55. He was born at 4-12 P.M. L. M. T. on 30–11–1858 Lat. 23° 38′ N. Long. 90° 81′ E. He died on 23–11–1937. The horoscope given is according to the Western System and has been recast after deducting Ayanamsa. House division is by trisection method. On the face of it this is seen to be a long life horoscope. Mars, Lord of 8th house is exalted. There are two benefics in 8th house. There is a trine between Sun and Saturn as also between Mars and Jupiter.

Jaimini Formula :

The chart which is usually adopted in India is known as Jaimini chakra and learned authorities assert that this is the chart to be used to interpret Jaimini, that is, without oblique ascension.

Fig. 3

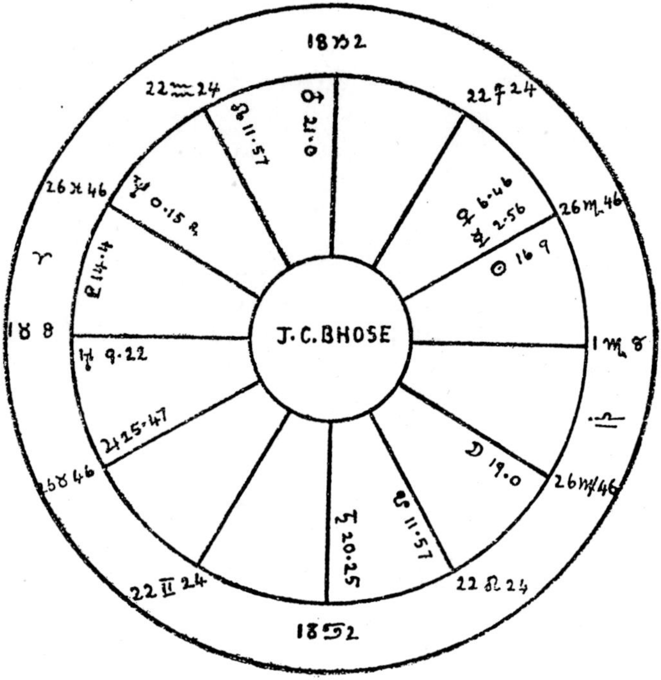

Lord of Asc. is Venus who occupies Sagittarius	—Common sign	Long
Lord of 8th is Jupiter Taurus	—fixed sign	
Lagna falls in Taurus	—fixed sign	Long
Moon occupies Virgo	—Common sign	
Lagna falls in Taurus	—fixed sign	Short
Hora Lagna falls in Aquarius	do	

Thus there is majority indication for long life.

Maraka lords :

Moon's Longitude at birth is Virgo 19° 0°

		y	m	d
Balance of Moon's period at birth		3	3	0
Period of Mars		7	0	0
,, Rahu		18	0	0
,, Jupiter		16	0	0
,, Saturn		19	0	0
	Total	63	3	0
Period of Mercury till end of sub-period of Jupiter		14	3	21
	Total	77	6	21
,, ,, Sub period of Saturn		2	8	9
	Total	80	3	0

Thus death took place in the major period of Mercury in the sub-period of Saturn.

Applying the rules as to maraka lords, we find the period of Mercury has the first preference being a benefic planet in association with Venus lord of second house, the periods of other planets having preferential

a

maraka powers occurring in early or middle life. Mercury's period occurring between 63 and 80 years is opportune. Any student of Hindu Astrology will at once spot Jupiter, as the sub-lord, to cause death as he is lord of 8th & 11th houses from Lagna ordinarily and here situated in sixth from major lord. But he would be wrong as Jupiter in this nativity is really lord of ninth and twelfth houses and Saturn is lord of 10th and 11th houses. Saturn is aspected by Mars (opposition) lord of 7th & 8th and he is in eighth from the major lord, Rule (13) of L. T. I, applies.

II. NEW ERA DIRECTIONS

B.A. 78° 59′

(Maximum range one degree)

Directions	Difference in minutes	Total	Average	Time equivalent
Asc ☍ ♂	— 53′			
☌ ♄	— 18			
Zod □ ☽	— 10			
♄ ⊼ ♅	+ 2			
8th □ ☉	— 24			
♀ □ ♃	— 2			
♃ △ ☊	+ 42			
☋ △ ♆	+ 41			
MC △ ♀	+ 15			
♆ △ ☽	+ 14			
☊ ⊼ ☿	+ 7	136	$10\frac{6}{13}$	64 days
☋ ☌ 8th Zod	+ 56			
Zod ⊼ MC	+ 57			

Nine out of thirteen directions are evil and five of them are close to the event. The involvement of Asc, 8th house, 8th (Zod) or Scorpio, 8th house lord are apparent.

C.A. 46° 4′

(Maximum range 35′)

Directions	Exactitude in minutes	Total	Average	Equivalent in time
Zod ☍ ☉	— 5			
♃ ⊼ ☋	— 6			
♄ □ ♀	— 17			
☿ △ ☽	Exact	+1′	$\frac{1}{8}$′	one day
L □ ♆	— 7			after event
♂ □ ♀	+ 18			
♆ ⊼ ☉	+ 10			
L ⊼ 8th Zod	+ 8			

Seven out of eight directions are evil. The average reveals the validity of the measure beyond dispute. The directions too are highly characteristic of the event.

R. C. A. (135° 24′)

(Maximum range — one degree)

Directions	Exactitude in minutes	Total	Average	Equivalent in time
Zod □ ☉	— 45			
☿ ⊼ ☽	— 49			
L ☍ ♆	— 47			
L ⊼ Zod	— 32			
♂ ☍ ♀	— 22	— 208	— 20$\frac{4}{5}$	74 days
♃ ✱ ☋	— 46			
♆ △ ☉	— 30			
Asc ✱ ☉	+ 23			
8th △ ☋	+ 13			
MC ☍ ☿	+ 30			

Group Average

B.A.	64 days		
C.A.	1 day	— 9	
R.C.A.	—74	— 9	— 3 days

True Average

Class of Direction	Total	Rate	Eqivalent in B.A.	Average	Equivalent in Time
13 B.A.	+ 136′	× 1	+ 136′		
8 C.A.	+ 1′	× $\frac{12}{7}$	+ 2′	$\frac{17}{31}$	+ 3 days
10 R.C.A.	— 208′	× $\frac{7}{12}$	— 121′		
31	Total		+ 17		

Example No. 4

King Edward VII

I. PRELIMINARY

Having dealt with the three of the greatest sons of India who are no longer in the land of the living, I shall now take up the Kings of England in a series beginning from Edward VII to illustrate the measure of death. The data with regard to these cases are undisputed and when taken in a sequence leaves no choice to the author in the matter of selecting cases. As already stated, it was while investigating the directions for the King's death that I came upon the discovery of the measure of death of 35′ to the year and the other measures treated of here followed only thereafter. It is true that at that time the further developments with regard to the restriction of orbs and aspects or even the principle of averaging was not thought of. These are the results of subsequent investigations conducted over a period of several years.

The King was born on Nov 9, 1841 at 10—48 A.M. This is a long-lived horoscope in the technical sense only. No doubt Jupiter lord of ascendant is in the first house but that is not his own sign but Scorpio. He has got the trine of retrograde Pluto but he has also got the Square of Uranus. Jupiter has a sextile aspect from debilitated Venus. Moon is lord of 8th house and has got a close square from Saturn. Sun too is in his debilitation sign of Libra. These features do not confer real long life.

Jaimini Formula :

Lord of Lagna is Jupiter occupies Scorpio	– fixed sign	Life long
Lord of 8th house is Moon & he occupies Virgo	—Common sign	
Lagna falls in Sagittarius	—Common sign	Medium life
Moon occupies Virgo	—Common sign	
Lagna falls in Sagittarius	—Common sign	Long life
Hora lagna falls in Aquarius	—fiixed sign	

Maraka lords :

Moon's Longitude is Virgo 7° 49′

	y	m	d
Balance of Sun's Major period	0	11	24
Major period of Moon	10	0	0
,, ,, Mars	7	0	0
,, ,, Rahu	18	0	0
,, ,, Jupiter	16	0	0
Saturn to end of sub-period of Rahu	16	5	18
Total	68	5	12
do Jupiter	2	6	12
Total	70	11	24

Death took place in the sub period of Jupiter in the major period of Saturn. According to standard rules, Mars has got first preference as a malefic associated with Saturn lord of 2nd house. Next comes Rahu who is a malefic in occupation of second house. Both periods were passed in early life and Jupiter in ascendant is a strong antidote to early death. Saturn's major period occurs between 51 & 70 years of life and is the maraka period. The likely sub-periods are those of Mars, Rahu, and Jupiter. All three have first class maraka powers. Jupiter is associated with Saturn lord of 2nd house in the first ; but judging by first appearances, Rahu's sub-period appears the more likely.

New Era Directions

B.A. (68° 29′)

(Maximum range one degree)

Directions	Exactitude in minutes	Total	Average	Equivalent in time
Zod □ ☽	+ 40			
☊ ☍ Asc	+ 18			
♀ ☌ Asc	+ 6			
♃ ⊼ ☽	+ 30			
☿ ☍ 8th	+ 53	+ 72′	+ 8′	49 days
Zod ☍ ♄	— 2			after event
♅ △ ☽	— 21			
♃ ✶ ♄	— 12			
♄ ⊼ 8th	— 40			

Six out of 9 directions are 'evil'

C. A. 39° 57′

(Maximum range — 35′)

Directions	Difference in minutes	Total	Average	Time equivalent
Zod ☍ ☿	— 7			
L △ ☽	— 4			
8th ⊼ L	— 11			
♀ ✶ ☽	— 16	— 24	— 3 3/7	36 days
♅ △ ♄	+ 25			before event
☽ □ 8th	+ 6			
♃ ✶ ☿	— 17			

There are four 'good' directions and three 'evil'. The good directions are formed between Venus lord of 6th and 11th houses (both very evil) and Moon lord of 8th (evil) and between Mercuıy and Jupiter (Mercury very evil as being lord of quadrants). Mercury is the worst maraka for Sagittarius born persons. But here he is lord of 7th & 9th houses though in twelfth house. The only really favourable aspect is between Saturn and Uranus but it is rather wide.

R. C. A. (117° 24′)

☊	☍	☿	— 11
L	□	☉	— 4
♀	□	☉	— 16
☿	☍	☽	— 21
♃	☌	L	— 34
	☍	♀	— 22
Mc	✶	♂	— 4

Directions	Difference in minutes	Total	Average	Time equivalent
Zod △ ♇	— 24			
✱ ♀	— 12	— 208′	— $18\frac{10}{11}'$	66 days
♄ △ Asc	— 4			before event
☉ ✱ ♂	— 56			

Group Average

B.A.	+ 49			
C.A.	— 36	— 53	— $\frac{53}{3}$	18 days
R.C.A.	— 66			

Uniform Average

9 B.A.	+ 72′	× 1	+ 72′	
7 C.A.	— 24	× $\frac{12}{7}$	— 41′	— 90′
11 E.C.A.	— 208	× $\frac{7}{12}$	— 121	

27 average—$\frac{90}{27}$ = —$3\frac{1}{3}$ = $\frac{10}{3} \times \frac{365}{60}$ before event = 20 days

Naronic measure ($\frac{3}{5}°$ = one year)

Arc 41° 5′

(Maximun range 36′)

Directions	Difference in minutes	Total	Average	Time equivalent
♅ λ̄ ☿	Exact			
♇ λ̄ ♄	+ 22			
☉ ☌ Asc	+ 22	— 37′	— $5\frac{2}{7}'$	53 days
8th ☍ ♅	— 14			before event
Asc ☍ 8th	— 36			
Mc ✱ ♆	— 33			
Zod λ̄ MC	+ 2			

The directions are quite remarkable in themselves and reasonably close to the event. The majority are 'Evil' directions with involvement of the 8th house, Saturn and Mercury. Death can be inferred therefrom eventhough the measure itself does not indicate it as such.

Frankland's Measures ($\frac{4}{7}°$ = one year)

(Arc 39° 8′)

(Maximum range 34′)

Directions	Difference in minutes	Total	Average	Time equivalent
♄ ☍ 8th	— 1			122 days
♅ □ ♄	— 23	— 24	— 12	before event

Under the limits imposed for the New Era Measures, these appear to be the only directions. The exactness of Saturn's opposition to 8h house cusp is as much a first class argument for the validity of the measure as for the validity of the trisection method of house division. The directions Zod ⊼ ♄ + 37′ and Moon □ 8th house cusp–43′ which are a few minutes outside orbs if included will reduce the average still further to 81 days before event.

$\frac{4}{7}°$ + 70°

Arc 109° 8′

(Maximum range 34′)

Asc ⊼ ☉	— 9			
♄ ☌ L	— 9			
Mc □ Zod	+ 11	+ 8	+ 2	22 days
♂ □ ☊	+ 15			beyond

Fig. 4

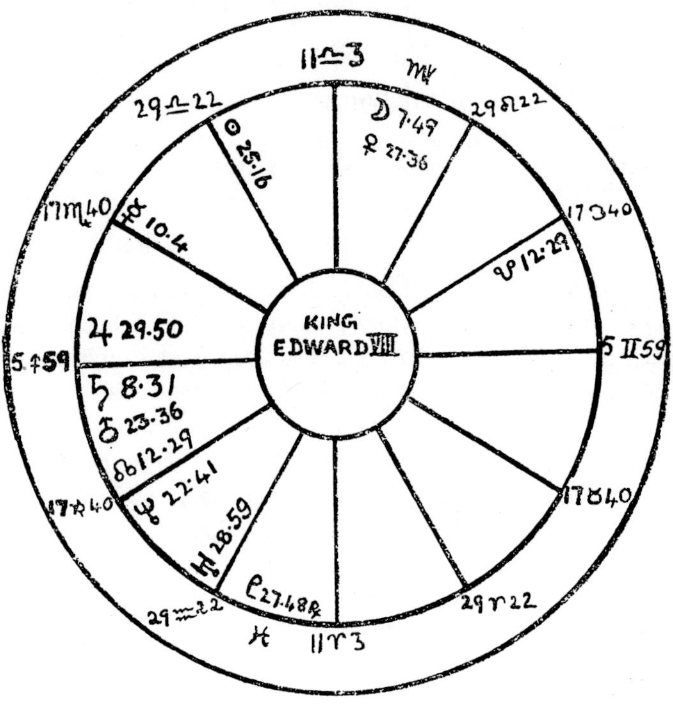

All are evil directions. So all these measures seem to thrive quite well under the restrictions and limitations imposed for New Era Measures.

Group Average

		Total		Average
As per $\frac{4}{7}°$	measure	— 122 days		
,,	$\frac{4}{7}°$ + 70 ,,	+ 32	— 90	— 45 days

This is the result ignoring the directions beyond orbs.

Carter's measure of death ($\frac{1}{4}°$ = one year)

Arc 17° 7′

(Maximum range 15′)

The only direction within orbs appears to be ☉ ✱ ☊ — 6 but if the range is extended to one degree as the author of the measure would doubtless have done nine, more directions appear but the average works to something like one year beyond event; but the directions as per reversed measure of death i.e. 4° = one year when averaged would point to nearly 66 days after event.

Example No. 5

King George V

I. LONGEVITY

George V was born on 3-6-1865 at 1-18 A.M. and died on 20-1-1936. His horoscope is given. The earlier books* give the ascendant (Sayana) as Aries 2° 4′ but

* Directions and Directing by H. S. Green.

the later books* give the ascendant (Sayana) as Aries 3° 19′ where the time of birth is givenas 1-20-6 A.M. Anyhow the difference is not much. It is the latter horoscope that has been adopted here. This horoscope is remarkable in many ways and furnishes very good confirmation of the validity of the measures herein employed.

This is a classical example of a long-life nativity. Saturn Ayushkaraka or conservator of vitality is in 8th with good aspects from Jupiter lord of ascendant and Uranus. Sun has good aspects from both Mars and Neptune. Jupiter is strong in tenth house. These are indications for long life. But Venus lord of 8th is Square Mars. Moon has Squares from Jupiter and Uranus and opposition from Neptune. So full period of long life will not be enjoyed and death may be expected early in the beginning of long life period.

Jaimini Formula :

Lord of Asc Jupiter in Sagittarius	—Common sign	Short life
Lord of 8th house Venus is in Aries	—Movable sign	
Lagna falls in Pisces	—a Common sign	Medium life
Moon occupies Virgo	—a Common sign	
Lagna falls in Pisces	—a Common sign	Medium life
Hora Lagna falls in Sagittarius	—a Common sign	

Medium life is indicated. This is a rather peculiar case in which promotion of class of life to next above

* Robson's Radix System.

is recommended by Jaimini. The conditions are that Mercury the Atmakaraka of the horoscope has benefics disposed in trine from him as also Jupiter. The addition of two more sets as suggested earlier does not help here.

Maraka Lords :

Moon's Longitude at birth Virgo 9° 7′

		y	m	d
Balance of	Sun's Major period at birth	0	4	23
	Moon	10	0	0
	Mars	7	0	0
	Rahu	18	0	0
	Jupiter	16	0	0
	Saturn	19	0	0
	Total	70	4	23
Mercury's major period and sub-period		2	4	27
	Total	72	9	20

Thus death took place in the sub-period of Mercury in the major period of Mercury and it will be seen that Mercury is the only appropriate maraka for the horoscope. First preference is for the planet in association with lord of 2nd house. There is no such planet in the horoscope. Next comes the turn of the planet (malefic) associated with lord of the 7th house. Venus and Kethu are with Mercury lord of 7th. But Venus is a benefic and Ketu's period comes after 87 years. Next come planet or planets in second house and these are Ketu, Venus and Mercury. The first has been already ruled out. Mercury is in addition a natural maraka for Pisces born natives (L. T.—II). No wonder that death took place as soon as his sub-period commenced.

II. NEW ERA DIRECTIONS

B. A. 70° 38′

(Maximum range one degree)

Directions	Difference in minutes	Total	Average	Time equivalent
Zod □ Asc	— 44			
△ 8thC	— 3			
♅ ⊼ ♆	— 55			
☽ ☍ ☉	— 44			
♄ ⊼ ♂	— 51			
8th ⊼ L	— 3			
8th △ ☿	— 13			
Mc □ ☉	— 32			
L □ ♄	— 9			
♅ △ ♀	— 32			
☿ □ ♄	+ 1	— 192	— $4\frac{10}{13}$	90 days
8th ⊼ ☉	+ 50			before event
♃ ⊼ ♂	+ 43			

Ten out of thirteen directions are evil and six of these are quincunx. There are four squares and one opposition and two trines. The Nirayana Zodiac figures two times and the eighth house cusp by trisection method four times.

Fig. 5

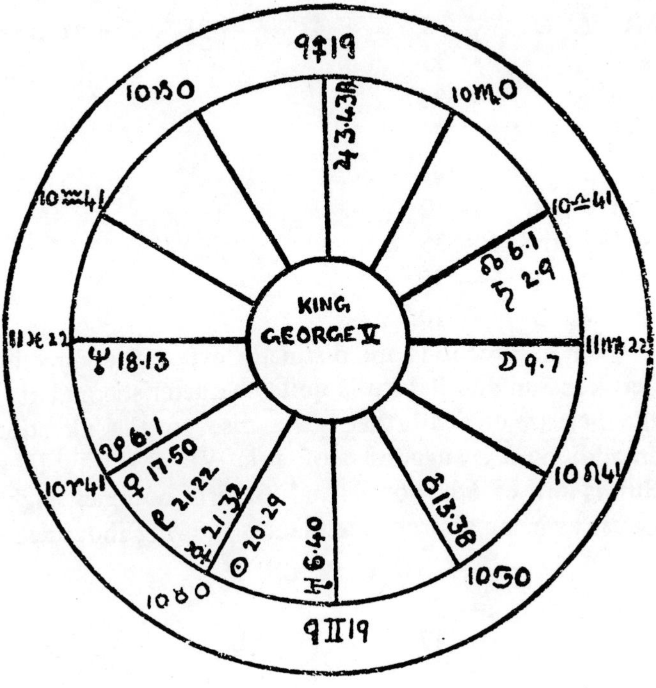
KING GEORGE V
9 ♐ 19
10 ♑ 0
10 ♏ 0
10 ♒ 41
10 ♎ 41
11 ♓ 22
11 ♍ 22
10 ♈ 41
10 ♌ 41
10 ♉ 0
10 ♋ 0
9 ♊ 19
♃ 3.43 R
☊ 6.1
♄ 2.9
♆ 18.13
☽ 9.7
☋ 6.1
♀ 17.50
♇ 21.22
☿ 21.32
☉ 20.29
♅ 6.40
♂ 13.38

C. A. 41° 12′

(Maximum range 35′)

Directions			Difference in minutes	Total	Average	Time equivalent
♅	□	♀	+ 2			
8th	Λ̄	L	+ 31			
	Λ̄	☿	+ 21			
MC	△	☉	+ 2	+ 47′	— $3\frac{11}{12}$′	47 days after event
☿	△	♄	+ 35			
L	△	♄	+ 25			
Zod	Λ̄	8thC	+ 31			
♄	△	♂	— 17			
Zod	✱	Asc	— 10			
♆	☍	8thZod	— 35			
☉	□	♄	— 28			
☽	Λ̄	☉	— 10			

Seven directions are distinctly evil. The direction between Sun and Saturn is quite characteristic and it is the measure of death that gives rise to the direction. In addition it is suggestive of rule VI of L. T. III as Sun is lord of 6th house and Saturn occupies eighth house as being appropriate planets to bring about death.

R. C. A. 121° 5′

Directions			Difference in minutes	Total	Average	Time equivalent
☽	□	8th	— 29			
MC	☍	8th	— 17			
♀	Λ̄	♆	+ 42			
L	△	☿	+ 55	+ 62′	+$7\frac{3}{4}$′	+ 27 days
☉	Λ̄	L	+ 12			
☉	Λ̄	☿	+ 2			
☋	✱	♅	+ 26			
♄	✱	♃	— 29			

Group Average

B.A	— 90			
C.A.	+ 41	— 22	— 7	7 days
R.C.A.	+ 27			before event

Uniform Average

13 B.A.	— 192′	× 1	— 192′	
12 C.A.	+ 47′	× $\frac{12}{7}$	+ 81′	+ 75′
8 E.C.A.	+ 62′	× $\frac{7}{12}$	+ 36′	

Average for 33 directions $= -\frac{75}{33}' = -5\frac{16}{31}$
= 14 days before event

Example No. 6

King George VI

I. LONGEVITY

George VI was born at 3-5 A.M. on December 12, 1895 and died on 6—2—52 at 56 years one month and twenty three days. Therefore this is a medium life horoscope. A lengthy article entitled " George VI's, Longevity" has been contributed by Mr. K. S. Jagannadha Rao to the Astrological Magazine of Bangalore*, giving the combinations for middle life.

Though Jupiter and Venus are in angles, they have a close square to each other.

Two malefics Neptune and Pluto occupy the 8th house with opposition from Sun and Mercury. Jupiter lord of 3 and 6th house is in an angle a familiar combination for medium life.

---

* May 1952 P. 367.

a

Jaimini Formula :

Lord of 1 Venus occupies Libra 8th do ,,	– Movable sign ,,	Long life
Lagna falls in Libra Moon occupies Scorpio	—Movable sign —fixed sign	Medium life
Lagna falls in Libra Hora lagna falls in Libra	—Movable sign —Movable sign	Long life

There is a provision in Jaimini's rules that if Atmakaraka joins lord of 2nd or 8th there should be a reduction of the class to the next lower. So here though long life is indicated by majority it will have to be reduced to medium group. Atmakaraka is inconjunction with Mars lord of 2nd house. But as per our suggestion to include two more items the result will be the same.

Lagna lord occupies Libra Lord of Moon's sign Mercury occupies Scorpio	—Movable sign —Fixed	Medium life
Lagna falls in Libra Atmakaraka Sun occupies Scorpio	—Movable sign —Fixed sign	Medium life

There is a majority of three in five for medium life.

Maraka lords :

Moon's Longitude at birth Scorpio 2° 27′

	y	m	d
Balance of Jupiter's major period at birth	1	0	22
Major period of Saturn	19	0	0
,, ,, Mercury	17	0	0
,, ,, Ketu	7	0	0
Total	44	0	22

„ Venus to end of sub-period of Rahu		10	2	0
	Total	54	2	22
„ „ Sub-period of Jupiter		2	8	0
	Total	56	10	22

So the King died in the sub-period of Jupiter in the major period of Venus period which comes as the fifth from birth, and so the one likely to prove maraka for medium life. When lord of the 8th house is the maraka, the lord of the 6th house will be one of the Sub lords to inflict death. In addition Jupiter is a natural maraka for Libra born persons.

New Era Directions

For purpose of New Era directions, the cusps of the houses as well as the planet's longitudes have to be calculated correct to the degree & minute to secure as accurate results as possible. While there appears to be no doubt as regards the time of birth of the late King which is uniformly given as 3-5 A.M. on 14—12—1895, the horoscopes given in western text books vary slightly from each other. In Lyndoe's Practical Astrology it is given as Libra 27°18′. In Louis de Wohl, The Secret Service of the Sky it is given as Libra 28°. But this may be an approximation though in that case it should have been given as Libra 27°. In Carter's Political Astrology it is given as Libra 27° 14′. But luckily I found the horoscope in Cyril Fagan's Zodiac's Old & New and by adding one degree was able to convert it to Chitra Zodiac without trouble. The ascendant given here is Libra 3° 47′ and after addition 4° 47′ (Niayana). The difference is not much.

Fig. 6

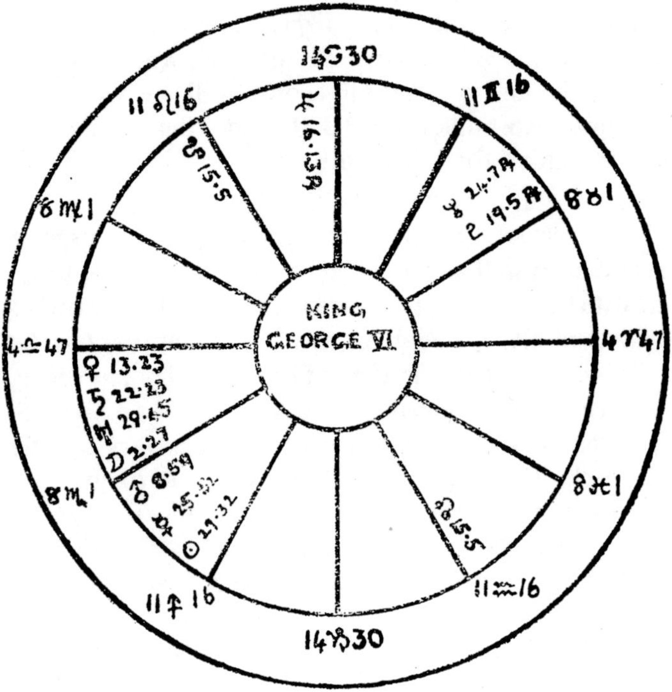

B. A. 56° 9′

(Maximum range one degree)

Directions			Difference in minutes	Total	Average	Time equivalent
Zod	☍	☿	+ 17			
♇	λ̄	☊	+ 9			
♄	λ̄	♇	— 33			
♂	□	Asc	+ 21	— 59′	— $6\frac{5}{9}$′	40 days
☿	□	♄	— 22			before event
8thC	□	Asc	— 37			
☉	✶	☿	— 11			
♇	☌	♃	— 59			
Asc	△	Zod	+ 56			

Seven out of ten directions are 'Evil' 8th cusp, Asc, Mars, Saturn are all involved. Jupiter and Pluto figure here but not Jupiter & Neptune.

C. A. 32° 45′

(Maximum range — 35′)

Directions			Difference in minutes	Total	Average	Time equivalent
Asc	☍	8thC	— 29			
♃	□	♇	— 7			
☉	✶	☽	— 10	— 41	— $5\frac{6}{7}$	48 days
♀	△	♃	— 5			before event
♇	△	♄	— 33			
Zod	☍	☽	+ 18			
☽	✶	Asc	+ 25			

'Good' directions are seen to be in the majority. But Jupiter is a maraka for Libra. Venus is also lord of 8th 'Sun is lord of Eleventh (Evil). Pluto trine Saturn is wide.

R. C. A. 96° 15′

(Maximum range one degree)

Directions	Difference in minutes	Total	Average	Time equivalent
♇ □ ☿	— 32			
♂ ☌ ☊	+ 9			
♂ ⊼ MC	+ 44			
☿ △ ☽	— 20			
♄ ⚹ ☉	— 54			
♃ ☌ ♄	+ 5			
☽ □ ♂	— 17	+ 98	+ $6\frac{7}{13}$′	23 days
☽ □ 8th	+ 47			after event
♆ ⊼ Zod	+ 22			
8th ⚹ ♀	+ 53			
♀ △ ♇	+ 33			
♂ ⊼ ♃	— 59			
☉ ⊼ Asc	+ 60			

Group Average

B.A.	— 40		
C.A.	— 48	— 65	22 days
R.C.A.	+ 23		

Uniform Average

9 B.A.	— 59	× 1	— 59′
7 C.A.	— 41	× $\frac{12}{7}$	— 70′
13 R.C.A.	+ 85	× $\frac{7}{12}$	+ 50′
29			— 79

Average —$\frac{79}{29}$ Time Equivalent 17 days before time

Example No. 7*

Carter's Case No. 2
(from Symbolic Directions in Modern Astrology)

I. LONGEVITY

To demonstrate the application of the measure of death of 35′ to the year the horoscopes of three of India's greatest men were first dealt with. Next the three Kings of England consecutively from King Edward VII were taken up. Now we shall take three cases from Carter's book ' Symbolic Directions in Modern Astrology'. The first case dealt with there is a case of accident and will be illustrated in the chapter relating to the measure of accidents. Case No. 2 is the case of a boy born at Sheffield Lat 53° 22′ Long 1°30′ W on February 17, 1911 at 1.15 P.M. and he died in March 18, 1926.

Mercury lord of Lagna posited in the 8th house cusp right in the middle of squares between Saturn and Rahu is enough to cause very early death (Vide Verse 40 Chap V of Hora Shastra by Pratyusas). Mercury has also got a square from Jupiter and Moon from Neptune. Moon has also got a close quincunx from Venus. Saturn lord of 8th is in his debilitation sign. Jaimini formula indicates long life but it is not designed for cases of early death (Balarishta). The formula also provides for reduction of class where as here, lord of 2 Moon becomes the Atmakarka.

* For Planetary Positions & Cusps Vide App. A. No 7.

Maraka lords :

Moon's Longitude at birth Virgo 25° 23′

	y	m	d
Balance of major period of Mars	5	11	3
Major period of Rahu, sub-period of Rahu	2	8	12
,, ,, Jupiter	2	4	24
Major period of Rahu sub-period of Saturn	2	10	6
Total	13	10	15
,, ,, of Mercury	2	6	18
Total	16	5	3

Death took place in the sub-period of Mercury in the major period of Rahu. Jupiter is a first rate Maraka for Gemini born persons as he is lord of 7th and 10th houses and he gives that power to Rahu by his opposition aspect which is very close. Mercury is the worst afflicted planet of the horoscope and occupies 8th house. Rahu is really at the fag end of eleventh house and the beginning of twelfth house and is conjoined with Saturn lord of 8th a maraka. So rule of (3) of L. T. III (c) will apply. Rule (6) also would apply as debilitated. Saturn who is lord of 8th is in conjunction with Rahu and Mercury is in closest aspect to Saturn by Square.

New Era Directions

B. A. 15° 5′

(Maximum range one degree)

Directions	Difference in minutes	Total	Average	Time equivalent
♂ ☌ ♅	+ 2			
8th ⊼ ♆	+ 54			

Directions	Difference in minutes	Total	Average	Time equivalent
☉ ☌ MC	+ 22			
✱ ♂	+ 47			
♄ ✱ Asc	+ 24	+ 118′	$+ 14\frac{3}{4}'$	90 days
Asc □ ♄	— 14			after event
♆ ☍ 8th	— 44			
MC ✱ ♅	+ 27			

There are four 'good' directions and four 'bad' directions. But the bad directions ♂ ☌ ♅, Asc □ ♄ are close and characteristic.

C. A. 8° 48′

(Maximum range 35′)

Directions	Difference in minutes	Total	Average	Time equivalent
8th □ ☋	— 5			
♅ ☌ ☿	— 9			
8th □ ♃	— 30			
L Λ̄ 8th	— 16			
☽ □ ♅	— 20	+ 14′	$+ 1\frac{3}{11}'$	13 days
Zod ☌ ♄	— 13			beyond event
☋ ☌ 8 Zod	+ 7			
♃ Λ̄ Zod	+ 32			
☿ □ ♃	+ 32			
♀ □ L	+ 21			
♆ Λ̄ ☉	+ 15			

Whatever evil elements may be considered lacking in the directions as per Basic Arc are amply supplied by the charateristic arc. All the directions are evil and terrific. No life could have survived the combined impact of such evil directions yielded by the measure of death. Perhaps Jupiter's conjunction ○ ♏ ○ may be termed good but for his being a first rate maraka for the horoscope. This is also quincunx Zodiac.

R. C. A. 25° 51′

(Maximum range one degree)

Directions			Difference in minutes	Total	Average	Time equivalent
Asc	⊼	♂	+ 5			
♆	□	♃	+ 44			
Zod	⊼	☽	+ 28			
♅	✶	Zod	+ 22			
☿	✶	♄	+ 18			
♄	△	♅	+ 21			
Zod	✶	♀	+ 56			
☽	☌	☊	— 5			
☽	☌	♃	— 30			
♀	⊼	♃	— 58			
♄	□	☉	— 18	— 17	— $1\frac{3}{14}$′	+ 4 days
Asc	⊼	MC	+ 20			before event
♀	⊼	☋	— 33			
L	□	Zod	— 47			

Group Average

Directions	Difference	Total	Average
B.A.	+ 90 days		
C.A.	+ 13 days	÷ 99	33 days
R.C.A.	— 4 days		before event

Uniform Average

Class of Direction	Total	Rate	Eqivalent in B.A.	Average	Equivalent in Time
8 B.A.	+ 118′	× 1	+118′		
11 C.A.	+ 14	× $\frac{12}{7}$	+ 24′	+132	$+\frac{132'}{33}$
14 R.C.A.	— 17	× $\frac{7}{12}$	— 10′		
33	= 24 days after event				

In discussing the Naronic measure Carter cites the following directions as per that measure for this event.

♀ □ ♅	— 33′
♅ ☌ ☿	+ 6′
☽ □ ♅	— 5′

While observing that Frankland's 4/7° measure is of the utmost value and a brilliant contribution to astrological science. Carter says that however, the choice between 3/5 and 4/7 must be left to the decision of the astrological world which had till then no time to test them. The values for 4/7, 7/12 and 3/5 with a denominator of 420 arc 240, 245, and 252 respectively and the middle one is selected as the measure of death here for reasons already stated.

III. CARTER'S MEASURE OF DEATH

Arc 3° 46′

The author cites the following directions.

Directions	Difference in minutes	Total	Average	Time equivalent
♂ ☍ Asc	— 28′			
♅ ☌ 8th	— 7′			
♅ □ ♄	— 44′	—125	—25	=1 year &
♄ □ ☿	— 41′		8 months before event	
☉ ✶ ♄	— 5′			

Three directions have been omitted and these are.

MC △ Asc	— 3			
♃ △ ♀	+ 35	—83	—10⅜	=8 months &
☊ ✶ ♀	+ 10			12 days before event

If the above arc is to be applied to the Nirayana horoscope here given, the direction ♅ ☌ 8th alone will be eliminated and the following additional directions will make their appearance.

☽ ☍ Zod	— 51
Zod ✶ Ł	+ 24
Zod △ ♅	— 45
♄ □ 8th	+ 21
♆ □ Zod	+ 23

The total for all the above **twelve** directions will be—104′ Therefore the average will be — $8\frac{2}{3}'$ = about 7 months before event.

But let us try by confining the directions as per this measure of death to the dimensions of this measure, that is 15′ **for purposes of averaging** and taking the other directions as only background influences, the following directions alone are relevant.

Directions			Difference in minutes	Total	Average	Time equivalent
☉	✶	♄	— 5			
MC	△	Asc	— 3	+ 2′	+ ⅔′	16 days
☊	✶	♀	+ 10			after event

All these directions however happen to be 'good' directions.

Example No. 8

(Carter's case No. 3 in Symbolic Directions in Modern Astrology)

Date of birth 8 P. M. on 11-5-1903 Lat. 39° 45′ Long. 105° W. The date of death is given as near the seventeenth birthday & death took place in a motorcar in a wind storm.

Directions			Difference in minutes	Total	Average	Time equivalent

B. A. 17°

(Maximum orbs one degree)

Asc	☍	♄	+ 56
	⚻	☉	— 51
♄	□	☽	— 34
☽	△	☋	— 25
♀	□	☊	+ 57
♅	⚻	☿	+ 29
☋	✶	♆	— 37
8th	⚻	♅	— 28
☿	☌	♀	+ 16
♂	☌	☊	+ 14
	13		

Directions	Difference in minutes	Total	Average	Time equivalent
☿ □ ♂	+ 59	+ 69′	+ 5¾′	35 days
Zod □ ♄	+ 13			beyond event

There are twelve directions within one degree range of which ‘ eight are distinctly evil. The good ’ direction ☿ ☌ ♀ is between lord of 8th and 11th houses and lord of 7th and 12th houses, the ownership in the case of either planet being very bad, bad for the latter according to the doctrine of change of nature by planets (an auspicious planet owning angles becomes malefic). The ownership of 8th, 11th and 12th houses is bad for all planets. The directions are formidable.

C. A. 9° 55′

(Maximum range 35′

Zod ⊼ Asc	+ 2			
MC ☌ ♂	+ 10			
Zod ✱ ♆	+ 32			
MC □ ♀	— 33			
8th △ ♃	— 7	— 15	— 1⅔	17 days
,, ✱ MC	— 20			before event
♂ ✱ 8th	— 5			
♃ ⊼ ♂	— 3			
L ☌ ♀	+ 9			

R. C. A.29° 9′

(Maximum range one degree)

Asc 8 ♆	— 21
MC ⊼ ♃	— 38
♂ ✱ ☽	— 12

Directions	Difference in minutes	Total	Average	Time equivalent
♀ △ ☽	+ 31			
♄ △ 8thC	+ 56	+ 46′	$+5\frac{1}{9}$	15 days
☉ ☌ L	+ 56			beyond event
♀ ✱ ♂	— 8			
L △ ♃	+ 4			
L ✱ MC	— 9			
☋ ⊼ ☊	— 51			
Asc ☍ ♆	— 21			

Group Average

B.A.	+ 35			
C.A.	— 17	+ 36	+ 12	12 days
R.C.A.	+ 15			

Uniform Average

12 B.A.	+ 69′	× 1	— 69		
9 C.A.	— 15′	× $\frac{12}{7}$	— 26	+ 51	$\frac{51}{31}$
11 R.C.A.	+ 46′	× $\frac{7}{12}$	+ 27		
$\overline{32}$				10 days after event	

This case is cited by Mr. Carter as an illustration of the fractional system of directing and he demonstrates how directions obtained by a series of fractions such as 1½°, 2°, 2½°, 3°, 3½° and 5° when averaged yield the result 17° 01′ which is the arc for death.

Carter's measure of death 15′ = one year

Arc 4° 15′

Directions for the Placidean map Sayana Zodiac given in the book.

Directions			Difference in minutes	Total	Average	Time equivalent
♆	☌	8th	+1° 7′			
♅	☍	♀	+1° 0′			
♀	☌	♆	+0°35′	+1°17′	+11′	8 months & 28 days
♂	□	♆	— 8′			beyond event
8th	Λ̄	♄	— 1			
⊙	Λ̄	♅	—29			
☽	Λ̄	♆	—47			

Arc 4° 15′

Directions for the Nirayana Zodiac are given here

(Maximum range one degree)

♅	☍	♀	+60			
☋	Λ̄	MC	+46			
♀	Λ̄	Asc	+ 5			
♄	✱	☋	—44			
♃	△	8thZod	—43	— 112	— 11$\frac{1}{5}$	9 months
Zod	Λ̄	☽	— 6			before event
Zod	Λ̄	♂	—45			
MC	Λ̄	Zod	—30			
♂	□	♆	— 8			
☽	Λ̄	♆	—47			

Arc 4° 15′

Directions under the limitations of New Era Technique

(Maximum range 15′)

♀	Λ̄	Asc	+ 4			
Zod	Λ̄	☽	— 6	— 10	— $\frac{1}{3}$	41 days
♂	□	♆	— 8			before event

The directions in force within orbs are quite characteristic as well as close to the event the directions within one degree range acting as background influences.

Example No. 9

Carter's case No. 4

(Symbolic Directions in Modern Astrology)

This is the case of a boy born July 24, 1911 at 2, P.M. at Lat. 44° 2′ N. 95° 45′ W. The boy died as the result of an automobile accident on December 18, 1920. In the nativity published in P. 43 of the book Mercury and Neptune arc shown as if both arc in Cancer and also interpreted as such (Vide remarks on Page 71 that Saturn is in good aspect to Mercury and Neptune). But the two planets are actually in different signs.

B. A. 9° 24′

(Maximum range one degree)

Directions	Difference in minutes	Total	Average	Time equivalent
Asc □ ☿	+40			
♅ □ ♂	+38			
♆ ☌ ☉ ..	+18			
♂ △ ♀	+28			
☋ △ ♀	+ 4	+27′	+3′	18 days
Asc △ ♆	+40			beyond event
Asc ☌ 8th Zod	—45			
♃ ✱ ♀	—10			
☽ ☍ ♅	—58			

Mars in Aries (Nirayana) is more characteristic of automobile accidents. The majority of directions are evil.

C. A. 5° 29′

(Maximum range 35′)

Directions	Difference in minutes	Total	Average	Time equivalent
☉ □ ♂	+ 14			
☽ □ Zod	— 15			
♆ ☍ ♅	— 6			
☿ ⊼ ♅	— 34	+ 9	+ $1\frac{2}{7}$	13 days
MC ✱ ♇	+ 34			beyond event
Zod ✱ ♇	— 5			
8th ✱ ☿	+ 21			

The average by death measure is staggeringly close. There are evil directions between Sun and Mars and there is also Mercury Uranus contact (Vide Example No. 15 of Astrology of Accidents by the same author).

R. C. A. 16° 7′

(Maximum range one degree)

Directions	Difference in minutes
♅ □ Asc	+ 54
Asc ⊼ ♇	+ 24
♀ ✱ ☉	+ 18
♃ □ ☿	+ 13
♂ ✱ ♆	+ 28
☊ □ ☿	+ 32
♂ □ ☿	+ 56
☊ ✱ ♆	+ 4
♄ ⊼ ♃	— 24
☊ ☍ 8thZod	— 53
♂ ☍ 8thZod	— 29

Direction			Difference in minutes	Total	Average	Time equivalent
♄	⊼	☋	— 38	+ 41	+ $2\frac{13}{14}$	10 days
L	⚹	♀	— 39			beyond event
♃	△	♆	— 10			

There are no less than ten 'evil' fateful directions for event, only four are 'good' directions. This should satisfy the most exacting critic both as regards the nature of the event, the manner in which death took place as also the timing of the event by average.

Group Average

B.A.	+ 18		
C.A.	+ 13	+ 41	14 days beyond event
R.C.A.	+ 10		

Uniform Average

9 B.A.	— 27′	× 1	= 27′	
7 C.A.	— 9′	× $\frac{12}{7}$	= $15\frac{1}{2}'$	+ $66\frac{1}{2}$
14 R.C.A.	— 41′	× $\frac{7}{12}$	= 24′	

Averagc $\frac{66\frac{1}{2}}{30}$ — equivalent in time 13 days beyond event

Carter's **Measure** of Death

(Arc 2° 21′)

The following directions are cited by the author

♅	☍	☉	— 1°10′			
♀	⚹	☽	+ 0°25′			
☽	⚹	♄	+ 22′	—49	—$9\frac{4}{5}$	7 months &
♄	⚹	♆	— 27			28 days before event
♄	□	☿	+ 1			

The good directions are surmised to have been turned into evil by Saturn being opposed to the rising degree.

Example No. 10

Three consecutive cases from Carter's Symbolic Directions in Modern Astrology have been taken up and illustrated with regard to New Era Measures and the new technique of working directions. Of course, all cases can be similarly dealt with and it will be only repetition. The diligent student can work the rest for himself. In fact, I had intended to include at least three more and made the record ready, but I thought it would be better to take them from other books. I shall take the next one from Carter's Principles of Horoscopic Delineation, one from Bradley's Solunars which recently came into my possession.

Case No. 4

In Carter's Principles of Horoscope Delineation

I. LONGEVITY

This is the case of a female born at 2-30 P.M. on Oct 17, 1867 at Geneva Lat. 46° 13′ Long. 6° 7′ E. She poisoned herself at 10-15 A.M. July 7, 1922. We need not go elaborately into the astrological causes for suicide as here we are mainly concerned with the directions for the event. But it may be mentioned in passing that Rahu has conjunction of 8th house cusp with quincunx from Neptune and Moon Square 8th cusp would appear to be the principal reasons. Sun Lord of 8th house is in debilitation and within the range of opposition from Neptune. It is doubtful if suicide could have been predicted as the manner of death. But proper attention to the location of Rahu should at least make it appear very probable according to the texts. In Hindu astrology the planets responsible for end by suicide are stated to be Rahu and Ketu. If they occupy 6th 8th or 12th houses and have connection with lords of angles or trines death by suicide is to be suspected. Here Rahu occupies 8th house according to the Hindu method of house division. He has a square from Moon Lord of 7th (an angle) sextile from Mercury lord of 5th (trine) and from Mars lord of 10th (angle). In addition there is the close quincunx from Neptune (not taken into account in the texts). Otherwise it is a clear case of medium life. Jaimini formula also confirms medium life whether three sets or five sets are employed. Death took place in the sub-period of Rahu in the major period of Saturn.

Moon's Longitude at birth Taurus 24° 36′

	y	m	d
Balance of Mars dasa at birth	6	4	1
Major period of Rahu	18	0	0
,, ,, Jupiter	16	0	0
Total	40	4	1
,, ,, Saturn to end of Sub-period of Mars	13	7	12
	53	11	13
,, ,, ,, of Rahu	2	10	6
Total	56	9	19

Snake bite and death through poison are given as distinct characteristics of this sub-period*. The major period is that of lord of 2nd house and planets in 6th, 8th, or 12th are the sub-lords to inflict death and Rahu is in 8th.

II. NEW ERA DIRECTIONS

B. A. 54° 43′

(Maximum range — one degree)

Directions	Difference in minutes	Total	Average	Time equivalent
☽ ⊼ ☋	— 47			
8th ☌ ♂	— 38			
♃ ⊼ ♄	— 27			
☽ ☍ Asc	— 22			
Zod ☌ ☽	+ 7	+ 15′	— 1½′	9 days
MC □ ♀	+ 18			after event
8thC ☌ ☿	+ 23			
♀ ⚹ ☉	+ 27			
♃ ☌ Zod	+ 28			
8th ☿ ♆	+ 46			

Note there is a train of evil directions involving Asc, 8th house and Sun, Mars and Neptune.

---

* यन्त्रसर्पाग्निमरणं (death through machinery, serpent or fire) Parashara.

C. A. 31° 55′

(Maximum range 35′

Directions			Difference in minutes	Total	Average	Time equivalent
♅	□	♇	— 32			
Asc	△	☿	— 13			
♆	☌	♇	— 3			
♅	□	♂	+ 2	+ 26	+ $3\frac{1}{4}$	34 days
♂	☍	☽	+ 9			after event
♃	⊼	☉	+ 11			
☿	⊼	♇	+ 20			
♆	☍	♂	+ 31			

Evil directions expressive of a violent end are unmistakeably present. The time indication is all that can be desired. There are three more directions beyond range ♇ ☌ ☽ + 43, ☿ ☍ ☽ — 52, ☋ ⊼ ♂ — 49 all evil and no doubt acted as background influences though technically excluded for averaging.

R. C. A. 93° 48′

(Maximum range one degree)

♂	⊼	8th	— 51			
☋	☌	☽	— 38			
8th	⚹	☉	— 24			
Asc	☌	♇	+ 9	+ 37′	+ $4\frac{5}{8}$′	16 days
♅	△	☾	+ 13			after event
☊	⊼	♇	+ 34			
Asc	☍	♂	+ 39			
☽	☌	8thC	+ 55			

Group Averge

B.A.	+ 9			
C.A.	+ 34	+ 59	— 20	20 days
R.C.A.	+ 16			before event

True Average

10 B.A.	+ 15′	× 1	+ 15′	
8 C.A.	— 22′	× $\frac{12}{7}$	+ 38′	— $\frac{19}{28}$
8 R.C.A.	+ 37′	× $\frac{7}{12}$	+ 22′	
21 directions total to			+ 75′	

Time equvalent 22 days after event

This result is certainly very close and the aspects quite characteristic. This speaks well for New Era directions as well as for New Era technique with the Nirayana Zodiac and the trisection method of domification all of which are brought into play in this illustration.

Example No. 11

Sigmund Freud

The horoscope of Sigmund Freud is given by the Mr. Bradley in his Solar and Lunar returns and the horoscope is there ready cast according to the Tropical Zodiac and also Hypsomatic Zodiacs. As it is Chitra Zodiac that is adopted here, it is necessary to recast it according to this Zodiac. This may be done by deducting the Ayanamsa for the date of birth from the tropical longitudes of ascendant and M. C. and the planets and by trisecting the eclipitic between M. C. and Asc. (The horoscope is No 11 in App. A). The directions in force for the death according to New Era measures are numerous and remarkable. Sigmund Freud was born at 9-23 A. M. L. M. T. on May 6, 1856. He died on September 23rd, 1939.

B. A. 83° 23′

(Maximum range one degree)

Directions			Difference in minutes	Total	Average	Time equivalent
♄	⊼	Zod	— 57			
☿	☍	8thC	— 44			
Zod	⚹	☉	— 44			
♂	☍	♄	— 42			
♃	⚹	☊	— 35			
MC	□	♃	— 35			
♀	△	♆	— 35			
♄	⊼	8th	— 14	— 94	— $\frac{94}{47}$	34 days before event
☿	□	♅	— 13			
♀	⊼	☿	— 12			
☉	⚹	☽	+ 8			
♄	△	♅	+ 17			
Asc	☍	Zod	+ 27			
☿	⊼	♆	+ 33			
♇	⚹	☿	+ 42			
☋	△	☉	+ 54			
♂	△	♀	+ 56			

C. A. 48° 38′

(Maximum range 35′)

Directions	Difference in minutes	Total	Average	Time equivalent
♇ ✱ ☊	— 31			
☿ ✱ ☉	— 19			
♄ □ ☉	+ 11	+ 23	+ $3\frac{5}{6}$	40 days
♂ ☌ 8thZod	+ 13			after event
☉ ✱ ♇	+ 16			
8thC ✱ ☽	+ 33			

R. C. A. 142° 57′

Directions	Difference in minutes	Total	Average	Time equivalent
♄ □ 8thC	— 40			
☿ ⊼ ♅	— 39			
♂ □ ☿	— 38			
☉ △ ☽	— 18			
♇ □ ♄	— 14			
♄ ☍ ♅	— 9			
Asc △ Zod	+ 1	+ 101	+ $6\frac{11}{15}$	24 days
☿ ⊼ ♆	+ 7			after event
♇ △ ☿	+ 16			
☋ ✱ ☉	+ 28			
♂ ✱ ♀	+ 30			
♄ △ ♆	+ 37			
♃ □ 8thZ	+ 37			
Asc ✱ 8th	+ 44			
Mc ✱ ♄	+ 59			

The 'good' and 'bad' directions in all the groups are nearly fifty-fifty. Saturn lord of 8th house figures in eight of them. Directions such as ♂ ☍ ♄, ♄ ⊼ 8th, ♀ ☌ 8th, ♄ □ ☉, ♄ ☍ ♆, ☾ □ ♄ are all remarkable.

Group Average

B.A.	— 34		
C.A.	+ 40	+ 30	10 days
R.C.A.	+ 24		after event

True Average

17 B.A.	— 94	× 1	— 94′	
6 C.A.	+ 40	× $\frac{12}{7}$	+ 39′	+ 4′
15 R.C.A.	+ 101	× $\frac{7}{21}$	+ 59′	

Average $\frac{4}{38}$ or $\frac{2}{19}$

Time Equvalent one day beyond Event

§ 2. Legacies, Gifts etc

The measure of 35′ to the year by reason of its being derived from the eighth division of the Zodiac represents not only the event of death but also all matters signified by the eighth sign or house. As 8th house stands also for legacies, sudden or unearned wealth, it is only natural to apply this measure to predict events, of such a nature.

Example No. 12

Nobelle Prize for Tagore

I have not been able to secure reliable published cases where natives have come into sudden wealth by legacies or otherwise. But in the articles on Dr. Tagore published in the Astrological Magazine, the time of his getting the Nobelle award for literature and also of his coming into a substantial annual endowment have been given and I propose to utilise these two instances for illustrating this measure in this respect.

Dr. Tagore came into the legacy of Nobelle by reason of his literary merit and the time of his receiving the award is stated to be 52 years and 5 months. This took place in the sub-period of Venus in the Major period of Moon :—

	y	m	d
Balance of Mercury's major period at birth	11	4	28
,, of Ketu	7	0	0
,, Venus	20	0	0
,, Sun	6	0	0
Total	44	4	28
Moon's period till end of ketu's sub-period	7	10	0
	52	2	28
Moon's period Venus's sub-period	1	8	0
Total	53	10	28

Sublord Venus is ruler of 8th house in the horoscope of birth in second house square Jupiter but trine Rahu. The latter aspect is an indication of the award proceeding from abroad. Rahu occupies the meridian of the horoscope in Sagattarius. The major lord Moon is in the first house trine Jupiter (exalted) and in exchange with him. Moon has also the close sextile of Uranus from the third house. Thus third, fifth, and eighth houses are all connected.

Fig. 7

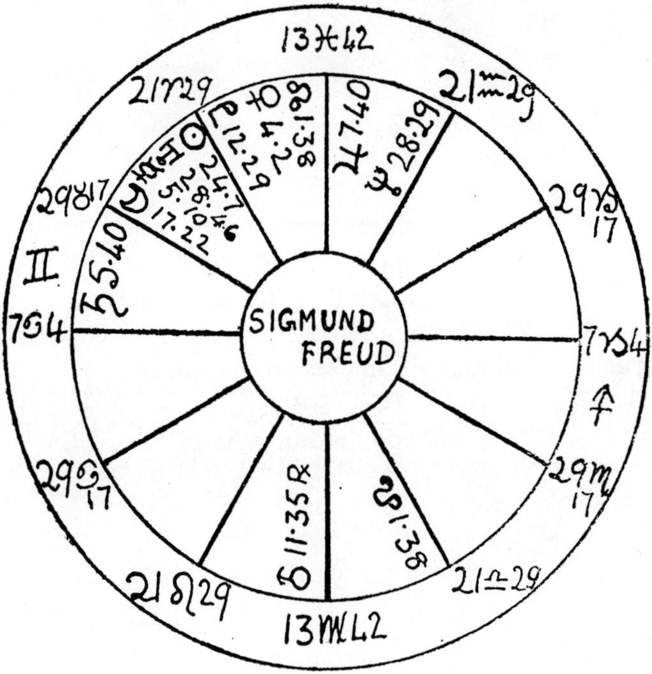

B. A. 52° 25′

(Maximum range one degree)

Directions			Difference in minutes	Total	Average	Time equivalent
♂	□	♀	— 25			
♃	△	♅	— 19			
☉	⚹	♇	— 11			
Zod	⊼	8th	+ 8			
☋	△	♇	+ 10			
☿	☌	♂	+ 15	+ 117′	+ $11\frac{7}{10}$′	71 days after event
♂	□	8thC	+ 24			
☿	⚹	Zod	+ 31			
♇	□	♆	+ 40			
MC	☍	♄	+ 44 (radical trine)			

The above directions notably ♃ △ ♅, ☿ ⚹ Zod, ☉ ⚹ ♇ are first rate indications for such an event. Also ☿ ☌ ♂ as Mars is not a malefic for this horoscope as he is ruler of 2nd and 9th houses but beneficial.

C. A. 30° 35′

(Maximum range 35′)

Directions			Difference in minutes	Total	Average	Time equivalent
☋	☌	♃	— 33			
Asc	△	☊	— 24			
8th	⊼	♀	— 14			
♀	⚹	Asc	— 11	— 69	— $8\frac{5}{8}$	90 days before event
☿	⚹	♆	— 10			
Asc	☌	☉	— 3			
♅	☍	MC	+ 12			
☉	⊼	☊	+ 14			

The directions ☉ ⚹ ♃ —54 and Pluto in 2nd ☌ ♅ —62 are also present as background influences though excluded for averaging.

R. C. A. 89° 51′

(Maximum range one decree)

Directions	Difference in minutes	Total	Average	equivalent in Time
8thC □ ♀	— 58			
♀ △ Asc	— 55			
Asc ✶ ☉	— 47			
♅ △ MC	— 32			
☉ ⊼ ☊	— 30			
♂ ✶ 8thZ	+ 7			
☋ ⊼ ☉	+ 12			
MC ✶ ♅	+ 14			
☉ △ Asc	+ 29			
♆ ✶ ☿	+ 36	+ 62	+ $4\frac{3}{7}$	16 days beyond event
Asc ✶ ♀	+ 37			
♀ □ 8thC	+ 40			
☋ ☍ Asc	+ 50			
♃ △ ☋	+ 59			

The R. C. A. directions are splendidly suggestive.

Group Average

B.A.	+ 71			
C.A.	— 90	— 3	— 1	one day before event
R.C.A.	+ 16			

True Average

10 B.A.	+ 117′	× 1	+ 119′		
8 C.A.	+ 69′	× $\frac{12}{7}$	— 118′	35	$\frac{35}{32}$
14 R.C.A.	+ 62′	× $\frac{7}{12}$	+ 36′		
32	+ 35				

$\frac{35}{32}$′=Time Equiv 7 days beyond Event

Example No. 13

Huge Annual Endowment For Dr. Tagore

I. PLANETARY PERIODS AND SUBPERIODS

Dr. Tagore came into a huge annual Endowment of Rs. 50,000 in September 1921. The actual date has not been given; the month alone being mentioned with the remark, 'Tagore was then aged 60 years and 4 months*.

	y	m	d
Balance of Major period of Mercury at birth	11	4	28
,, Ketu's	7	0	0
,, Venus	20	0	0
,, Sun	6	0	0
,, Moon	10	0	0
Total	54	4	28
Mars till end of sub-period of Ketu	4	10	24
Total	59	3	22
,, of Venus	1	2	0
Total	60	5	22

Sublord Venus is ruler of 8th house in 2nd. Note that the Nobel award came to him also in the sub-period of Venus. Mars is ruler of 2nd and 9th houses and Zodaical 8th.

II. NEW ERA DIRECTIONS

B. A. 60° 20′

(Maximum range one degree)

Directions	Difference in minutes	Total	Average	Time equivalent
☽ ⊼ 8thC	— 54			
☊ ⊼ ♃	— 48			

* P. 28 Astrological Magazine Jan. 1942.

Directions			Difference in minutes	Total	Average	Time equivalent
Asc	⊼	☊	— 39			
8thC	△	♀	— 29			
♀	□	Asc	— 26			
☿	□	♆	— 25			
♅	⊼	MC	— 3	— 43′	— $\frac{43}{13}$	20 days before event
☉	☌	☋	— 1			
Zod	☌	♂	+ 4			
♂	△	Zod	+ 36			
☊	✱	☉	+ 41			
MC	□	♅	+ 43			
☉	□	Asc	+ 58			

C. A. 35° 12′

(Maximum range 35′)

Directions			Difference in minutes	Total	Average	Time equivalent
☉	☌	♂	— 34			
MC	⊼	☋	— 33			
☉	✱	Zod	— 18			
☋	✱	♂	— 13			
MC	□	☉	— 12			
☋	△	Zod	— 3			
♄	⊼	8thC	+ 1	— 67	— 6$\frac{7}{10}$	70 days before event
♅	□	Asc	+ 3			
☽	□	♃	+ 16			
MC	✱	Asc	+ 26			

R. C. A. 103° 26′

(Maximum range one degree)

Directions			Difference in minutes
☉	⊼	♆	— 55
♆	✱	♀	— 49

a

Directions	Difference in minutes	Total	Average	Time equivalent
Asc □ ☿	— 48			
☿ □ 8thC	— 45			
♄ Λ̄ ☋	— 38			
☋ Λ̄ ♆	— 34			
♄ Λ̄ ☉	— 17			
☉ △ ☿	— 10	— 153	— $10\frac{3}{15}$	36 days before event
♆ △ 8thC	Exact			
☋ ☍ ☿	+ 11			
L ✶ ♂	+ 16			
♄ △ Asc	+ 21			
☿ △ ☽	+ 29			
ℸ △ Zod	+ 32			
♃ △ ♆	+ 34			

Group Average

B.A.	— 20		
C.A.	— 70	— 126	42 days before event
R.C.A	— 36		

True Average

13	B.A.	— 43′	× 1	— 43′
10	C.A.	— 67′	× $\frac{12}{7}$	— 115′
15	R.C.A.	— 154′	× $\frac{7}{12}$	— 90′
38				— 248 Average $6\frac{10}{19}$′

Time Equiv=40 days before event

The results are close enough for all practical purposes. Perhaps it may be closer if the actual date is known.

CHAPTER IX

MEASURE OF ACCIDENTS, SICKNESS ETC.

§ I. BASIS OF MEASURE

This measure which is related to the sixth house is to be used in connection with all affairs pertaining to that house, such as illness, accidents, operations, etc not ending in death but in recovery. Sickness whenever serious lasts for a period of time and no particular date can be referred to or taken up for purposes of demonstrating the measure, but operations and accidents are referrable to a single date and will serve to illustrate this measure. It is not to be inferred therefrom that this measure is of no use for the prediction of illness, but the technique suggested for the use of this measure in connection with such illness is slightly different and will be dealt with in its proper place.

Carter's Astrology of Accidents deals with accidents exclusively as the name implies and a great mass of material and data are found collected there which have been of great use to this writer in many respects. The measure to be used for direction for this category of events is of course the proportion which the sixth sign of the Zodiac bears to the entire Zodiac of 360 degrees, that is 150° : 360° or 5/12 or 25′ to one year. I believe that 35′ to the year measure may also be considered in this connection as a complementary measure as all the directions formed with the latter measure cannot mean death as this can happen but once. Directions as per death measure, good and bad, will be scattered throughout life and will no doubt influence events in the same manner as the measure of 25′ to the year. Still, much of research has not been done in this direction and the matter is still under investigation. So that aspect is not dealt with here. The measure of accidents taken by itself yields sufficiently satisfactory results.

As for illustrations, I cannot do better than use the materials already collected in Carter's works as the horoscopes are also found there ready cast. Here, therefore, I shall take up the non-fatal cases from the two books of Carter; Symbolic Directions in Modern Astrology and Astrology of Accidents.

§ II. PROCEDURE

The method of working is the same as for the measure of death. The aspects and points for direction are the same except with regard to the cusps and Zodiacal points. In the case of the measure of death, in addition to ascendant and M. C. and the planetary bodies, the cusps of 8th house and O ♍ O were taken. Here the points to be taken instead are the cusps of 6th house and O ♍ O (or 6th Zod). The orbs and method of averaging are the same.

§ III. EXAMPLES

Example 14. (No. 12 in App. A)

Case No. 1 in Carter's Symbolic Directions in M.A. is a case of accident and concerns the nativity of a man born in Wiltshire, England at 8–10 A.M. on 25–6–1891. The information is that in an accident sustained through machinery in the factory in which he was employed, his arm was torn off, there was great danger to life through sepsis and though his life was saved, his career was ruined. He got damages from the Company. This accident took place on 30–10–1923.

B. A. 32° 21′

(Maximum range one degree)

Directions	Difference in minutes	Total	Average	Time equivalent
♃ ✱ ☿	+ 23			
☽ ☌ ♃	— 37			
♄ △ ☽	— 33			
♃ △ Asc	— 10			
☿ □ Zod	— 14			
☉ □ MC	— 3	+ 91	+ $7\frac{7}{12}$	45 days
Asc ⊼ Zod	+ 19			beyond event
♄ □ ♂	+ 2			
MC ☌ ♆	+ 39			
MC ☌ [	+ 18			
☋ △ MC	+ 27			
♀ ✱ ♄	+ 60			

The directions that are very close to accident are ♄ □ ♂ + 2 and ☉ □ MC — 3. The former for the accident and the latter for the career being ruined may be noted. The directions to and from the Zodiacal points, I have found in many instances, to have an element of inescapability, that is, are found to be responsible for events over which the native has no control.

C. A. 13° 29′

(Maximum range 25′)

Directions	Difference in minutes	Total	Average	Time equivalent
☋ □ ♃	— 21			
☿ ☌ ☉	— 13			
Asc □ ☊	— 10	+ 12	+ $1\frac{5}{7}$	25 days
Zod ☌ MC	— 2			after event
♅ ⊼ ♀	+ 17			
Asc ✶ ☉	+ 20			
♂ □ ♅	+ 21			

It is significant that ♂ □ ♅ is in evidence here also, and is a violent direction. Mars is in twelfth house in sign Gemini (arm). Jupiter is ruler of the 6th house and occupies 8th house and the square direction of Rahu to Asc and Ketu to Jupiter indicate septic complications. Asc ✶ ☉ preserves life. Uranus is opposition M. C. in the radix. Venus ruling 4th and 11th houses is evil for the horoscope.

R. C. A. 77° 38′

(Maximum range one degree)

Directions	Difference in minutes
☽ ✶ ☉	— 60
6thC ✶ ☊	— 50
☋ ⊼ 6thZ	— 45
☿ □ L	— 31
♅ ☌ 6thC	— 29
6thC □ ☉	— 20
☿ □ ♆	— 10
Asc ⊼ L	+ 2

Directions	Difference in minutes	Total	Average	Time equivalent
Asc ⊼ ♆	+ 23			
♅ ☍ ♂	+ 46	— 124	$-11\frac{3}{11}$	29 days
♀ ✶ ♅	+ 50			before event

A violent direction between Uranus and Mars is present here also. Directions to the cusp of 6th house and to O ♍ O are also to be found. Ascendant too is badly involved.

Group Average

B.A.	+ 45		
C.A.	+ 25	+ 41	14 days
R.C.A.	— 29		after event

True Average

12 B.A.	+ 91′	× 1	+ 91′	
7 C.A.	+ 12′	× $\frac{12}{5}$	+ 29′	
11 R.C.A.	— 124′	× $\frac{5}{12}$	— 52′	
30			— 68	Average $2\frac{2}{15}$′

Time Equiv ⊙ = 14 days after event

It would be a useful study to compare the positions of planets and cusps according to the Sayana (Western) and Nirayana (Hindu) horoscopes in all the cases dealt with here but it will occupy too much space. Such a comparison will be made with regard to this horoscope alone.

Tropical			Sidereal		
(Placidean cusps)			(Trisection Method)		
6th cusp falls in ♑			6th cusp falls in ♐		
Mars occupies ♋			Mars occupies ♊		
,,	,,	11th house	,,	,,	12th house
Sun	,,	11th house	Sun	,,	12th house
	,,	Cancer		,,	Gemini

and so on. The positions according to the Nirayana horoscope appear more characteristic of the accident and the involvement of the arm which was torn off.

Example 15 (Case No. 2 in A. A.)

The first case in Carter's Astrology of Accidents is one that ended fatally. We shall take up the second case which was a case of accident only. A lady born 0-8 P.M. on Aug 24, 1867 Washington D. C. became unconscious from geyser fumes in connection with a bath at Zurich on Oct. 30, 1927. The Nirayana converted horoscope is given here (No. 13 in App. A) with the cusps worked out correct to the minute as is necessary for the New Era directions.

B. A. 60° 11′

(Maximum range one degree)

Directions	Difference in minutes	Total	Average	Time equivalent
☋ ☌ ☾	— 52			
MC ⚹ ☉	— 49	— 14	— $4\frac{1}{6}$	25 days
Zod ⚹ ♀				before event
♆ □ ☊	— exact			
♀ ☍ Zod	+ 36			
6thC ⚹ ♀	+ 54			

The directions Neptune Square Rahu (Exact) and Ketu conjunction Pluto are characteristic of the nature of the accident. Carter gives Mercury opposition Neptune which is necessarily omitted here as beyond the orbs for averaging as it is—84′. Apparently the direction between Neptune and Rahu is overlooked though the longitude of the Node is given in the map, perhaps because recognition of the influence of nodes is still lukewarm in Western Astrology. The Nodes account for a great deal of poisoning cases, suicides, narcosis, etc.

C. A. 25° 5′

(Maximum range 25′)

Directions	Difference in minutes	Total	Average	Time equivalent
Asc □ ☊	— 9			
6thC ☍ ♄	— 8			
MC □ ♅	— 3	— 3	— $\frac{3}{5}$	9 days
Asc ⊼ ♆	+ 2			beyond event
♄ △ ☿	+ 15			

R. C. A. 144° 26′

(Maximum range one degree)

Directions	Difference in minutes
Asc ⊼ ☊	— 48
6thc ✱ ♄	— 47
MC ⊼ ♅	— 42
Asc ☌ ♆	— 37
♄ △ ☿	— 24
♅ ☌ Asc	— 7
⊙ ⊼ ♅	+ 18
Zod △ ♇	+ 27

Directions	Difference in minutes	Total	Average	Time equivalent
☊ △ ♂	+ 42			
♀ △ ☾	+ 52			
Asc △ ☿	+ 57			

Mercury is ruler of 8th and 11th houses making him very evil. Mars is ruler of 6th house. Venus is ruler of 12th also and hence Venus too is not good.

Group Average

	Days		
B.A.	— 25		
C.A.	— 9	— 12	12 days
R.C.A.	— 2		before event

True Average

6 B.A.	— 25′	× 1	— 25′	
5 C.A.	— 3′	× $\frac{12}{5}$	— 7′	
11 R.C.A.	— 9′	× $\frac{5}{12}$	— 4′	
22			— 36	Average $1\frac{7}{11}'$

Time Equiv = 10 days before event

Example 16 (No. 14 in App. A)

I shall take up one more case from Carter's Astrology of Accidents before passing on to other cases. The next case of accident in that book for which the horoscope also is given is No. 8 but the date of accident is not available which is necessary for being dealt with here. So also case No. 13. I shall pass on to case No. 19 which is that of Carter's own daughter. She was born at 6-40 A. M. on March 20, 1916. London. This girl had a severe fall on 16–8–1926 while on a holiday when she fell through a skylight to stone-steps 13 feet below and was found unconscious on a heap of glass. Employing the New Era measures for the Event, I find that there is no necessity for any rectification of birth time though it is stated that this horoscope has figured in the never ending controversies regarding the Pre-Natal Epoch ; and I have no idea as to what the controversy was about. A small correction was however found necessary with regard to the longitude of Jupiter. In the chart given in that book (P. 102 it is given as Aries 8° 40′ whereas I think it should be Aries 8° 34′ according to Ephemeris (Raphael).

B. A. 10° 25′

(Maximum range one degree)

Directions	Difference in minutes	Total	Average	Time equivalent
☉ △ ♂	— 35			
♀ △ 6thZ	— 19			
☾ ✱ ♀	— 16	— 1′	— $\frac{1}{8}$′	one day
♆ ☌ ♂	+ 4			before event
☉ □ ♄	+ 9			
♃ ✱ ♅	+ 56			

'Good' directions are four and 'evil' directions are only two. The evil directions are closest for the event. The planets concerned in the good directions are Venus, Jupiter and Uranus. Venus is quite evil because of his rulership of 3rd and 8th houses. Jupiter is the ruler of angles and Uranus of 12th house! It is to be noted that though the danger was great "no lasting ill effects ensued."

C. A. 4° 20′

(Maximum range 25′)

Direction	Difference in minutes	Total	Average	Time equivalent
♅ □ 6thZ	— 17			
♄ ⚹ 6thC	— 10			
L ⊼ ☊	+ 3	+ 21′	+ 3½′	51 days beyond event
☽ ⚹ ♂	+ 11			
☿ ⚹ ♀	+ 11			
6thC □ ♅	+ 23			

R. C. A. 20° 59′

(Maximum range one degree)

Direction	Difference in minutes	Total	Average	Time equivalent
Asc ⚹ ♄	— 53			
♅ ☍ ♄	— 34			
☿ ☌ ☉	— 34			
6thC △ ☊	— 27			
Zod △ 6thC	— 27	— 131′	— $13\frac{1}{10}$′	33 days before event
L □ Zod	— 26			
♂ ⚹ L	+ 4			
♄ ☌ ♆	+ 36			
Asc ⚹ ☿	+ 56			

Group Average

B.A.	— 1		
C.A.	+ 51	+ 17	6 days after event
R.C.A.	— 33		

True Average

6 B.A.	— 1′	× 1	— 1′
6 C.A.	+ 21′	× $\frac{12}{5}$	+ 50′
10 R.C.A.	— 131′	× $\frac{5}{12}$	— 55′
22			— 6 Average $\frac{3}{11}$′

Time Equiv = 2 days before event

Example No. 17

From accidents we shall pass on to operations the exact date of which also can be taken up for illustration of this measure. Gandhi was operated on for appendicitis on 12-1-1924. Since the date of birth is Oct. 2, 1869 B. A. is 54° 17′. This occurred in the sub-period of Rahu in the major period of Rahu itself. The very combination is evil enough.

चोराग्नि विषशस्त्रार्ती राहोन्तर्गतेऽप्यहो—" Affliction through thief, fire, poison or instrument (Parashara) " Rahu is square Asc and Mercury and Mercury is ruler of Virgo the sign on the cusp of the twelfth house. Sun sextile Rahu (Radix) was a life-saver.

B. A. 54° 17′

(Maximum range one degree)

Direction	Difference in minutes	Total	Average	Time equivalent
⊙ △ ☊	— 58			
ℓ ⊼ ♄	— 33			
♅ ✱ ♀	— 24			
Zod ⊼ ♀	— 9			
Asc ⊼ ♃	— 5			
6thC ☌ ♃	— 3	— 93′	— $6\frac{3}{15}'$	57 days
MC △ ♃	+ 1			before event
Asc △ ☽	+ 7			
6thC □ ☽	+ 9			
♆ 8/15 ♄	+ 22			

C. A. 22° 37′

(Maximum range 25′)

Directions	Difference in minutes	Total	Average	Time equivalent
Asc ⚻ ♆	— 1			
Asc ☌ ♂	+ 1			
6thC ☌ ♅	+ 1			
,, ⚻ ♂	+ 3	+ 38′	+ $4\frac{3}{4}$′	99 days
MC △ ♆	+ 5			after event
,, □ ♂	+ 7			
♀ ✶ ☉	+ 8			
☽ □ ♄	+ 14			

Asc ☌ ♂ is very close and very characteristic. Mars has a radical opposition to Pluto and Jupiter, Jupiter being ruler of 6th house. Venus ruler of 8th is conjunct Mars. Mars is also square Moon and quincunx Neptune in Pisces.

R. C. A. 130° 17′

(Maximum range one degree)

Directions	Difference in minutes	Total	Average	Time equivalent
☉ □ ♃	— 57			
☉ ☍ ☽	— 45			
♄ ☌ Zod	+ 37			
☉ ✶ ♆	+ 47	+ 191′	$23\frac{7}{8}$′	61 days
☉ □ ♂	+ 49			after event
♀ △ MC	+ 50			
♀ ☌ 6thC	+ 54			
♀ ⚻ Asc	+ 56			

Group Average

B.A.	— 57		
C.A.	+ 69	+ 73	24 days after event
R.C.A.	+ 61		

True Average

10 B.A	— 93′	× 1	— 93′
8 C·A	+ 38′	× $\frac{12}{5}$	+ 91′
8 C.A	+ 191′	× $\frac{5}{12}$	+ 80′
29			+ 78′ Average $\frac{78}{26}$′

Equiv in time : 22 days after event

The result yielded by averaging leaves nothing to be desired. The transits on 12–1–1924 are also remarkable, and Nirayana longitudes are employed. Neptune transits square of radical Mars (same degree). Venus square radical Jupiter (within one degree). Mercury square radical Uranus (almost exact). According to Tropical longitudes Neptune transits Moon and Uranus opposition Sun (exact degrees).

Example No. 18

King Edward VII.

The operation for appendicitis took place on 24-6-1902. Birth Nov. 9, 1841. Therefore Basic Arc is 60° 38′.

B. A. 60° 38′

(Maximum range one degree)

Directions	Difference in minutes	Total	Average	Time equivalent
♄ □ ☿	— 55			
MC ⊼ ☋	— 48			

Directions	Difference in minutes	Total	Average	Time equivalent
♀ □ ♅	— 45			
L □ ♅	— 33			
♅ △ 6thZ	— 23			
☿ □ MC	— 21			
♆ □ ♂	— 17			
♅ ⊻ ♃	— 13			
♀ □ L	+ 26			
♃ ✶ Z	+ 28	— 151′	— $13\frac{8}{11}'$	= 83 days after event
L △ ♀	+ 50			

C. A. 25° 16′

(Maximum range 25′)

Directions	Difference in minutes	Total	Average	Time equivalent
♃ □ ☉	— 10			
☊ ⊼ ♇	— 4			
Zod ☍ ☉	Exact	+ 37′	+ $6\frac{1}{6}'$	90 days after event
♀ □ ♆	+ 11			
♆ □ 6th	+ 17			
L □ ♆	+ 23			

R. C. A. 145° 31′

(Maximum range one degree)

Directions	Difference in minutes
♅ □ ☉	— 46
♀ ✶ ♂	— 29
☿ △ Asc	— 24
L △ ♂	— 17
☊ □ ♇	+ 11
Zod ✶ ☉	+ 15
MC □ Asc	+ 35

Directions	Difference in minutes	Total	Average	Time equivalent
℄ ☌ ♆	+ 38			
6thC□ ☊	+ 42	+ 82′	+ $8\frac{7}{11}$′	20 days
♃ ☍ ☉	— 45			after event
♅ ⊼ ♂	+ 54			

Group Average

B.A.	— 83 days			
C.A.	+ 90 ,,	+ 27	=	9 days
R.C.A.	+ 20 ,,			after event

True Average

11 B.A. direction total to	— 151′ × 1	+ 151′	
6 C.A.	+ 37′ × $\frac{12}{5}$	+ 89′	
11 R.C.A.	+ 82′ × $\frac{5}{12}$	+ 34′	
28		— 28′	Average–1′

Time Equiv = 6 days before event

In a total of 28 directions 21 are distinctly evil. No further comment is necessary as to their appropriateness; and they are sufficiently severe and numerous enough to satisfy the most exacting critic.

Example No. 19

King George V. (operation)

On Nov. 21, 1928, the King's illness was announced. On the 25th pleurisy had set in and on Dec. 12, the operation for drainage was performed. As the King was born on 3-6-1865 the basic arc for 12-12-28 is 63° 32′.

a

B. A· 63° 32′

(Maximum range one degree)

Directions			Difference in minutes	Total	Average	Time equivalent
♄	☍	♅	— 59			
☽	△	♂	— 59			
MC	⊼	♂	— 47			
δ	⊻	♂	— 40			
♅	☌	6th C	— 29			
♄	✱	☊	— 20	— 112′	— 8′	49 days
Z	☍	♃	— 10			after event
♀	✱	☿	— 10			
♀	✱	L	Exact			
☋	☍	M.C	+ 14			
☋	□	☽	+ 26			
6th	□	♂	+ 35			
♃	△	♅	+ 35			
♅	△	M.C	+ 53			

C. A. 26° 28′

(Maximum range 25′)

Directions			Difference in minutes	Total	Average	Time equivalent
L	✱	♆	— 23			
MC	□	☊	— 14			
☿	✱	♅	— 13			
♃	□	Zod	+ 11	— 19′	— 3⅘′	— 55 days
☋	⊼	♄	+ 20			before event

R. C. A. 152° 29′

(Maximum range one degree)

Directions			Difference in minutes
♆	△	☿	— 50
☋	□	MC	— 49

Directions	Difference in minutes	Total	Average	Time equivalent
♆ △ Ł	— 50			
☋ ☌ ☽	— 37			
6thc ☍ ♂	— 28			
♀ △ ☉	— 10	— 52′	— $\frac{1}{3}$′	11 days before event
♅ ✶ ☽	+ 2			
♃ Ā ☊	+ 11			
♆ □ ☉	+ 13			
MC ✶ Asc	+ 26			
♄ □ ♃	+ 55			
☽ ☍ 6htc	+ 55			

Group Average

B.A.	— 49		
C.A.	— 55	— 115	38 days before event
R.C.A.	— 11		

True Average

14 B.A.	— 112′	× 1	— 112′
5 C.A.	— 19′	× $\frac{12}{5}$	— 46′
12 R.C.A.	+ 341′	× $\frac{5}{12}$	+ 142′
31			— 163 Average $\frac{163}{31}$′

Time Equiv = 38 days before event

Example No. 20

King George VI. (Serious Lung operation)

The King underwent a major operation in which a portion of the lung tissue was resected on 24-9-1951. As the King was born on 14-12-1895 the Basic Arc is 55° 47′.

B. A. 55° 47′

(Maximum range one degree)

Directions	Difference in minutes	Total	Average	Time equivalent
6thC ⊼ Asc	— 59			
♄ ⊼ ♇	— 55			
♀ □ ♄	— 44			
☉ ✱ ☿	— 33			
♇ ♇ ☊	— 13			
Zod ☍ ☿	— 5	— 105′	— 10½′	64 days
♂ □ Asc	— 1			before event
♇ ☌ MC	+ 22			
Asc △ Zod	+ 34			
♆ ✱ ♇	+ 49			

C. A. 23° 15′

(Maximum range 25′)

Directions	Difference in minutes	Total	Average	Time equivalent
MC ⊼ 6thC	— 17			
☽ ☌ ☿	— 11	— 4	— 1	15 days
☿ ⊼ ♇	+ 1			before event
☉ ✱ ♄	— 23			

The closest direction is ☿ ⊼ ♇ ☉ Mercury is in 3rd house (trisection method). Pluto is in 8th house. Mercury in 8th sign. Moon conj. Mercury of course takes place in 3rd house in Scorpio ☉ Sun Sextile Saturn is indicative of the vitality that sustained the royal native through the serious operation.

R. C. A. 133° 53′

(Maximum range one degree)

Directions	Difference in minutes
♅ △ MC	— 52
☊ △ ♅	— 47

Direction	Difference in minutes	Total	Average	Time equivalent
☊ ⊼ ☉	— 34			
6th ✱ ♄	— 29			
Asc □ ıL	— 25			
♆ ⊻ 6th	— 1			
☉ ☍ ♀	+ 2			
♃ □ 6thC	+ 6	— 19′	— $\frac{19}{14}$′	3 days
☽ △ ♃	+ 7			beyond event
♅ ⊼ ♀	+ 15			
♂ ⊼ ♄	+ 29			
Zod ✱ ♀	+ 30			
☉ ☌ ☉	+ 34			
☿ ⊼ ♂	+ 46			

Group Average

B.A.	— 64			
C.A.	— 15	— 82	Or	27 days
R.C.A.	— 3			before event

True Average

10	B.A.	— 105′	× 1	— 105′
4	C.A.	— 4	× $\frac{12}{5}$	— 10′
14	R.C.A.	— 19	× $\frac{5}{12}$	— 8′
28				123′

Time Equiv = 27 days before event

Example No. 21

King Edward VII. (Typhoid fever)

Under the measure representing the sixth house, we have dealt first with cases of accidents, and next with cases of operations both of which can be referred to a particular date as the date of occurrence and the measure of 25′ to the year has been found to apply remarkably well to such cases. This measure is none the less useful in charting the events in the course of an illness that is prolonged, whether acute or chronic. As an illustration of an acute illness, I shall take up the horoscope of King Edward VII who suffered from typhoid fever towards the end of 1871. Particulars of the course of this illness are available with dates in Casting the Horoscope by Alan Leo and are copied from that book (P. 99.)

Dates	Particulars	Age		
23-11-1871	Illness announced	30	0	14
29-11-1871	Declated serious (typhoid)	30	0	20
31-11-1871	Slight rally	30	0	22
8-12-1871	Life despaired of	30	0	29
16-12-1871	Crisis of illness surmounted	30	1	7
25-12-1871	Danger over	30	1	16

The period of illness thus ranged from 30° 2′ to 30° 8′ B. A. The basic arc is general and common for all events and the key to the interpretation of events in connection with sixth house lies in its characteristic measure, namely 25′ to the year. According to this measure the range is from 12° 31′ to 12° 33′ We have all along proceeded on the basis of a maximum range of 25′ to this measure for calculation of directions to be averaged. We shall allow the same range now also and calculate the directions within that range, namely, from 12′ 6′ — 12° 58′. The following are found to be in operation.

6thC	8	♃	12° 10′ B	
♇	⊼	☿	12° 16′ B	
6thC	M	6 (Zod)	12° 20′ B	Average
Zod	□	☊	12° 29′ B	12° 29′
☉	✶	☽	12° 33′ G	
M.C	✶	♂	12° 33′ G	
☿	✶	♆	12° 37′ G	
☊	□	☉	12° 47′ B	

The average of directions formed with C. A. for 6th house within a period of two years points to 12° 28′ which is equal to 29° 55′ B. A. or 29 years 11 months This is just before the announcement of illness and could have been clearly predicted. In the first four *evil* directions Jupiter, Mercury, Pluto, Rahu and 6th house are involved. Mercury and Jupiter occupy the 8th sign of the Zodiac, Scorpio. Pluto occupies Pisces, twelfth sign. Mercury being ruler of an angle is a malefic. Rahu represents infection and the measure itself relates to illness. The four *evil* directions are succeeded by three *good* directions. Recovery from illness also could have been safely predicted. The period of transition from danger to safety should naturally be expected to be about the time when the first good direction began to take effect. ☉ ✶ ☽ 12° 33′ C. A. is equal to 30° 7′ B. A. which indicates 30 years 1 month and 13 days by which time the crisis had been announced and the danger was declared to be over shortly thereafter.

CHAPTER X

THE MEASURE OF PARTNERSHIP AND MARRIAGE

§ I. MARRIAGE

We have thus far dealt with in order, the measure of death and the measure of sickness, accidents and operations representing 8th and 6th houses in a nativity. Lying on either side of the descendant, these two houses are complementary to each other just as 2nd and 12th houses lying on either side of the first house representing gain or acquisitions (2nd) and loss (12th). The seventh house is complementary to the first house, and this house traditionally represents the life partner, business partner and their affairs. By the same parity of reasoning as in the case of the other houses such as 8th and 6th, it follows that the measure appropriate to the seventh house is the half-degree or 30′ to one year.

In Chapter III entitled the 'Prediction of Marriage' in his Symbolic Directions in Mundane Astrology, Mr. Carter demonstrates that the one degree measure affords a valuable guidance in this respect. As usual in this scheme of directing the one degree measure yields the 'Basic' Arc and is retained as such. But the characteristic Arc. is 1/2 degree to the year and this with the appropriate reversed Characteristic Arc 2° to the year are utilised to indicate the events of the seventh house such as marriage, death of partner, etc.

Example No. 22

QUEEN VICTORIA'S MARRIAGE

This is the first case dealt with in Prediction of Marriage by Mr. Carter. Queen Victoria was born at 4-15 A.M. on 24–5–1819 at London. The Nirayana horoscope is given in the Appendix. She was married at 20 years and 9 months and the basic arc is given as $20\frac{3}{4}°$. The comparatively early marriage is justified by the author on the ground that in the radical horoscope Jupiter, lord of the seventh house is sextile Mars. The directions for the event of marriage given by the author according to one degree measure are.

> Venus $\frac{3}{4}°$ past the Square of Jupiter.
> 7th house cusp exactly trine Venus
> Sun opposition Uranus.

The horoscope of the Queen is not given in that work and the one given here is that found in Harwood's 'Primary Directions by the Polar Angle Method' converted into terms of Nirayana Zodiac, and the cusps determined by the trisection method of house division. The seventh house cusp given by Harwood as Sagittarius 5° 4′ and the direction 7th house cusp trine Venus is 25° 49′. Longitude of Venus is Aries 26° 35′ and so is — 46′. Direction Sun opposition Uranus is 28′ short.

verse 51 of Chapter VII of Jataka Sarvartha Chinthamani as follows, "If the lord of the seventh house is near the ruler of the ascendant or in near signs, the marriage of the native will take place early". In this horoscope we find Mars ruler of 7th house (Nirayana) in Pisces 26° 19′ and Venus (ruler of ascendant) in Aries 5° 16′. Really they are within nine degrees of each other. The rulers will be the same according to Tropical longitudes also.

Moon's Longitude at birth is Taurus 12° 22′

	y	m	d
Therefore balance of Moon's Major period at birth is	8	2	21
Major period of Mars	7	0	0
Major period of Rahu sub-period of Rahu	2	8	12
,, ,, ,, of Jupiter	2	4	24
Total	20	3	27
,, ,, ,, of Saturn	2	10	6
Total	23	2	3

Thus the marriage took place in the sub-period of Saturn in the Major period of Rahu. In the horoscope Rahu is in close association (same degree) with Mars lord of 7th house and takes on his functions. Saturn receives the sextile of both luminaries located in the first house. Saturn being lord of 10th, an angle, is auspicious for the horoscope and himself and major lord being in the same sign has brought about marriage in accordance with the very letter of Parashara's Text :—

तद्भुक्तौ वाहनं सेवा......................विवाहोत्सवकार्याणि

We shall now proceed to apply New Era Technique.

Procedure

The procedure is the same as was adopted for the other houses.

1. Work all directions by one degree measure (maximum range one degree for one planet or sensitive point to all other points and planets.
2. Work out directions to and from O° ♈ as also for O ♎ O and also from 7th house cusp.
3. Repeat the same procedure with C. A. and R. C. A.
4. Average.

B. A. 20° 45′

(Maximum range one degree)

Directions			Difference in minutes	Total	Average	Time equivalent
♀	⊼	☋	— 48			
♂	☌	☿	— 33			
MC	⚹	♅	— 29	— 96	— $13\frac{5}{7}$	8 days
☉	☍	♅	— 28			before event
Asc	⚹	♀	— 10			
☋	☍	☿	— 3			
☿	⚹	♄	+ 55			

C. A. 10° 23′

(Maximum range 30′)

Zod	□	MC	— 24
☋	⊼	♄	— 15

Direction	Difference in minutes	Total	Average	Time equivalent
☋ ⚹ ♆	— 1	— 39	— $7\frac{4}{5}'$	94 days
♆ △ ☿	— 1			before event
♅ ⊼ ☽	— 2			

R. C. A. 41° 30′

(Maximum range one degree)

Direction	Difference in minutes	Total	Average	Time equivalent
Asc □ ☊	— 58			
☿ ⚹ Zod	— 53			
Zod ☌ ☽	— 52			
♅ △ Asc	— 50			
Asc □ ♂	— 28			
♃ ☌ ♄	— 19			
♃ □ ♆	— 5			
Asc ⊼ ♃	+ 13			
♂ ⚹ ♄	+ 22			
♂ △ ♆	+ 36	— 99	— $8\frac{1}{4}$	25 days
Zod △ MC	+ 43			before event

Group Average

B.A.	— 83		
C.A.	— 94	— 202	67 days
R.C.A.	— 25		before event

True Average

7	B.A.	— 96′	× 1	— 96′
5	C.A.	— 39′	× 2	— 82′
12	R.C.A.	— 99′	× $\frac{1}{2}$	— 49′
$\overline{24}$	Direction	— $\frac{223}{24}$	Time equivalent	59 days before event

N. B. This is much more than usual for New Era directions though by no means excessive by any other standard. Ordinarily some rectification may be called for. But Pluto is missing in the map and when taken into account may reduce the average.

Example No. 23

The next case of marriage dealt with in that work* is that of King Edward VII. His marriage took place on 10-3-1863. As he was born on 9-11-1841 the basic arc for marriage is 21° 20′. This is also a case of early marriage and the reason for this is stated to be that Venus in the King's nativity is sextile to the ruler. According to Hindu Astrology, the ruler of 7th and 1st house are together in the same sign, and so near each other. He married in Rahu's major period and sub-period. Rahu is in the sign of Capricornus ruled by Saturn who is posited close to the ascending degree. The ruler of 7th house is Mercury and he throws a sextile to Rahu. Rahu is also trine Moon. Rahu who by nature reflects the nature of these planets brought about the marriage of the native. Rahu is in 2nd house which in Hindu Astrology is known as 'Kudumbam' or family and the native sets up family when marriage takes place. Carter's directions for the event are:—

Moon part ruler of 7th house conjunction Venus

Cusp 7th close Square Venus.

The first direction is 1° 33′* and the second 17′—

* Symbolic Directions in Modern Astrology by Carter.

while the second is close enough, the first is far wide and though it has undoubted background influence can scarcely be called a direction which will help in the prediction of such an event. The direction Ascendant trine Venus by the duodenary measure is also given and this is not close being + 1° 50′ or 268 days beyond event.

New Era Directions

B. A. 21° 20′

(Maximum range one degree)

Directions			Difference in minutes	Total	Average	Time equivalent
☽	☍	Zod	— 51			
☽	△	♃	— 41			
Asc	□	L	— 29	— 85	— 12$\frac{1}{7}$	74 days
Asc	□	♀	— 17			before event
♄	□	Zod	— 9			
☽	⊼	♅	+ 10			
♄	✱	♅	— 52			

C. A. 10° 40′

(Maximum range 30′)

Directions			Difference in minutes	Total	Average	Time equivalent
☊	⊼	♂	— 27			
♅	△	☿	— 25			
Zod	☍	MC	— 23			
☿	✱	♄	— 15	— 42	— 5$\frac{1}{4}$	64 days
☉	⊼	7th	— 3			before event
L	△	♄	— 3			
♃	✱	☿	— 26			
☋	☌	♆	— 28			

R. C. A. 42° 40′

(Maximum range 60′)

Directions	Difference in minutes	Total	Average	Time equivalent
☿ ☌ ♂	— 52			
♅ □ ☊	— 50			
♆ □ Asc	— 38			
☉ ☌ ♄	— 35			
ℓ ⊼ MC	— 35			
☊ △ ☉	— 7	— 109	— $8\frac{5}{13}$	25 days before event
♃ ☌ ☊	+ 1			
☉ □ ☽	+ 7			
Zod △ ☋	+ 11			
☿ ☌ ☿	+ 12			
♂ ⚹ Asc	+ 17			
ℓ ☍ ☿	+ 24			
♅ ☍ MC	+ 36			

Group Average

B.A.	— 74		
C.A.	— 64	— 163	54 days before marriage
R.C.A.	— 25		

Uniform Average

7 B.A.	— 85	× 1	— 85	
8 C.A.	— 42	× 2	— 84	— 223½
13 R.C.A	— 109	× ½	— 54½	
28 Directions		Average	— $\frac{447}{56}$	

Time Equiv = 49 days before event

Example No. 24

King George V was married on 6–7–1893. Therefore the Basic Arc is 28° 5′. Jupiter lord of Ascendant and Mercury lord of 7th house are farther apart (nearly 138 degrees between them). In accordance with the Hindu rule marriage took place comparatively later than in either of the above two cases. Marriage took place in the sub-period of Kethu in the major period of Rahu. Mercury Venus and Rahu aspect each other and Rahu has the sextile of Jupiter, ruler of ascendant. Rahu is in the seventh sign of the Zodiac trine Uranus. Ketu occupies second house, and necessarily has the trine of Jupiter and sextile of Uranus. No wonder marriage was brought about.

New Era Directions

B. A. 28° 5′

(Maximum range one degree)

Directions	Difference in minutes	Total	Average	Time equivalent
☿ ☌ ☉	— 52			
♃ □ ♄	— 21			
Asc △ MC	+ 8			
♄ ⊼ Zod	+ 14			
☉ □ ♅	+ 11			
Asc ⊼ ☽	+ 20	+ 165	+ 13¾′	84 days beyond event
☉ □ ♆	+ 21			
♂ ⊼ Asc	+ 21			
☊ ⊼ ♃	+ 23			
☽ □ ♅	+ 32			
☉ ✶ ♀	+ 44			
MC ⊼ ♅	+ 44			

C. A. 14° 3′

(Maximum range — 30′)

Directions	Difference in minutes	Total	Average	Time equivalent
♃ □ ♆	— 27			
☿ ⊼ ☊	— 26			
☊ ⊼ ☉	— 25			
♀ ⊼ ♄	— 16	— 66	— $9\frac{3}{7}$	115 days before event
♃ △ ♀	— 4			
♆ ☍ ♄	+ 7			
Zod □ ♂	+ 25			

R. C. A. 56° 11′

(Maximum range one degree)

Directions	Difference in minutes	Total	Average	Time equivalent
♅ △ ♃	— 52			
☽ ⊼ ☋	— 43			
L □ ♆	— 40			
MC ✱ ☋	— 31			
☿ □ ♆	— 30			
L ✱ ♀	— 17			
☿ ✱ ♀	— 7	— 10	— $\frac{5}{7}$	2 days before event
♃ ✱ Zod	— 6			
☋ △ ♄	+ 3			
♂ □ MC	+ 30			
♅ ✱ ♄	+ 42			
♂ ☌ ☽	+ 42			
♆ ✱ ♂	+ 46			
7thC ⊼ ♅ a	+ 53			

True Average

B.A.	+ 845			11 days
C.A.	— 115	+ 33	+ 11	before event
R.C.A.	— 2			

Uniform Average

11 B.A.	— 165	+ 165	
6 C.A.	— 66×2	— 132	
14 R.C.A.	— 10×½	— 5	
31	$\frac{28}{31}$		5 days
Average			beyond event

Remark can be made in connection with this case that there are more evil directions than 'good' directions in B. A. and C. A. groups. But the principle stated elsewhere that the directions within range here allowed are for purposes of averaging with a view to fix the time limit. The nature of the event is always to be Judged as usual with the help of directions that are near enough. For example in one degree progresssion, Neptune conjunction Venus, Pluto sextile Neptune Mercury sextile Neptune and by the characteristic measure meridian trine Pluto and Mercury, Sun trine midpoint between Rahu and Saturn, Uranus sextile Pluto and Mercury, Saturn opposition Neptune, Sun opposition Saturn. In R. C. A. good directions preponderate. When the directions are considered especially by the characteristic measure, the prediction of marriage becomes quite possible.

Example No. 25

Queen Mary's Marriage

Queen Mary's age at the time of marriage was 26 years one month and ten days. So she was married in the sub-period of Mercury in the major period of Saturn. Saturn is the ruler of the horoscope and Mercury is in the fourth house, an angle, conjunction Sun and trine ascendant. The effects attributed to this position in the texts are auspicious celebrations, happiness etc.

B. A. 26° 7′

(Maximum range one degree)

Direction	Difference in minutes	Total	Average	Time equivalent
MC △ ♀	— 50			
☽ ✶ ☉	— 39			
♅ □ ♀	— 41			
Asc ✶ ♀	+ 8	+ 11	+ $1\frac{4}{7}$	10 days
♀ ☌ ☿	+ 11			before event
☋ △ ♂	+ 19			
♄ △ ♂	+ 11			

Of these Venus conjunction Mercury and Saturn trine Mars alone have been referred to by Mr. Carter. The other directions are no less characteristic. Kethu in conjunction with Moon ruler of 7th in second house (setting up family), Ascendant sextile Venus, very close are all noteworthy as also Moon ruler of 7th sextile Sun.

C. A. 13° 3′

(Maximum range 30′)

☽ ⊼ 7th Zod— 29

7th(Z) ⊼ ☉ — 11

Directions	Difference in minutes	Total	Average	Time equivalent
MC △ ☊	— 8	— 9	$12\frac{1}{3}$	74 days
♅ △ ♄	— 1			before event

♃ △ ♄ — 36 and Zod ✱ ♃ — 64

are no doubt background influences for marriage.

R. C. A. 52° 13′

(Maximum range one degree)

♆	△	Asc	— 52			
MC	△	☿	— 40			
♂	⊼	☽	— 47			
♅	□	☿	— 31	— 90′	—$7\frac{1}{2}$′	23 days
☿	□	Zod	— 25			before event
♇	⊼	Asc	— 15			
Zod	✱	♆	— 9			
♆	☍	MC	+ 6			
♂	△	Asc	+ 14			
♆	□	♃	+ 32			
♇	☌	♅	+ 34			
♇	⊼	MC	+ 43			

Group Average

	Days		
B.A.	+ 77		
C.A.	+ 74	+ 157	58 days
R.C.A.	+ 23		before event

True Average

7	B.A.	— 89′	× 1	— 89′
4	C.A.	— 49′	× 2	— 98′
12	R.C.A.	— 90′	× $\frac{1}{2}$	— 45′
23	Direction			— $133\frac{1}{2}$′

Average—$\frac{232}{23}$ — 61 days before event

§ 2. DEATH OF PARTNER

Marriage is only one of the events pertaining to 7th house. Partnership, dissolution of partnership, divorce, death of partner are all matters that come within the purview of the house and so under the measure of $\frac{1}{2}°$ to one year.

Example No. 26

DEATH OF MRS. GANDHI

Mrs. Gandhi died on 24-2-1944, when Gandhi was 74 years 4 months and 24 days old. She died in the major period of Rahu and the sub-period of Venus in Gandhi's horoscope. This combination is notorious for causing death of wives in the male horoscope. Venus is Kalatrakaraka (signifies wife in a male horoscope) and Rahu is a malefic. Venus is actually in the second house. The texts declare that the sub-period of Venus in the major period of Rahu, if Venus occupies 2nd or 7th houses, the loss of wife, or son, or accidental death will take place*.

---

* Directional Astrology of the Hindus by Rele P. 87.

B. A. 74° 24′

Directions			Difference in minutes	Total	Average	Time equivalent
♂	□	☿	— 57			
♆	△	☿	— 55			
☿	△	♆	— 17			
☿	✱	♇	— 15	+ 142	+ $10\frac{12}{13}$	66 days
☊	⊼	♆	+ 9			beyond event
☋	⊼	♂	+ 11			
☽	□	☊	+ 11			
♃	☌	☊	+ 23			
☽	☌	☿	+ 37			
☿	△	L	+ 38			
♃	□	☿	+ 49			
♄	⊼	MC	+ 51			
♄	△	Asc	+ 57			

Moon Square Rahu — An evil direction between the ruler of seventh house and a malefic in 8th, and quite close ! Ketu quincunx Mars — Mars in 7th house and Ketu in second (house of death) and also quite close.

C. A. 37° 12′

(Maximum range 30′)

Directions			Difference in minutes	Total	Average	Time equivalent
♆	△	Asc	— 10			
♂	✱	Asc	— 12			
♂	⊼	MC	— 18	— 84′	— $16\frac{4}{5}$′	204 days
☉	☌	♀	— 19			before event
♄	⊼	☽	— 25			

R. C. A. 144° 48′

(Maximum range one degree)

Directions	Difference in minutes	Total	Average	Time equivalent
♃ ✶ ☽	— 60			
Zod ✶ ♅	— 57			
☋ △ ☿	— 46			
♆ △ L	— 17			
☽ △ ♆	+ 20			
☽ ✶ ♂	+ 22	+ 85′	+ 7$\frac{1}{12}$	22 days before event
♅ ⊼ ♃	+ 24			
♃ ☍ ♆	+ 32			
♅ △ ☽	+ 36			
Zod △ ♃	+ 39			
♂ ⊼ ♀	+ 45			
♆ ✶ ♀	+ 47			

Group Average

B.A.	+ 66			
C.A.	— 204	— 116	— 39	39 days before event
R.C.A.	+ 22			

True Average

13 B.A.	— 142′	× 1	+ 142	
5 C.A.	— 85	× 2	— 170	
12 R.C.A.	+ 85	× ½	+ 42½	
30	— 14½		123′	
		Time Equivalent		3 days after event

Example No. 27.

Dr. Tagore (wife's death)

The information available in the article of Mr. Ghatak referred to is that Dr. Tagore's wife died when he was 41 years 6 months and odd days. The B. A. is therefore taken as 41° 30′. Death took place in the sub-period of Saturn in the major period of Sun. Sun is lord of 6th house (12th from 7th) in second house (eighth from 7th). Sun is square Jupiter ruler of Ascendant in close association with Venus lord of 3rd and 8th houses from Ascendant. He is also in conjunction with Pluto with an exact Semi-Square from Neptune. Saturn occupies 6th (twelfth from seventh) with square from Uranus and quincunx from Neptune and trine from Mercury who is malefic by reason of owning angles fourth and seventh.

Could this event have been predicted with these materials. To any student of Hindu Astrology with some experience this should be pretty obvious With the system of aspects herein recommended it should be more obvious still especially if Uranus, Neptune, and Pluto are also taken into account. Saravali gives for the combination of Saturn and Sun as sub-lord and major lords. स्वकळत्रनाशं (death of one's own wife). Mercury ruler of seventh is without house strength as he is located at the very end of first house and the beginning of second house ; whereas Jupiter ruler of ascendant is placed near the centre of fifth house where he is exalted, trine Moon, and in exchange with him. The native survives his wife.

NEW ERA DIRECTIONS

B. A. 41° 30′

(Maximum range one degree)

Directions	Difference in minutes	Total	Average	Time equivalent
♄ ⊼ ♀	— 49			
♃ ⊼ ☿	— 37			
♅ □ Zod	+ 13	+ 109	+ $13\frac{5}{8}$	83 days
MC △ ♂	+ 20			beyond event
☿ ⊼ MC	+ 30			
MC ✱ Zod	+ 36			
Zod □ ♄	+ 43			
☿ ☌ ♅	+ 53			

The above are very appropriate directions.

C. A. 20° 25′

(Maximum range 30′)

Directions	Difference in minutes	Total	Average	Time equivalent
♆ ☌ Zod	— 24			
♃ △ ♇	— 22			
7htZ ⊼ ☽	— 18	— 66	— $16\frac{1}{2}$	200 days
♂ □ ☽	— 2			before event

It has been observed that directions to and from the Zodiacal point have an element of inescapability or fatalistic significance good or bad.

R. C. A. 83° 0′

(Maximum range one degree)

Directions	Difference in minutes
♀ □ ♇	— 60
Zod □ Asc	— 52
☋ △ ♅	— 52

Directions	Difference in minutes	Total	Average	Time equivalent
♂ ⊼ Asc	— 36			
Asc ✶ ☾	— 14	— 76′	— 6⅓′	19 days
♃ ✶ MC	— 7			before event
Zod ✶ ♀	— 6			
♂ △ ♀	+ 10			
♃ ⊼ ♅	+ 16			
☉ □ ☾	+ 24			
☋ ⊼ ☾	— 45			
♅ ☌ ♄	— 56			

Group Average

B.A.	+ 83 days			
C.A.	— 200 ,,	— 136	45 days	
R.C.A.	+ 19 ,,		before event	

True Average

8 B.A. direction total to	+ 109′	× 1	+ 109′
4 C.A.	— 66′	× 2	— 132′
12 R.C.A.	— 76′	× ½	— 38′
24			— 61

Average — $\frac{16}{24}$ Time Equivalent — $\frac{61}{24} \times \frac{365}{60}$
= 15 days before event.

Example No. 28

Queen Mary (King George V's death)

The King died when the Queen was nearly 68 years and six months old and the event took place in the sub-period of Moon in the Major period of Venus. Moon is ruler of seventh house and occupies 2nd house

(8th from 7th) square Sun ruler of 8th house. Death of a near relative and danger to spouse are the effects listed for this combination.

B. A. 68° 39′

(Maximum range one degree)

Directions	Difference in minutes	Total	Average	Time equivalent
♃ □ ♂	— 46			
☉ △ ♆	— 29			
☿ ⊼ ♇	— 27			
MC ☍ ♂	— 20	— 28	— $3\frac{1}{2}$	21 days
♅ △ ☽	+ 18			before event
♃ ☌ ☽	— 17			
Asc △ ♂	+ 38			
♅ ⊼ ♆	+ 55			

C. A. 34° 20′

(Maximum range 30)

Directions	Difference in minutes	Total	Average	Time equivalent
☽ □ ☊	— 21			
♂ ✱ ♄	+ 6			
♂ ☌ ☊	+ 8	+ 28	+ $5\frac{3}{5}$	68 days
☿ ✱ ♀	+ 16			after event
♀ △ Asc	+ 19			

R. C. A. 137° 18′

(Maximum range one degree)

Directions	Difference in minutes	Total	Average	Time equivalent
♂ △ ♀	— 40			
☊ ☍ Asc	— 29			
♄ ✱ Asc	— 27	+ 8	+ $1\frac{1}{3}$	4 days
♄ □ ♅	+ 22			after event
☉ ⊼ Zod	+ 32			
Zod ☍ ♇	+ 50			

Group Average

B.A.	— 21		
C.A.	+ 68	+ 51	= 8 days
R.C.A.	+ 4		after event

True Average

8 B.A.	— 28×1′	=	— 28′	
5 C.A.	+ 28×2′	=	+ 56′	
6 R.C.A.	+ 8×½′	=	+ 4′	— 4′
19				+ 32

Average — $\frac{32}{19}$ Time Equivalent × $\frac{32}{19}$ × $\frac{365}{60}$

= 10 days after event

CHAPTER XI

MEASURE OF VOYAGES

Ninth house represents various things including religion, philosophy, long voyages and journeys, etc. Of these, voyages alone can generally figure as events to which the measure pertaining to this house, namely, $\frac{2}{3}$ degree to the year can be applied and demonstrated. This fraction represents the proportion which the beginning of the ninth sign bears to the entire Zodiac. We shall take up for illustration cases which have already figured in connection with other measures.

Example No. 29

Gandhi's Voyage to England

Mahatma Gandhi undertook only one voyage beyond the shores of India in his later life and that was when he sailed to England for the Second Round Table Conference from Bombay on May 29th, 1931 and came back to Bombay on December 28th, 1931 acknowledging the failure of his mission. The Basic Arcs for the beginning and end of the voyage are 61° 54′ and 62° 15′ respectively. The journey took place in the sub-period of Mercury in the major period of Rahu which began at 60 years 6 months and twenty-three days and ended at 63 years 4 months and twenty-nine days. For this combination of sub-lord and major lord, where Mercury occupies an angle, Parasara says "voyage to the West and interview with the King there"! Well may Sepharial exclaim that he was surprised at the literal exactness of the predictions according to this system of planetary periods and sub-periods. Both Mercury and Rahu are in cardinal signs and Mercury is ruler of the ninth house (long journeys) and twelfth (wanderings far from home). The journey lasted for just four months and thus is a 'duration', rather than an 'event' happening on a particular date. So we will adopt the method we have been following for such cases. In reality there is no difference between the two methods.

Voyage B. A. 61° 54′ — 62° 15′

Extended by orbs of one degree — B. A. 60° 54′—63°15

Directions	Difference in minutes	Total	Average
L △ ♂	60° 53′		
♀ △ L	61° 4′		
♆ ✱ ☽	61° 32′		
♂ Λ̄ ☽	61° 34′		
♃ ☌ ♅	61° 36′		
♂ △ ♃	61° 46′	617° 52′	61° 47′
☽ □ ♃	61° 48′		
♃ □ Zod	61° 51′		
♀ □ ♆	61° 59′		
☽ ☍ ♃	62° 3′		
L ☍ ♃	62° 39′		
♂ ✱ ♅	63° 22′		

But including the first and last directions slightly beyond orbs, the average will be 61° 51′. The average of directions with the one—degree measure over a period of two years and four months points to a date within one month of the start of the voyage. Jupiter ruler of Zodaical ninth and third house of the nativity figures in five out of the eleven directions. Mercury ruler of the ninth house though not in evidence here does so in the directions as per characteristic measure of 40′ to the year.

C. A. 40°36′ — 42° 10′ (extended orbs)

Directions	Arc	Total	Average · Equivalent in B. A.
☉ □ ☽	41° 02′		
☉ ☍ ♃	41° 14′		
Zod ⊼ ☿	41° 44′	208° 9′	$\frac{41°38 \times 3}{2} = 62°27'$
♅ ✱ ☿	41° 59′		
Zod △ ☋	42° 10′		

R. C. A. 91° 51′ — 94° 22′ (Extended orbs)

Directions	Arc	Total	Average · Equivalent in B. A.
♃ △ Zod	91° 51′		
♀ ✱ ♅	91° 59′		
☽ ☍ Zdo	92° 3′		
L ☌ ☽	92° 27′		
♂ ⊼ ♅	93° 22′	930°14′	$93°1\frac{2}{5}' \times \frac{2}{3} = 62°1'$
♀ ☍ ☽	93° 31′		
♆ ✱ Zod	93° 35′		
♂ □ Zod	93° 37′		
♀ □ ♃	93° 43′		
♄ △ ♀	94° 6′		

Group Average

B.A.	61° 47′		
C.A.	62° 27′	186° 15′	62° 5′
R.C.A.	62° 1		

Voyage began	61° 54′
ended	62° 15′
Total	124° 9′
Average	62° 4½′

True Average

10 B A	directions total	to 6170° 52′	× 1	= 617° 52′
5 C A	,, ,,	to 208° 9′	× $\frac{3}{2}$	= 312° 14′
10 R C A	,, ,,	to 930° 14	× $\frac{2}{3}$	= 620° 9′
			Total	1550° 15′
25	,,	Average		62° 1′

Example No. 30

The information available in the article in the Astrological Magazine already referred to is that Dr. Tagore went to Iran by air and that great homage was paid to him there and that this event happened in April-May 1932 when he was just 71 years old. Thus this event happened also in the sub-period of Mercury in the major period of Rahu, same combination as in the case of Gandhi for which Parasara was quoted. Here also Mercury occupies an angle in a cardinal sign. Rahu's inherent power to send a man abroad is well recognised in Hindu astrology. Here, he occupies Sagittarius, the ninth sign of the Zodiac. Mercury has the sextile from Mars ruler of the ninth house and a trine from Saturn ruler of the 12th house. Saturn is ordinarily connected with journeys to the west. The phrase used in Saravali मानलाभश्च is very characteristic of the tremendous ovation he received there. The word used by Parasara is even more appropriate :— महद्यशः

Tagore's Aerial flight to Persia

B. A. 71°

(Maximum range = one degree)

Directions	Difference in minutes	Total	Average	Time equivalent
♆ ☍ 9thC	— 50			
♅ △ Zod	— 17			
MC □ ♂	— 10			
☿ ☍ MC	Exact			
MC □ 9thZ	+ 6	+ 60′	+ $6\frac{2}{3}$′	= 41 days after event
Zod ✱ ♄	+ 31			
♂ ☌ ♄	+ 29			
♄ Λ̄ ☽	+ 44			
♆ Λ̄ MC	+ 45			

R. C. A. 47° 20′

(Maximum range 40)

Directions	Difference in minutes	Total	Average	Time equivalent
☽ ✱ ♆	— 28			
♀ ✱ ♄	— 21			
9thc □ ☿	— 5			
☿ ✱ ♃	— 3	+ 33′	= $4\frac{5}{7}$′	= 43 days after event
Asc □ ♄	+ 25			
♂ □ L	+ 30			
☿ Λ̄ ☊	+ 35			
a				

R. C. A. 106° 30′

(Maximum range one degree)

Directions	Difference in minutes	Total	Average	Time equivalent
Zod □ ♃	— 36			
☽ □ ☿	— 33			
♂ ⊼ ♃	— 20			
☿ □ ☉	+ 6			
☉ ☌ ♄	+ 13			
♆ ☌ ☊	+ 30			
☊ ✶ ♄	+ 34	+ 90	+ 10	37 days
♀ ⊼ ♆	+ 45			after event
♆ ✶ ☉	+ 51			

Group Average

B.A.	+ 41		
C.A.	+ 43	+ 121	= 40 days
R.C.A.	+ 37		after event

There is a persistent indication of about 40 days plus in all the groups.

True Average

9 B.A.	+ 60′	+ 1	=	60
7 C.A.	+ 33	+ $\frac{3}{2}$	=	$49\frac{1}{2}$′
9 R.C.A.	+ 90	+ $\frac{2}{3}$	=	60′
25				$169\frac{1}{2}$′

Average $6\frac{4}{5}$′ = 41 days after event

It is to be noted that the correct timings for the journey are not available. Though there are bad directions, most of the planets concerned in such directions are well aspected at birth. Rahu trine Venus, Pluto; and Mars sextile Jupiter and Mercury; Moon sextile Uranus, trine Jupiter, and 9th house cusp.

Example No. 31

Nearly all but the chapter relating to the voyage measure had been printed when the commonwealth tour of Queen Elizabeth II was announced; and so, it has been found possible to put it in here. The Queen was born on 21-4-1926 at Bruton street, London W. C. 1 at 1-20 A.M. G. M. T. The horoscope of the Queen is given at Page 53 of Carter's Introduction to Political Astrology according to the Tropical Zodiac with Placidean cusps. It has got to be recast according to the Sidereal Zodiac with cusps by the Trisection method (Fig 8). The Queen and the Duke of Edinburgh started from London by air in the Royal strato-cruiser Canopus on 23-11-1953 at 9-1 P.M. that is 27 years and 216 days which works to B. A. 27° 36′.

Moon's Longitude at birth Cancer 19° 19

		y	m	d
Therefore the balance of Mercury's period at birth was		13	7	14
Ketu's major period		7	0	0
Major period of Venus till end of sub-period of Moon		6	0	0
	Total	26	7	14
,, ,, sub period of Mars		1	2	0
	Total	27	9	14
,, ,, of Rahu		3	0	0
	Total	30	9	14

Fig. 8

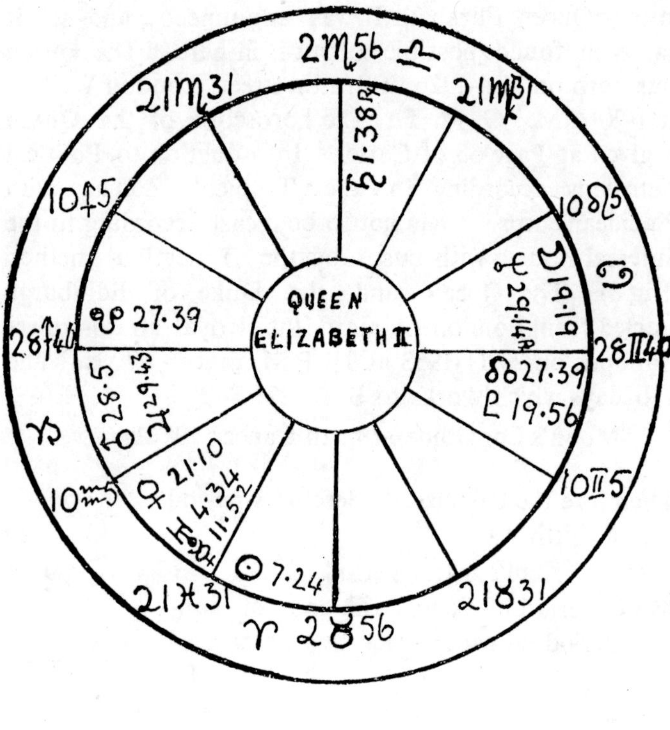

Thus the tour started towards the end of the sub-period of Mars when it had yet two months and eight days to run. The greater part of the tour occurs in the sub-period of Rahu§. The major period is that of Venus who is ruler of fifth and ninth houses and the appropriateness of the voyage is thus borne out. Both Venus and Mars occupy the second house with Mars in Capricornus where he is exalted and in association with Jupiter who rules the ascendant. This association is stated to lead to seeing ' rare sights ' in the sub-period of Mars in the major period of Venus in the texts. Rahu's sub-period is still more appropriate. The effects attributed are long journeys towards south-west, and return to native land with success in the objects of the journey " § Rahu occupies the ascendant with a sextile from Saturn.

B. A. 27° 36′

(Maximum range one degree)

Directions	Difference in minutes	Total	Average	Time equivalent
9the △ [	— 49			
♆ △ ☊	— 49			
♅ ⊼ MC	— 46			
♀ △ ☽	— 33			
♃ ✱ ☊	— 25	— 92	— $9\frac{1}{5}$	= 56 days
Zod △ ☊	— 3			before event
♄ △ ♆	Exact			
♅ ⊼ ♄	+ 32			
MC △ 9 (Z)	+ 32			
MC ✱ ♃	+ 49			

---

§ नैर्ऋतीं दिशमाश्रित्य प्रयाणं यातुकार्यसिद्धिः स्यात्स्वदेशंपुनरेष्यति

C. A. 18′ 24°

(Maximum range one degree)

Directions			Difference in minutes	Total	Average		Time equivalent
MC	✱	9thC	— 11				
♄	⊼	L	+ 6				
MC	□	♀	+ 10	+ 73′	+ $12\frac{1}{6}$′	=	111 days
☿	☌	Zod	+ 16				after event
☽	△	☉	+ 19				
☿	✱	♃	+ 33				

R. C. A. 41° 24′

(Maximum range one degree)

☽	✱	♄	— 55				
♃	☌	☿	— 45				
☉	✱	☽	— 31				
Zod	✱	☿	— 28	— 139′	— $19\frac{6}{7}$′	=	79 days
♀	⊼	MC	— 22				before event
L	□	♄	— 18				
☽	△	♃	+ 60				

Group Average

B.A.	— 56				
C.A.	+ 111	— 24	— 8	or	eight days
R.C.A.	— 79				before event

True Average

10 B.A.	— 92′×1	— 92′	Average
6 C.A.	+ 73′×$\frac{3}{2}$	+ $109\frac{1}{2}$′	— 3′
7 R.C.A.	— 139 ×$\frac{2}{3}$	— $92\frac{2}{3}$	
23		— 70′	

= 18 days before event

No more striking or appropriate directions can be conceived of : 9th house cusp, Rahu, Mercury, Jupiter, Zodiac, Pluto all figure prominently in harmonious aspects which are in the majority (16 out of 23) and the time indication is certainly very close.

CHAPTER XII

THE MEASURE OF THE MERIDIAN

§. 1. GENERAL

Events pertaining to the meridian are to be related to their characteristic measure of 270′ to 360 or $\frac{3}{4}$ to the year and directions calculated on this basis are found to work remarkably close to events of the tenth house. Though directions beyond the range fixed here are excluded for averaging and timing events, directions outside this range have certainly efficacy in shaping the nature of events and should also be generally considered and not ignored for all purposes.

The tenth house stands for honour, credit, father, ruling power etc. In Western Astrology there is a difference of opinion not yet settled as to whether M.C. is to be taken to indicate the father or the mother. In the latest text book on Astrology by M. Hone, it is stated that the fourth house generally refers to the mother as the older books imply* and again later on§ that both the fourth and tenth houses may show the parents from the angle of vision of the children. Carter doubts § whether any house shows the parents of

---

* P. 93. \$ P-95. \$ Principles of Astrology P. 85. but see P. 91 where it appears that he is inclined to prefer 4th house for father when he says in \$ 2. "Thus father's money is 2nd from 4th i.e., the fifth."

the native very clearly. However, it appears that now there is a chance for this matter to be finally settled if sufficient research is brought to bear on this point in the light of the New Era measures by taking $\frac{1}{4}^\circ$ = one year measure and $\frac{3}{4}^\circ$ measure for the father and working out directions in a large number of cases and tabulating the results. To do so here would be obviously outside the scope of this work.

§ 2 DEATH OF MALE PARENT

Example No. 32

As the first case for illustration of this measure of $\frac{3}{4}^\circ$ to the year, I shall take up the Example Nativity in the above Text book of M. Hone,— the case of 'John Smith' The horoscope cast according to the Western System with the tropical longitudes for the planets and Placidean cusps of houses is available in that book. The same recast with trisection cusps and Nirayana longitudes is given in the Appendix (App. A. No. 17) 'John Smith' was born on 21-6-1924 at 2-27-52 P.M. L. M. T. Lat 51° 34 N. Long 1° 47′ W. The death of the father is stated to have taken place on 17-10-1944. Before proceeding to work directions for the event with the meridian measure I shall take the indulgence of the reader to relate an incident that took place within a few days after the purchase by me of a copy of that book. On page 256, there is a query "Whether it would have been possible to foretell the death of the father from the directions ?" and the answer given there is "it is much to be doubted". This observation induced me to make the following test. When a friend of mine learned in both systems of astrology* called on me, I handed to him a copy of the horoscope of 'John Smith' cast in Indian fashion rather,' South Indian fashion containing only the nine planets of the Hindu system including Rahu and Ketu and excluding the three trans. Saturnine planets, Uranus, Neptune and Pluto thus.—

Nirayana

Native born 21-6-1924 at 2-28 p. m.

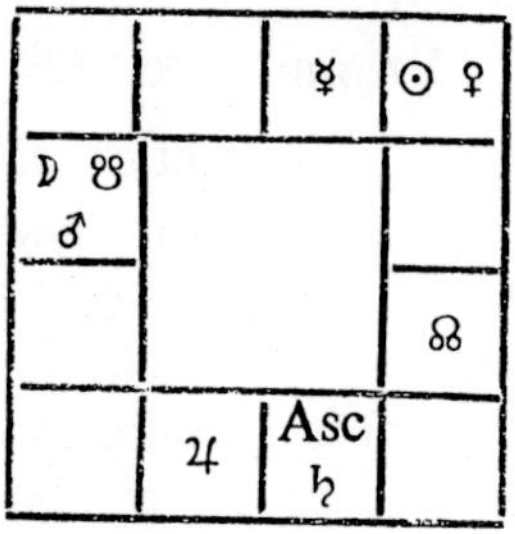

Balance of Rahu dasa at birth 17 years 6 months and 10 days and put him the Query "what is the father's longevity", a very common question in Hindu Astrology. From the way in which the question was put he could have inferred that the death was a past event, and he did. Whatever calculations were required for the answer he made mentally and as I was watching by the clock opposite to me, the answer came in less than five minutes when he rapped out "Guru dasa Sani Bukti" (major period of Jupiter and sub-period of Saturn). This is to be worked out as follows :—

* K. Sivasubramaniya Iyer referred to in the preface as well as in Chapter on Aspects.

	y	m	d
Balance of Rahu dasa at birth	17	6	10
Jupiter's period, Jupiter's sub-period	2	1	18
Total	19	7	28
„ „ Saturn's sub-period	2	6	12
Total	22	2	10

that is between 19-7-28 year and 22 years 2 months and 10 days. The death of the father actually took place when the native was 20 years and three months old. So the answer was correct. This is not mentioned as an exceptional instance but as a sample of the kind of predictions that are being made daily by hundreds of Astrologers all over the country with the aid of the system of planetary periods and sub-periods mentioned by Parasara and described in this work briefly.

New Era Directions

B. A. 20° 20′

(Maximum range one degree)

Directions	Difference in minutes	Total	Average	Time equivalent
♃ ⊼ MC	— 34			
Zod ⊼ ♃	+ 1			
♅ □ ☾	+ 16	+ 90′	+ 18′	= 109 days after event
♂ ⊼ ♆	+ 49			
Asc △ ♀	+ 58			

C. A. 15° 15′

(Maximum range 45′)

Directions	Difference in minutes
Asc △ ☾	— 45
♄ △ ☾	— 39
☿ ☌ ☉	— 34

Directions			Difference in minutes	Total	Average	Time equivalent
☋	⚹	L	— 26			
♃	⚹	♂	— 29			
☿	△	☽	— 28			
☽	△	♀	+ 7			
♂	□	☿	Exact	— 135′	— $12\frac{3}{11}$	= 100 days
☉	☌	♀	+ 13			before event
♀	⊼	☽	+ 23			
☿	△	♂	+ 30			

R. C. A. 27° 6′

(Maximum range one degree)

☿	☌	L	— 23			
Asc	⊼	Zod	— 7			
♀	⊼	Zod	— 1			
♂	⊼	☊	+ 3			
♅	△	♆	+ 15			
♂	⊼	♄	+ 16	+ 66	+ 7	= 32 days
♂	⊼	Asc	+ 22			after event
♆	⚹	♀	+ 31			

Group Average

B.A.	+ 109	
C.A.	— 100	Total 41 days; average 14 days
R.C.A.	+ 32	after event

True Average

9	B.A.	— 90′	× 1	= 90′		Total
11	C.A.	— 135	× $\frac{4}{3}$	— 180′		48′
8	R.C.A.	+ 56	× $\frac{3}{4}$	+ 42′		

Average for 24 Directions 2′

Time Equive. 12 days before event

This event has been already demonstrated to be capable of being predicted by the system of planetary periods and sub-periods. Could the same prediction have been done with New Era Measures ? It is important to note that these measures are advised to be used in connection with and as an adjunct to the system of planetary periods. **Yet it has also been averred that these can stand by themselves as a separate system self-sufficient by itself.** Ample justification for this state, ment will be found in the directions above averaged. The characteristic arc provides a direction which is adverse and also exact to the event, namely Mars Square Mercury. Mars is in close association with Moon ruler of M. C. and Mercury occupies 8th house no doubt the majority of the C. A. directions are 'good' but the evil directions in the other groups are greatly in majority. It is also to be noted that the planets figuring in the good directions Sun, Mars, Jupiter etc rule evil houses.

Let us compare at least with regard to this case the results with the measure of the house (4th house) or $\frac{1}{4}°$ to the year for the event, though there can be no final adjudication on the matter from this case alone. The B. A, of course, is common to all the measures. The only directions for that is, 5° 5′ within orbs are Jupiter trine Neptune — 10′ and Mars quin-cunx M C — 5′. Though M. C. is included as a sensitive point in all cases, we should expect some direction to I. C. also if it is characteristic of the father. Then Mars would have only a Semi ⊖ sextile to I. C.

Even extending the orbs to one degree range which would mean a total of directions for 8 years (four years on either side) the directions are as follows :—

C. A				R. C. A.			
♆	△	Zod	+ 39′	Zod	☌	♀	— 49′
Asc	△	☉	+ 45′	☽	✶	♅	— 22′
♄	△	☉	+ 51′	☉	□	♅	— 16′
☽	⊼	MC	+ 53′	♅	☍	♃	— 16′
♅	△	♄	+ 55′	1-C	☍	♄	— 20′

With C. A. directions so overwhelmingly **favourable**, the two or three 'evil' directions in R. C. A. do not mean much. The directions as per C. A. in this case at any rate leave no room for doubt as to the measure to be applied in the case of the father.

Example No. 33

We shall take the next example from the horoscopes already dealt with. The death of King George V had no additional significance for King George VI than the death of a father as he was not next in succession, though he became King later on. The event took place when he was 40 years one month and 6 days old in the sub-period of Saturn in the major period of Mars. Both planets occupy second house though in second and twelfth signs from each other. Note that in the previous example, the sub lord and major lords were also in second and twelfth signs from each other, as here—Parashara gives for this combination. पित्रमात्रवियोगश्च (death of father or mother).

New Era Directions

B. A. 40° 6′

(Maximum range one degree)

Directions			Difference in minutes	Total	Average	Time equivalent
☽	✱	♀	— 50			
ℓ	□	Zod	— 49			
☊	△	☿	— 41			
♀	☍	♆	— 38			
ℓ	△	♅	— 34			
♆	□	Asc	— 34			
ℓ	⊼	☉	— 21			
Ase	□	☋	— 12	— 161′	— $12\frac{5}{13}$	= 75 days before event
♂	⊼	ℓ	Exact			
Asc	△	MC	+ 23			
♃	□	☿	+ 27			
MC	□	♆	+ 29			
☉	✱	♂	+ 39			

C. A. 30° 5′

(Maximum range 45)

Directions			Difference in minutes	Total	Average	Time equivalent
MC	☌	☋	— 30			
☉	□	Zod	— 23			
♅	△	Zod	— 10			
☉	✱	♅	— 8			
♅	☌	☉	+ 18	+ 7	+ 1	= 6 days after event
Zod	☍	♅	+ 20			
☋	✱	MC	+ 40			

Directions	Difference in minutes	Total	Average	Time equivalent
	R. C. A. 53° 28′			
	(Maximum range one degree)			
♅ ⊼ ♆	— 54			
L □ ♀	— 50			
Zod ☌ ♆	— 39			
☊ ⊼ ♂	— 26			
♄ ⊼ ♃	— 22			
♂ ✱ ☽	Exact	— 1′	— $\frac{1}{11}$′	= one day before event
☿ △ L	+ 15			
☉ □ ♄	+ 37			
♃ ✱ ♂	+ 42			
♄ △ ☋	+ 46			
♅ ✱ ♄	+ 50			

Group Average

B.A.	—	75 days	— 70	— 23 days before event
C.A.	+	6		
R.C.A.	—	1		

True Average

13 B.A.	— 161	× 1	— 161′	
7 C.A.	+ 7′	× $\frac{4}{3}$	+ 9′	
11 R.C.A.	— 1	× $\frac{3}{4}$	— 1	
31			153	Average—$\frac{153}{31}$ = 5′

Time Equivalent 30 days before event.

Example No. 34

Two Examples for the meridian measure have been already dealt with. In allotting a total of half a dozen illustrations for this measure, we had originally selected some others for the remaining four, but recent events have induced us to make a change and select them from current history and these are :—death of King George VI for the horoscope of the present Queen, and three events relating to the meridian of President Eisenhower, namely his assumption of supreme command in the Second World War, the Victory, and his Election for Presidentship. Beyond being events of current history, there is one other reason, the horoscopes of the Queen and P. Eisenhower are available ready cast, the former by Mr. Carter and the latter by Cyril Fagan.

DEATH OF KING GEORGE VI

The King died on February 2, 1952 and this meant to the present Queen not only the death of the father but also accession to the throne. This event remarkable to her in a two-fold way happened in the sub-period of Moon in the major period of Venus. The effects for this combination are " The native will hold a responsible and administrative post "* Moon is in 7th house a kendra and strong in her own sign trine' Mercury. But both major and sub lords are Quincunx to each other a position which is worse even than 2nd and 12th for each other we saw was the case in the two prior examples of death of father. Moon is also square Sun, opposition Mars ruler of M. C. These indicate the death of the father.

a

B. A. 25° 48′

(Maximum range one degree)

Directions	Difference in minutes	Total	Average	Time equivalent
MC ✱ ♃	— 59			
♄ ✱ ♂	— 39			
MC △ ♆	— 30			
♄ ⊼ ☊	— 13			
☉ ☍ MC	+ 16	— 9	— 1	= 6 days
☿ ☌ ☉	+ 16			before event
♅ ☌ Zod	+ 22			
♅ ✱ ♃	+ 39			
MC ✱ ♂	+ 39			

A glance at the above list of directions and the closeness of the result indicated by the average should silence all opposition to the efficacy and validity of the one—degree measure. How simple to calculate also if confined to definite limits!

C. A. 19° 21′

(Maximum range 45′)

Directions	Difference in minutes	Total	Average	Time equivalent
Zod ✱ ♇	— 35			
☿ ⊼ ♄	— 25			
♃ ⊼ ☽	— 15	— 84	— 16$\frac{4}{5}$	= 102 days
♄ □ ♀	— 11			before event
Zod □ ☽	+ 2			

R. C. A. 34° 24′

(Maximum range one degree)

Directions	Difference in minutes	Total	Average	Time equivalent
♆ ☍ ♅	— 56			
☊ □ MC	— 53			

Direction	Difference in minutes	Total	Average	Time equivalent
♃ ☌ ♅	— 27			
♂ △ MC	— 27			
Zod ✱ ♅	— 10			
MC △ ☉	— 4	— 55	— 5	= 30 days
☉ ✱ ☿	— 4			before event
Asc □ MC	+ 8			
☊ □ ♄	+ 25			
♆ ✱ MC	+ 42			
♂ △ ♄	+ 51			

Group Average

B.A.	— 6 days		
C.A.	— 102 „	— 138	= 46 days
R.C.A.	— 35 „		before event

9 B.A.	$-\ 9' \times 1$	— 9′
5 C.A.	$-\ 84' \times \frac{4}{3}$	— 112′
11 R.C.A.	$-\ 55' \times \frac{3}{4}$	— 41
25		— 162′ Average $-\frac{162}{25}$

Time Equiv. 39 days before time

This occurred in the major period of Venus. Venus rules 5th and 9th houses (and not 6th and 11th) and is trine Pluto and Rahu. The sub lord Moon is ruler of Cancer intercepted between 7th and 8th house cusps, occupies the end of 7th house, is trine Mercury, opposition Mars and Jupiter and conjunction Neptune. The combination of Venus and Moon has been declared in the texts as capable of conferring the insignia of royalty. The opposition of Mars ruler of M. C. to Moon and

Moon being quincunx with major lord indicate the death of the male parent. In the B. A. directions M. C. ⚹ ♃ ; M. C. △ ♆, M. C. ⚹ ♂, ♅ ⚹ ♃ are all outstanding and unmistakable directions. On the other hand ♄ ⊼ ☋, and ☉ 8 M. C. are quite evil. The C. A. and R. C. A. directions are also very significant of the double nature of the event. If the M. C, reduced by even as much as 5'* (putting the recorded birth time back by 15 seconds) the time equivalent will be reduced to within one month. Even as it is the event is close to the time indicated by the average of the directions.

$ 3. ASSUMPTION OF DIGNITY & POWER

Example No. 35

Coronation of Queen Elizabeth

The Coronation of Queen Elizabeth II on 2-6-1953 is too recent and colourful an event in modern history to be ignored in such a context as this and though it means the inclusion of one more Example than originally intended it is dealt with here. The coronation took place in the sub-period of Mars in the major period of Venus. The major lord is the ruler of two trines and the sub lord of two angles. The latter is common but the former is not and such a combination is quite unique.

शुक्रस्यान्तर्गते भौमे केन्द्रकोण समन्विते ।
स्वोच्चेवा स्वर्क्षगे भौमे लाभे बल समन्विते ॥

---

* which will be the case when birth time is rectified by Hindu methods.

लग्नाधिपेन संयुक्ते कर्मभाग्याधिपान्विते ।
तद्भुक्तौ राजयोगादि संपदं शुभशोभनं ।।

वस्त्राभरण भूम्यादे रिष्टस्यप्तिः सुखागमः ।
पुत्रोत्सवो भूमिलाभो गृहे कल्याणसिद्धितः ।।

"If in Mars sub-period in the major period of Venus, Mars is located in an angle, or trine, or Exaltation sign or if he is powerful or in conjunction with ruler of ascendant or with lords of 9th and 10th houses, he gets Raja Yoga (becomes King or assumes Kingly powers) auspicious celebrations, clothes, ornaments, gain of lands, desired objects, happiness, birth of children etc".

Nothing bad being involved in this event such as death of father, the directions reflect the auspicious nature, 'evil' directions being comparatively rare.

B. A. 27° 7′

(Maximum range one degree)

Directions	Difference in minutes	Total	Average	Time equivalent
[illegible] ✱ ♃	— 58			
Zod □ ♂	— 58			
♃ ✱ ☋	— 49			
Zod △ ☋	— 32			
♄ △ ♆	— 29			
☉ ✱ ♅	— 3			
♅ ⊼ ♄	+ 3			
MC △ Zod	+ 3			

Directions	Difference in minutes	Total	Average	Time equivalent
MC ✱ ♃	+ 20			
♄ ✱ ♂	+ 40	— 114	— $10\frac{4}{11}$	= 62 days
MC △ ♆	+ 49			before event

In Eleven directions, nine are good and only two are bad.

C. A. 20° 20′

(Maximum range 45′)

☿ λ̄ MC	— 44			
♆ ✱ L	— 22			
♀ ☌ ☿	— 22			
☉ □ ♂	— 21			
Asc ☍ ⌓	— 19	— 14	— $1\frac{2}{5}$	= 15 days
☉ △ ☋	+ 5			before event
♃ △ L	+ 7			
Zod ✱ L	+ 24			
☿ λ̄ ♄	+ 34			
♃ λ̄ ☽	+ 44			

N. B. ♄ □ ♀ + 48   are background
Zod ✱ ♀ — 50   influences

R. C. A. 36° 39′

(Maximum range one degree)

♀ ✱ ♂	— 46
☊ λ̄ ♅	— 45
♀ □ ☋	— 20
♂ ☌ ♅	— 20

Directions	Difference in minutes	Total	Average	Time equivalent
♄ △ ☉	+ 23	— 8	— $1\frac{1}{7}$	= 5 days before event
♆ ☍ ♅	+ 49			
☋ □ MC	+ 52			

Group Average

B.A.	— 62	— 82	— 27	or 27 days before event
C.A.	— 15			
R.C.A.	— 5			

True Average

11	B.A.	— 114	× 1	— 114′
10	C.A.	— 14	× $\frac{4}{3}$	— 19′
7	R.C.A.	— 8	× $\frac{3}{4}$	— 6
28				139′ Average — $4\frac{27}{28}$

Time Equiv 30 days before event

Example No. 36

Assumption of Supreme Command by Eisenhower

"Horoscope of Eisenhower" was the subject matter of an article by the Editor of the Astrological Magazine in February 1953 issue. Pisces has been fixed as the Lagna (rising sign) and from the Navamsa chart appended we are led to infer that the ascending degree is between 0° — 3° 20′ of Pisces, the date of birth being Oct 14, 1890. Lat 33° 46′ N. Long 96° 32′ W. In the March issue of the same magazine an article entitled "General Eisenhower's Birth time" by Cyril Fagan has been published. Cyril Fagan with his usual thoroughness investigates the available data with regard to the birth time and with the help of Quotidians and Solunars has tentatively fixed the birth time at 5.11 P.M. on that date. I am wholly indebted to the above articles for data for the examples given here. Cyril Fagan writes in Page 262 Col. 3 " Lack of biographical data precludes me from making further Quotidian or directional checks. The time 5-11 P. M. is only a first approximation and may be in error by "+ or —" 4 minutes. When more adequate biographical detail is to hand a more rigorous rectification could be attempted. Whether such will confirm or disprove the present preliminary determination remains to be seen". My own investigations with the available data have enabled me to fix the birth time as 5-9-40 P. M. with Nirayana Chaitra ascendant as Pisces 24° 8′.

The General was appointed Supreme Commander of the Allied Forces on 24-12-1943. Moon's Longitude at birth was Libra 11° 20′ and the balance of Rahu's major period at birth was 11 years 8ms and 12 days. Therefore this event occurred : in

	y	m	d
Rahu	11	8	12
Jupiter	16	0	0
Saturn	19	0	0
Total	46	8	12
Mercury's Major period till end of Venus period	6	2	24
Total	52	11	6
Sun's Sub-period	0	10	6
Total	53	9	12

Fig. 9

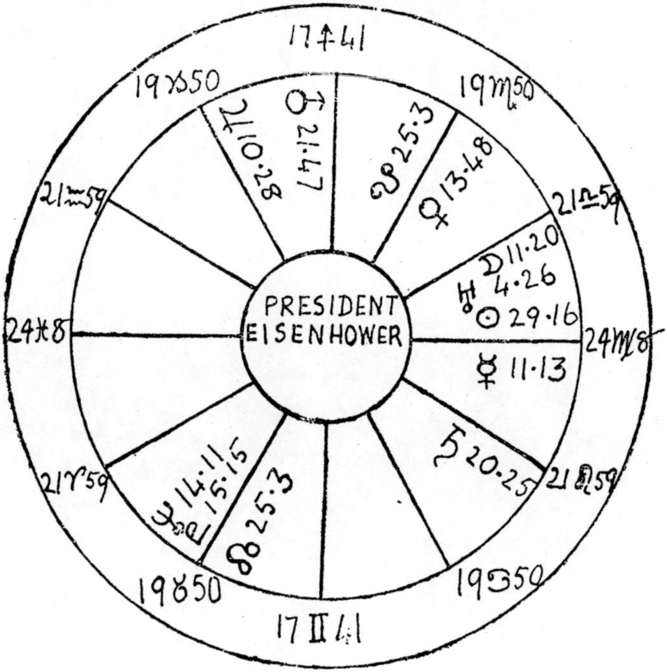

the sub-period of Sun in the major period of Mercury. One is struck at once with the appropriateness of the direction. The traditional effects attributed to this combination are "Favour of Kings", "Attainment of high position", "Journey to East of birth place and destruction of enemies and Victory".

Directions

B. A. 53° 12′

(Maximum range one degree)

Directions	Difference in minutes	Total	Average	Time equivalent
Zod ✱ Asc	— 56			
♃ ⊼ ♅	— 46			
♄ ⊼ ♆	— 34			
MC △ ☽	— 27			
Asc ⊼ MC	— 21			
MC ⊼ ☿	— 20	— 132	13⅕	— 80 days
♂ □ ♇	— 16			before event
☽ ✱ ♅	— 6			
☊ ⊼ MC	+ 34			
♂ △ ♆	+ 48			

The predominence of Evil directions is to be noted and bears out the suggestion of Carter* that the presence of such directions and transits is more likely to point to the attainment of a high post which carries heavy responsibilities with it.

C. A. 39° 54′

(Maximum range 30′)

Directions	Difference in minutes
☿ ✱ ♂	— 40
Zod △ ♃	— 34

* Astrology Vol. 26 No. 3 P. 67.

Directions			Difference in minutes	Total	Average	Time equivalent
♀	□	Asc	— 26			
Asc	⊼	♅	— 24			
♆	□	Asc	— 3			
♃	☍	♄	— 3			
Ł	⊼	☊	+ 6	+ 9	+ $\frac{3}{4}$	= 5 days beyond event
♅	☍	♆	+ 9			
♄	☍	Zod	+ 19			
☋	□	♅	+ 31			
♅	☌	♀	+ 32			
☿	✱	♄	+ 42			

R. C. A. 70° 56′

(Maximum range one degree)

Directions			Difference in minutes	Total	Average	Time equivalent
MC	⊼	⊙	— 39			
Zad	△	☽	— 24			
♃	□	♂	— 23			
♀	△	☊	— 19			
Zod	□	☿	— 17			
♆	✱	☊	+ 4			
♇	⊼	Ł	+ 7			
Zod	⊼	♃	+ 28			
☽	☌	♃	+ 29	+ 122	+ $10\frac{1}{6}$	= 62 days beyond event
Asc	△	♅	+ 38			
♃	⊼	♄	+ 59			
♆	△	Asc	+ 59			

Group Average

B.A.	— 80		
C.A.	+ 5	— 13	= 4 days before event
R.C.A.	+ 62		

True Average

10 B.A.	— 132′	× 1	— 132′	
12 C.A.	+ 9′	× $\frac{3}{4}$	+ 12′	
12 R.C.A.	+ 122′	× $\frac{4}{3}$	+ 92′	
$\overline{34}$ directions total to			— $\overline{28}$	Average — $\frac{28}{24}$

Time Equiv. = 5 days before event

Example No. 37

(Allied Victory 30-4-1945)

B. A. 54° 32′

(Maximum range one degree)

Directions	Difference in minutes	Total	Average	Time equivalent
☋ ⊼ ♄	— 50			
L ☍ ♄	— 41			
Zod ☌ ☊	— 31			
☉ △ Asc	— 20			
♄ ⊼ L	— 18			
♅ ✱ ☉	— 18			
Zod ✱ Asc	+ 24			
♃ ⊼ ♅	+ 34			
♄ ⊼ ♆	+ 46			
MC △ ☽	+ 53	+ 98	+ $8\frac{1}{6}$	= 50 days beyond event
Asc △ MC	+ 59			
MC ⊼ ☿	+ 60			

C. A. 40′ 54°

(Maximum range 45′)

MC △ ☉	— 41
Zod ⊼ ☽	— 26

Directions	Difference in minutes	Total	Average	Time equivalent
♃ ✱ ♂	— 25			
☿ ⊼ ☊	— 21			
Zod △ ☿	— 19			
☉ ✱ ♃	— 18			
♆ ⊼ ☋	+ 2			
♅ ☍ L	+ 5			
☿ ✱ ♂	+ 20	— 27	— 2¼	= 18 days before event
Zod △ ♃	+ 26			
♀ □ Asc	+ 34			
Asc ⊼ ♅	+ 36			

R. C. A. 72° 43′

Maximum range one degree

Directions	Difference in minutes	Total	Average	Time equivalent
☽ ☌ ☋	— 60			
♃ ☌ Asc	— 57			
♅ ☌ MC	— 32	— 53′	— $5\frac{8}{9}'$	= 27 days before event
☿ △ Asc	— 12			
☽ □ Asc	— 5			
♂ ⊼ ♅	+ 4			
MC ✱ MC Z	+ 24			
☉ ✱ ☽	+ 39			
☉ □ ☿	+ 46			

Group Average

		Total	Average	Time equivalent
B.A.	+ 50			
C.A.	+ 18	+ 5	+ $1\frac{2}{3}$	= 2 days before event
R.C.A.	— 79			

True Average

12 **B.A.**	$+ 98'$	$\times 1$	$+ 98'$
12 C.A.	$- 27'$	$\times \frac{4}{3}$	$- 36'$
9 R.C.A.	$- 53$	$\times \frac{3}{4}$	$- 40$
33			$+ 24$ Average $\frac{2}{3}\frac{2}{3}'$

Time Equiv. 5 days before event

Example No. 38

President Elect (5-11-1952)

His Election as President took place in the sub-period of Saturn in the major period of Mercury. Saturn is in 6th, an evil house. He is also in twelfth from major lord. This requires explanation and has apparently been slurred over by other Astrologers dealing with this matter. Ordinarily one would not be led to expect Victory under such conditions. No doubt the major lord is exalted, sextile Venus, Trine Neptune, Pluto and Jupiter and Saturn is Trine Mars and M. C. These are all excellent. But Saturn is in 6th and this fact would ordinarily negative victory but this case comes under an exception. Sixth though an evil house, its occupation by a planet who is lord of 6th, 8th or 12th houses gives rise to Vimala Yoga and a native born under this yoga "will be happy, independent, and will hold a respectable position and be renowned for his good qualities". Here Saturn is ruler of 12th house and occupies 6th and with such powerful help from the major lord and other aspects was able to confer this in his sub-period. Moreover Saturn, a natural malefic, is powerful in 6th an Upachaya house (3, 6, 10 and 11 are known as Upachaya houses).

B. A. 62° 4′

(Maximum range one degree)

Directions	Difference in minutes	Total	Average	Time equivalent
☿ ☍ ♆	— 54			
☽ ⊼ ♆	— 47			
MC ☍ ♄	— 40			
☿ ☌ ♀	— 31			
L ⊼ MC	— 22			
♀ △ L	+ 37	— 55	— $5\frac{7}{8}$	= 42 days before event
♄ ✱ ♂	+ 42			
♆ ✱ L	+ 60			

C. A. 46° 33′

(Maximum range 45′)

Directions	Difference in minutes	Total	Average	Time equivalent
Asc ☍ ☽	— 39			
Asc △ ☿	— 32			
MC △ ♅	— 12			
Asc △ ♃	+ 13			
☋ □ ☽	+ 16			
♀ ☌ MC(Z)	+ 21			
☋ △ ☿	+ 23			
☉ ☍ L	+ 34	+ 102	+ $10\frac{1}{5}$	= 83 days after event
♅ □ ♄	+ 34			
♆ □ Zod	+ 44			

R. C. A. 82° 45′

(Maximum range one degree)

Directions	Difference in minutes	Total	Average	Time equivalent
MC ⊼ ☽	— 54			
Asc ☍ MC	— 48			
MC ☍ ☿	— 47			
♂ ✱ L	— 43			
♄ ☌ ♀	— 38			
☿ ✱ ♅	— 28			
☽ □ ♅	— 21			
MC ✱ ♃	— 2			
☋ △ MC	+ 7			
☉ ☌ ♂	+ 14			
♂ ✱ ♆	+ 21	— 137	— $10\frac{7}{13}$	= 48 days before event
☉ △ ♀	+ 44			
Zod ☍ ♂	+ 58			

Group Average

B.A.	— 42			
C.A.	+ 83	— 7	— $2\frac{1}{3}$	or 2 days before event
R.C.A.	— 48			

True Average

8 B.A.	— 55′ × 1	— 55′	
10 C.A.	+ 102 × $\frac{4}{3}$	+ 136	
13 R.C.A.	— 137 × $\frac{3}{4}$	— 103	
31		— 22	Average — $\frac{22}{31}$

Time Equiv. 4 days after event

CHAPTER XIII

THE MEASURE OF CONFINEMENT AND INCARCERATION

Next to meridian, stands the eleventh house with its characteristic measure of $\frac{300}{360}$ or $\frac{5}{6}^{\circ}$ to the year; but no events pertaining to the house are capable of easy demonstration, except very rarely. So we shall proceed next to the measure which represents the events of twelfth house which is related to imprisonment, true or false, losses, etc. I have started with the nativity of Gandhi in this book. Now, the sentence of imprisonment which he received for a period of seven years in 1922 at the beginning of his Satyagraha movement in India is a sufficiently important event to be taken up in this connection for purposes of illustrating this measure.

This sentence was passed on Gandhi on March 18, 1922 while Gandhi was undergoing the subperiod of Moon in the major period of Mars. Moon is the most afflicted planet of the horoscope. He receives close squares from Jupiter, Pluto, Venus, and Mars; a trine from Neptune and from Saturn. His association with Rahu enhances the evil and the period of sentence continues into the subperiod of Rahu in the major period of Rahu.

Directions

B. A. 52° 28′

(Maximum range one degree)

Directions	Difference in minutes	Total	Average	Time equivalent
Asc △ ♆	— 10			
12thc ⚻ ♆	— 8			
,, ☌ ♂	— 6			
MC ⚻ ♆	— 4			
,, ⚹ ♂	— 2			
♀ □ ☉	— 1			
☽ ⚹ ♄	+ 5			
♃ ⚻ ♄	+ 17			
☿ ⚻ MC	+ 19			
☿ □ 12thc	+ 23			
☿ □ Asc	+ 25			
♄ ⚻ ☊	+ 38	+ 384′	+ $21\frac{1}{3}$′	= 130 days after event
☋ △ MC	+ 45			
12thc ☍ ♇	+ 47			
☋ ☍ 12thc	+ 49			
☋ ⚻ Asc	+ 51			
MC △ ♇	+ 51			

C. A. 48° 6′

(Maximum range 55′)

Directions	Difference in minutes
☽ ☌ ☉	— 52
♃ □ ☉	— 40
☿ △ Zod a	— 10

Directions	Difference in minutes	Total	Average	Time equivalent
☿ ⚻ ♅	+ 5	— 11′	— $1\frac{4}{7}$	= 10 days before event
☊ ⚻ Zod	+ 16			
♀ ⚻ ☊	+ 22			
♀ ✶ ☿	+ 48			

R. C. A. 57° 14′

Directions	Difference in minutes	Total	Average	Time equivalent
♃ △ ♂	— 60			
12(Z) ♄ ☌ ♃	— 55			
♂ ✶ ♀	— 49			
♆ ⚻ ♀	— 47			
Zod ✶ ☽	— 43			
☽ △ ♇	— 19			
♃ ✶ ♇	— 7			
♅ ⚻ ♆	+ 34			
♅ ✶ ♂	+ 36	— 14′	— $1\frac{1}{13}$	= 6 days before event
♄ △ ⊙	+ 39			
Zod ✶ ♆	+ 49			
Zod ⚻ ♂	+ 51			
♃ △ ♀	+ 57			

Group Average

		Total	Time equivalent
B.A.	+ 130		
C.A.	— 10	+ 97	= 32 days after event
R.C.A.	— 23		

True Average

18 B.A.	+ 384′	× 1	+ 384′	
7 C.A.	— 11′	× $\frac{12}{11}$	— 12′	
13 R.C.A.	— 14′	× $\frac{11}{12}$	— 13′	
38 directions total to			+ 359	Average + $\frac{359}{38}$

Time Equiv. = 55 days after event

Example No. 40

The same measure of 55′ to the year should naturally operate for the release from prison also. This happened on 5–2–1924 close upon the operation for which he was removed from jail to hospital.

B. A. 54° 21′

(Maximum range one degree)

Directions	Difference in minutes	Total	Average	Time equivalent
⊙ ✱ ☋	— 54			
L ☍ ♄	— 29			
♅ ✱ ♀	— 20			
Zod ⊼ ♀	— 5			
Asc ⊼ ♃	— 1			
12thc ⊼ □ ♃	+ 3			
MC △ ♃	+ 5	— 49	— $4\frac{9}{10}$	= 30 days before event
12thc □ ☽	+ 13			
Asc △ ☽	+ 15			
♆ ☍ ♄	+ 26			

C. A. 49° 49′

(Maximum range one degree)

Directions	Difference in minutes	Total	Average	Time equivalent
♅ △ ♄	— 47			
12thc ☌ ♀	— 46			
MC ✱ ♀	— 44			
♂ □ ⊙	— 43			
♆ △ ⊙	— 41			
Zod ☍ ♄	— 31	— 232′	— 29′	= 192 days before event
12thZ ⊼ ♄	— 31			
☽ ☌ ⊙	+ 51			

R. C. A. 59° 17′

(Maximum range one degree)

Directions	Difference in minutes	Total	Average	Time equivalent
♂ △ ♆	— 45			
☋ ⊼ ☋	— 43			
♆ ⊼ ♂	— 41			
MC ☌ 12thc	— 39			
♂ ☍ L	+ 10	— 35	— $4\frac{3}{8}$	— 24 days before event
L △ ♀	+ 21			
☽ ☍ ♆	+ 49			
♅ △ ♃	+ 53			

Group Average

B.A.	—	30 days		
C.A.	—	192	— 246	= 82 days before event
R.C.A.	—	24		

True Average

10 B.A.	— 49′	× 1	=	49′	
8 C.A.	— 232′	$\times\frac{12}{11}$	=	253′	
8 R.C.A.	— 35′	$\times\frac{11}{12}$	=	— 32′	
26				— 334	— 13′

= 79 days after event

It was exactly 24 days before the official order of release that Gandhi was taken from prison to hospital for operation and he never returned to jail though he was sentenced for 6 years.

———

CHAPTER XIV

AN EXAMPLE OF DIRECTIONAL INVESTIGATION

§ I. GENERAL

To work out directions for any given event in a horoscope according to set rules is one thing. To predict an event from the directions is quite different. The former is easy and only some rudiments of knowledge of mathematics and of astrology are required. But, for the latter, deep knowledge and ripe judgment and Experience will be found necessary. The difficulties are :—

First, with a mere list of directions worked out for a particular period of time, nothing can be done. For, the directions are derived from the natus, which is the foundation. The directions can find fulfilment in results that are only appropriate to the nativity. Same directions give rise to different effects or events in life in different nativities or even in different stages of the same life, The promise and capabilities of the radix have first got to be grasped and judged before predictions can be ventured. The probable length of life, nature and extent of success in business, profession or service, which department is most favoured, whether marriage is likely or not and if probable, whether early or late marriage, whether more than one marriage is indicated, likelihood of issue, etc all this will have to be gleaned from the nativity and the question 'when'? arises only thereafter.

Secondly : the operation of directions is conditioned by the age of the native ; e. g., directions by the measure of death will occur almost from birth onwards for every year of life but it is obvious that death can take place but once. Therefore directions sufficiently powerful should occur at the proper age to be able to cause death. Good directions between Sun and Venus, ascendant and Venus etc., even by the measure of partnership cannot cause marriage when the native is in his teens or too advanced in age.

Thirdly : the interpretation of directions : This is the most difficult task in any system of directions. But in the system here devised, there is much greater facility because of the fact that the measure employed, itself gives a clue as to the sphere of life in which it will take effect. Though this is decidedly a help, this cannot supersede the difficult task of judging what shape the events will take, whether good or bad, and how it will affect the native and so on.

Example No. 41

To demonstrate how to set out to decide the nature and time of a future event, I cannot do better than take the very case dealt with by Carter for the same purpose that is, to try to judge the time of death in the case of a nativity of a male born on 9-4-1900 at 11-5 P.M. Lat 55° 58′ N, Long 3° 12′ W. As already pointed out, there is no use resorting to the measure of death at the outset as directions can always be found that are likely to cause this event at all ages.

In this horoscope (Appendix A. Serial No. 20)

Neptune is in the 8th house according to the view adopted here that cusp is the centre of the house with a range of half the extent of house space on either side. He is square to Mars ruler of the horoscope in twelfth sign of the Zodiac and also square to Mercury ruler of eighth house. Mercury is evil because of rulership of eighth and eleventh houses. Mercury is in conjunction with Mars in fourth house and Mars has squares from both Saturn and Neptune. This is a reputed combination for short life* No doubt Jupiter is in Lagna (ascendant) but he is in conjunction with malefics Uranus and Neptune with opposition from Pluto and Venus. Jupiter therefore cannot prolong life and there is no use of looking beyond 33 or 34 years for the native (Alpayu or short life limits).

Jaimini Formula

Lord of Ascendant Mars in Pisces, Common Sign ,, eighth house Mercury in Pisces do	} Medium
Lagna (Ascendant) in Scorpio, Fixed Sign Moon occupies Leo , do	} Short
Lagna (Ascendant) in Scorpio, Fixed Sign Hora Lagna falls in Taurus do	} Short

Maximum life — 33 years

* Vide verse 8 of Chap VI of Horasara by Pratyusas.
,, 84 of Chap XIV Sarwarthachintamani

§ III. CAUSE OF DEATH

Eighth house has to be looked to principally and Neptune is found in occupation with squares from Mercury and Mars from Pisces. There is also a sextile from Sun from the same sign. Saturn also aspects the eighth house. According to Hindu Astrology the Navamsa in which eighth house cusp falls is also to be taken into account. The Navamsa is Pisces in this case for which death is declared to be due to "dysentery' fever, burning, disease of belly, poison, beatings, discontinuance of food etc."* 'The eighth from Moon falls also in Pisces. Planets Sun, Mercury and Mars who also figure have connection with poison § Turning to Western Astrology, a planet exactly on the seventh house cusp in its own sign will partly indicate the nature of death†. In this horoscope Venus is in Taurus (own sign) very close to seventh house cusp and Venus can cause death by poison. He is afflicted by the opposition of Jupiter and Uranus and by a quincunx of Saturn. Carter shows by statistical analysis the 11-12 degrees of common signs notably Sagittarius and Pisces are specially involved in poisoning cases‡ ; and the planets figuring in these areas in the case are curiously enough the same planets as find mention in Phaladeepika. Carter also observes that Neptune is a

---

* Verse Chap XXVI Horasara.

§ Verses 4 and 5 Chap XIV Phaladeepika.

† Robson Text book of Astrology P. 172.

‡ Astrology of Accidents P. 109.

common afflictor; with Neptune in 'eighth square Mercury ruler of 8th, Mercury himself weak and afflicted by Saturn and Mars in watery signs, the inference that poison is the most likely element in causing death is pretty obvious. Saturn opposing eighth house from Sagittarius indicates privation also as an element.

§ IV NATURE OF DEATH

The nature of afflictions in connection with eighth house suggests that death will be unnatural. Lord of 8th house being afflicted by malefics, two malefics attacking the same luminary, malefics in first and eighth houses, afflictions to fourth and eighth houses and their rulers are all independent indications. In this case, Neptune is in 8th, lord of 8th afflicted by Mars Saturn, and Neptune. Moon has got quincunx from both Mercury and Mars. Jupiter, Uranus, and Rahu are all quincunx cusp of 8th. Mercury and Mars are in fourth and Jupiter ruler of fourth (malefic) is conjunction with Uranus, Rahu is opposition Pluto and Venus.

Robson's Text book P. 170—1 gives the following table.

Jupiter in Scorpio — Liable to tragic death, due to Society or politics.

Uranus in Scorpio — Liable to sudden end.

Sun in Pisces — Danger of violent death from secret enemies.

Neptune in 8th — Death through drugs.

Here Mercury ruler of 8th is weak because of his occupying his debilitation sign and is afflicted by both

Saturn and Mars in watery signs and also by Neptune in addition.

Thus unnatural death by poison appears fairly conclusive from the above investigation.

§ 5. Will it be Accidental, Homicidal or Suicidal

We can rule out homicidal at the outset as there are no indications. for a violent end that way. As for accidents there is a very instructive little book written by Carter giving tabulations that are the result of collation of laborious statistics and none of the signs, houses, or planets figuring here have any connection with the areas mentioned therein as maximum except Uranus who scores by being in first house. So accidents too may be ruled out.

Suicide alone remains : Is suicide to be fixed upon only as a desideratum or are there positive indications for it in the horoscope ? Carter deals with this very case in his Principles of Horoscopic Delineation and gives causes not only for this one being a case of suicide but also gives the chief indications for suicides in general and they are :—(P 79).

1. Neptune in some relation to eighth
2. Mercury in familiarity with Mars
3. Jupiter in familiarity with Saturn
4. Sun in familiarity with Saturn or Neptune
5. An element of desperation (often an Aries group or a Uranus affliction).

and the reasons for this one being a case of suicide as applicable to the tropical horoscope given are :—

1. Moon rules eighth sextile Neptune
2. Mercury conjunct Mars
3. Jupiter has no familiarity with Saturn, perhaps here Uranus substitutes Saturn
4. Sun sextile Neptune
5. Mars Saturn constitutes the desperate element

The reasons that are applicable to the Nirayana horoscope given here are as follows and compare more favourably.

1. **Neptune occupies eighth house.** The reason given by Carter applies to this horoscope also as Cancer is intercepted between 8th and 9th houses.
2. Mercury conjunct Mars
3. Jupiter and Saturn in mutual reception
4. Sun Sextile Neptune
5. Uranian affliction to the eighth house is partile (only 4′ difference) and Mars square Saturn is alsc present. Therefore a careful examination of the relevant factors reveals suicide by poison as the most probable method of end.

§ 6 **When**?

We have already settled the group of life as belonging to short life and life span will not exceed 34 years.

		y	m	d
Moon's Longitude at birth Leo 1°32′ and so the balance of Ketu dasa at birth was		6	2	10
Period of Venus		20	0	0
	Total	26	2	10
„ of Sun		6	0	0
	Total	32	2	10

Sub-periods in Sun's Major period

			y	m	d
Sun's period begins			26	2	10
Sub-period of Sun			0	3	18
		Total	26	5	28
,,	Moon		0	6	0
		Total	26	11	28
,,	Mars		0	4	6
		Total	27	4	4
,,	Rahu		0	10	24
		Total	28	2	28
,,	Jupiter		0	9	18
		Total	29	0	16
,,	Saturn		0	11	12
		Total	29	11	28
,,	Mercury		0	10	6
		Total	30	10	4

Ketu's Major period ends with 6th year which is too early to kill. So the choice is between Venus and Sun. In cases of short life it is the third dasa (period) from birth that usually kills*. Therefore Sun's major period is an easy choice. Venus becomes malefic enough to become a maraka by ruling 7th and 12th houses and occupying seventh, a maraka house. But when he occupies seventh any planet aspected by him also becomes a maraka for persons born under Scorpio § Jupiter is aspected by Venus. Jupiter is already a maraka for the horoscope as ruler of 2nd house and 4th house (angle).

* Verse 16, Chap VIII Sarvarthachintamani

§ G. Srinivasamurthy Span of Life Chap X.

Sun is ruler of the third asterism and Jupiter of seventh which makes him even more powerful in this respect. Jupiter is the most likely sublord to inflict death. Saturn though in second and a malefic is not so powerful. With the above materials before us it is not difficult to choose Jupiter's sub-period in Sun's major period between 28 years two months and 28 days and 29 years 0 month and 16 days, that is between **B. A. 28° 15′** and 29° 3′. This is a **duration** and New Era Directions can be worked out on that basis with the range of one year on either side.

B. A. 27° 15′ — 30° 3′

Directions			Arc	Directions			Arc
☿	⊼	☽	27° 14′	♄	△	MC	28° 32′
♀	□	♆	27° 17′	♇	⊼	☊	28° 48′
MC	⊼	♂	27° 51′	♄	△	♀	29° 6′
♆	□	Zod	27° 54′	♀	□	MC	29° 26′
8thc	△	♃	28° 16′	Asc	△	♂	29° 40′
☋	☍	8thc	28° 25′	8thc	△	♅	29° 56′
☽	⊼	Zod	28° 28′	♅	☍	8th	30° 4′

Total 428° 44.′ Average $\frac{428° 44'}{15} = 28° 35'$

C. A. 15° 54′ — 17° 32′

MC	☍	☉	16° 6′	♇	⊼	Asc	16° 37′
♃	□	☿	16° 9′	☿	△	☊	17° 10′
♇	□	♂	16° 17′	♄	□	Zod	17° 26′
☽	□	♃	16° 37′	☋	□	♂	17° 29′

Total 133° 51′. Average 16° 44′ $\times \frac{12}{7}$ = 28° 41′

R. C. A. 47° 26′ — 50° 48′

Directions			Arc	Directions			Arc
♄	□	8thc	47° 26′	♆	△	☊	49° 22′
☊	✱	♂	47° 29′	8thc	□	Asc	49° 24′
♆	△	♅	47° 43′	♅	✱	Asc	49° 28′
☊	✱	Asc	47° 49′	♄	△	♆	49° 32′
Asc	□	☉	47° 55′	☊	△	MC	49° 83′
Zod	☍	♃	48° 9′	Zod	☍	♅	49° 49′
☽	✱	♅	48° 17′	♇	⊼	♄	49° 54′
♀	□	Zod	48° 20′	☽	△	☋	49° 56′
☽	□	8thc	48° 21′	☊	△	♀	50° 12′
♇	✱	MC	48° 26′	MC	□	☽	50° 26′
MC	⊼	♂	48° 54′	♀	☌	♆	50° 26′
♄	☍	☽	48° 58′	♆	⊼	♇	50° 34′
♇	✱	♀	49° 0′	Asc	□	Zod	50° 43′
8thc	⊼	♂	49° 4′	♃	✱	♂	50° 48′
♅	✱	♂	49° 8′				

Total 1425° 11.′ Average 26 = 49° 9′ × $\frac{7}{12}$ = 28° 40′

Group Average

B.A.	28° 35′		
C.A.	28° 41′	85° 56′	28° 39′
R.C.A.	28° 40′		

True Average

16 B.A.	457° 20′	× 1	= 457° 20′
8 C.A.	133° 51′	× $\frac{12}{7}$	= 228° 0′
29 R.C.A.	1425° 11′	× $\frac{7}{12}$	= 831° 21′
53			1516° 41′

Average 28° 38′

Arc for death 28° 46′ Difference 8′

The next case dealt with in that chapter for purposes of demonstration is that of King Edward VII. This case has already been dealt with. But, for purposes of investigation the student can assume that the sub-period for his death would be that of Mars, or Rahu or Jupiter and he will not be far wrong. He can work the directions for this duration of time and arrive at the correct time of death within very close range. It has already been shown that the average as per New Era technique is close to the event. The process of averaging in a duration in this case is too long to be given here and there is nothing new. The student can work it out for himself and verify. One example has already been given which will suffice.

CHAPTER XV

OBITER DICTA

§. 1.

It is not to be supposed that the final word on 'Directions' has been said with the inauguration of New Era Measures, and the technique suggested for working them. Rather it may be said to have only begun. Whenever new ground is broken in any science, there is always scope for further improvements and extensions. Further investigations have already proceeded along certain lines that are promising but by no means complete yet.

When the characteristic measure and its reversed measure are found to furnish valid directions that are appropriate for the event, it should not be surprising if the characteristic measure further reduced in the same manner should exhibit similar properties.

Example No. 42

Taking the first example in this book namely that of Mahatma Gandhi, the C. A. by measure of death was 45° 42′. If this arc is further reduced by the same measure of death i.e., 45° 42′ $\frac{7}{12}$, the F. C. A. (Further reduced characteristic arc) will be 26° 40′ and for this arc the directions in force for the tragic event are (within orbs 20° 25″). Uranus and Neptune were in radical square.

Directions			Arc	
♅	△	♆	— Exact	
♅	□	♂	+ 2	
♄	□	☉	+ 5	
♃	✱	♀	+ 11	Total 35 Average 7′
Zod	☍	♂	+ 17	

This and the direction ♅ □ ♂ so close to the event cannot be ignored by any student of astrology. Robson gives the following effects for an evil direction between Mars and Uranus* "Sudden illness and operations, danger of violence, accidents by fire, electricity explosions etc." Alan Leo gives more or less the same effects: "This is one of the most unfortunate aspects that can be experienced either causing the native to behave with insane rashness or overwhelming him with some great trouble from an entirely unexpected quarter ..Accident by fire, electrical installations, or explosives are occasional concomitants of this influence and all unnecessary exposure to risk in such matters should be avoided..It is a very dangerous aspect and can only be contended against by the power of the spirit."

The directions given above are those within orbs of dimension (20′ 25″). Many other directions come in if one degree is to be allowed as done by the Astrologers of the West for even slower measures than this one, such as Jupiter Quincunx Venus, Ascendant conj. 8th Zod M. C. Square 8th Zod Moon Square Pluto, Ascendant Square Uranus, eighth house cusp sextile Zod., Uranus square Pluto.

---

* Radix system P. 93 § Progressed Horoscope P. 171-2.

Example No. 43

Yet the case of Gandhi is by no means a solitary instance of the application of F.C.M. (Further Contracted Measure) For Tagore's death F. C. A. (Further Contracted Arc) is 29° 19′ and the direction ♄ ⊼ ☿ is exact and characteristic. Mercury is in the second house (maraka). Another direction is Jupiter trine Venus + 12′ both planets being in radical square. Jupiter is ruler of angles and Venus ruler of 3rd and 8th houses. Just beyond orbs is ☉ ⊼ 8th house cusp —28′, no doubt a background influence.

Example No. 44

In the case of J. C. Bose next dealt with (Ex. 3) the F. C. A. for death is 26° 53′ and Mercury Square Zodiac — 11. and Neptune Quincunx:8th C. + 22′ are the directions in force. Several more will come in if one degree is allowed.

Example No. 45

In the case taken up for directional investigation (Ex. 39) the F. C. A. is 9° 48′ and the following directions are seen to be present.

Directions			Arc	Directions			Arc
♀	☌	☊	— Exact	8thC	□	Zod	— 19
☋	△	☽	— 16	Ł	☌	♆	÷ 22
♄	⊼	L	— 18	☽	□	♀	— 20

Is there a lesson to be learnt from the direction in force closest for the event as per F. C. A.? We will advert to this later after taking some more examples to illustrate F. C. M.

Example No. 46

Queen Victoria : This case is cited by Harwood to illustrate the method of working directions by the Polar Angle Method which is really simpler than Primary directions worked by any other method. Queen Victoria was born on 24-5-1819 and died on 22-1-1901.*

The reasons for the death of the Queen given there need not be gone into as they are given for a wrong date. The F. C. A. is 27° 47′ and the directions within orbs are :—

Directions	Arc	Directions	Arc	Average
♄ ☌ ♀	— 2′	♅ □ Zod	— 12′	— $9\frac{1}{4}$′
♀ ⊼ 8thC	— 7′	♆ □ ♀	— 16′	

Example No. 47

John Ruskin : This case is the one taken by Sepharial as the Example in his Directional Astrology. John Ruskin was born on 8-2-1819 at 7-30 A.M. in London and died on 20-1-1900. The F. C. A. for death is 27° 33′. Directions are (within orbs)

☋ ☍ 8th (Zod)	— 1′	♅ □ Zod	— 21	— $\frac{11}{4}$′ — $2\frac{3}{4}$′
☽ ⊼ ☿	+ 5′	Zod □ ☉	+ 6	

The Primary Directions worked out by Sepharial for this event are :—

---

* (but wrongly given in the above book as 22-1-1902 Age 82y 8 m).

Directions				Arc	Average
☉	P	♅	Zod	80° 10′	
Asc	□	♄	Mundo	81° 2′	
Asc	S.Q.	☉	Zod	81° 11′	81′ 4′
Asc	P	♅	Zod	81° 27′	
☽	□	♂	Zod Con	81° 30′	

Arc for Death 80° 57′

Quite close! But working them? How to fix the limits for the directions for which average is to be taken? On the other hand with the horoscope ready cast, the matter of working B. A., C. A. and R. C. A. as also F. C. A. is a question of minutes for each arc with no great mathematical skill involved. The directions by F. C. M.:—Zod □ ☉, ☊ ☍ 8th Zod, ♅ □ Zod are all characteristic and within orbs of dimension.

Example No. 48

Ivar Kreuger : This is case No. 2 in Principles of Horoscopic Delineation by Carter. The relevant data and horoscope are given there. Born 2-3-1880 Lat 56° 45′ N Long 16° 15′ shot himself 12-3-1932. F. C. A. for death 17° 42′.

The directions are ♂ □ ☿—11′ Zod ☌ ♆ + 6′

Example No. 49

Girl born in London at 4 A. M. on 11-1-1903. Suicide on 26-12-1930 for no known reason (case No. 5 in P. H. D.) F. C. A. for death is 9 31′. The directions are ☉ ☌ ♄ + 17′, ♄ △ ♂—20′; ☋ □ ♀ + 3′;

Zod ✶ ♆ + 10; ♂ □ ☾ + 23′

Example No. 50

German born 25-10-1879 named Haarınan Executed on 15-5-1925 (case No. 8 of P. H. D) F. C. A. for death is 15° 26′. The directions are ☽ ✱ M.C. — 2′ ; ♆ ☌ ♂ 10′ ☌ ♆ ☌ L — 22′; Zod △′ ♅ — 18′.

Example No. 51

Female born 21-3-1890. Committed suicide by poison on 25-4-1909. (Case No. 6 of S. D. of M. A. by Carter). F. C. A. 6° 30′. The directions are ♅ ⊼ ♆ Exact ; ☊ ☍ ♃ — 16′ ; ♄ ⊼ ♃ —19′ ; M C △ ☿ + 15 (Mercury a maraka for the horoscope) ; ♄ □ L—18 ;′ ☊ ⊼ L — 15′

These cases have been taken up as ready cast horoscopes are available and a review of the directions nearest to the event would be instructive.

Review

Ex. No. 45	♀ ☌ ☋ Exact	Suicide by poison
,, 49	☋ □ ♀ + 3′	Suicide (cause not stated but probably poison)
,, 51	♅ ⊼ ♆ Exact	Suicide by poison
,, 43	{ ♅ □ ♂ + 2 ♅ □ ♆ Exact	Gunshot (homicidal)
,, 48	{ Zod ☌ ♆ + 6′ ♂ □ ☿ — 11′	Gunshot (suicidal)
,, 50	{ ☽ ✱ MC — 2′ ♆ ☌ ♂ — 10′	Executed
,, 46 ,, 47	{ ♄ ☌ ♀ — 2′ ☋ ☍ 8th — 2′	Lingering illness

Anyhow this aspect of the problem merits further investigation.

§ 2

Just as F. C. A. in the case of the death measure furnishes directions that are appropriate to this event, F. C. A. for meridian measure of 45′ to the year i.e., 33′ 45′ should indicate events that are referrable to the meridian. We will again take up the case of John Smith.

Example No. 52

The C. A. for death of father was 15° 15′. F. C. A. would therefore be 15° 15′ × $\frac{3}{4}$ = 11′ 26 and the directions within orbs (34′) are :—

Directions

Directions	Arc	Directions	Arc	Total	Average
☽ △ ℒ	— 20′	☿ □ Asc	— 3′		
☉ ☌ ℒ	— 14′	♆ ☍ ☽	— 1′		
☿ □ ♄	— 9′	ℒ □ Zod	+ 13′	—28′	—3½′
♆ ✶ ☉	— 7′	Zod □ MC	+ 13′		

The nearest aspect is ♆ ☍ ☽ — 1 and Moon is ruler of M. C.

§ 3

What is true for a reduced measure should also by analogy apply to an expanded measure. So it appears worthwhile investigating what the result will be for R. C. A. expanded on the same scale, which we will call E. M. We shall first experiment with cases where the Basic Arc is small one and take up cases for which the

CHAPTER XVI

NEW ERA MEASURES AND RECTIFICATION

§ 1 GENERAL

The methods of rectification of birth time can be divided into two classes (i) Rectification from the principal incidents of life (ii) Rectification by formulæ. Rectification by Epoch belongs to the second group and is the only method of this group that has attained some distinction and following in the West even where its validity is being questioned nowadays. There are also methods of rectification by epoch in Hindu astrology but it is not our object to elaborate them here.

The method of predicting events in Hindu astrology is principally by the system of planetary periods and their subdivisions. This depends on the longitude of Moon at birth and so the birth time cannot be rectified correct to the minute or second by this method as there will be no appreciable change in the directional influences within a few minutes or even half an hour. On the other hand there are a great variety of methods of rectification by formulæ by which the correct birth time can be fixed quite easily.

a bath of boiling water and died on 23-10-1920 (Ex. No. 7 in that book). E. A. 16° 17′. The directions are ☊ ☍ M.C. + 1; ♃ ☌ ☿ + 13′; M.C. ☍ ♂ + 9′; Beyond the orbs there are many more directions. According to Carter's analysis, common signs figure largely, in scalding cases, Pisces being the most frequently occurring sign. 'Scalding is a Piscean misfortune' (P 65). In the Sidereal map used here, Mercury, Mars and Sun are in Pisces and Mercury is ruler of 8th house. Saturn and Pluto are close to 8th house cusp (Trisection), 8th cusp as well as Saturn being in watery Navamsas. Mars in watery sign has been considered to be necessary 'to boil the water'. Rahu reflects the effect of Saturn in whose sign he is placed. His closest aspect (quincunx) is from Neptune from a watery sign, and the closest direction to the event being Rahu opposition M.C.

CHAPTER XVI

NEW ERA MEASURES AND RECTIFICATION

§ 1 GENERAL

The methods of rectification of birth time can be divided into two classes (i) Rectification from the principal incidents of life (ii) Rectification by formulæ. Rectification by Epoch belongs to the second group and is the only method of this group that has attained some distinction and following in the West even where its validity is being questioned nowadays. There are also methods of rectification by epoch in Hindu astrology but it is not our object to elaborate them here.

The method of predicting events in Hindu astrology is principally by the system of planetary periods and their subdivisions. This depends on the longitude of Moon at birth and so the birth time cannot be rectified correct to the minute or second by this method as there will be no appreciable change in the directional influences within a few minutes or even half an hour. On the other hand there are a great variety of methods of rectification by formulæ by which the correct birth time can be fixed quite easily.

§ 2. DIFFICULTIES

Rectification by events though widely practised in both schools of astrology is by no means easy. There are very many systems of direction and naturally the results as per one system may not tally with those arrived at by another system. Then the question arises which system should be given the preference. Even employing one system exclusively, it is almost impossible to arrive at a birth time that accounts for all the events of life with uniform exactitude. When the birth time is so adjusted as to show the exact time for one event, it will be usually found that it is rather wide as regards other equally important events. The difficulty is not even purely mathematical either, for it would call for great nicety of judgment to select one direction appropriate for a particular event and vice versa.

Moreover rectification by events alone is based on a fallacy. It proceeds on the assumption that one particular direction alone has caused a particular event. No doubt, events are caused by appropriate directions but when they are worked out for well — authenticated horoscopes where there is abosolutely no doubt regarding the accuracy of the time of birth it is very often found that events do not happen as per schedule. Yet the reverse rule is adopted for fixing the time of birth! Yet this is successfully being done by astute astrologers who allow a margin for events and choose that time which is most satisfactory. Still this is no guarantee that the time so fixed is the correct birth time.

§ 3 AVERAGING — ONLY WAY

An event is more often the result of a parallelogram of forces at work—forces proceeding from several directional influences operating to produce an effect. No direction however powerful operates completely dissociated from other directional influences before and after, both as regards the nature of the event and as regards the time of precipitation. Hence the principle of averaging is the best solution possible for the vexed problem of rectification by events. It has been demonstrated already that averaging of directions in force within a prescribed period of time works close to the time of events in a large number of cases so as to preclude all chances of coincidence.

The principle of averaging for rectification can be adopted for any system of directions. Primary directions are now rarely in use because of the difficulties in computing them. Moreover they are so numerous that choice becomes extremely difficult. This difficulty is stressed by more than one astrologer. Alan Leo says* "It is one of the especial purposes of this chapter to draw attention to the immense number of these and to emphasize the unsatisfactoriness alluded to as due less to their number or to any difficulty in their calculation (which is nearly a matter of time and patience) than to the extreme subtlety of judgment required to decide just what event is signified by any particular aspect."

---

* Casting the Horoscope P. 101.

Example No. 55

Case of King Edward VII

The case of King Edward VII is taken up in that work as an example for rectification of birth time and R. A. M. C. suggested for adoption tentatively is 13 hrs. 57 min. 47 seconds, the R. A. M. C. for the bulletin time being' 14 hrs. 1 min. 11 seconds. Other possible R. A. M. Cs., each within a reasonable margin of the bulletin time suggested are :—

(1) 13. 58. 28	M.C.	Death of Duke of Clarence
(2) 13. 52. 24	M.C.	Birth of Prince Edward of York
(3) 14. 1. 7	Asc	Birth of Duke of Saxe-Coburg

The rectification of King Edward VII's birth time has been effected by E. H. Bailey in his Prenatal Epoch* with directions for the principal events of life from the Epochal horoscope. Why rectification should have been thought at all necessary in the case of a birth time which can be reasonably assumed to have been correctly noted is not explained by anybody showing how the bulletin time is unsatisfactory. But Mr. Carter has made the observation that a slightly different time than the recorded one would give better results but it is wise to abstain from too ready interference with recorded time. This is perfectly understandable. We have dealt with the principal events in the life of that monarch in this book and we have found no reasons for interfering

* P. 184–6.

with the birth time as sufficiently satisfactory results have been obtained by the application of New Era Measures.

Events	Group Average	True Average
Death	18 days before	20 days before
Operation for Appendicitis	9 days after	one day before
Marriage	54 days before	49 days before

About 50 days is not such a big difference as to call for rectification especially when other events are very closely indicated and the birth time may well be left alone; but we will utilise this case as an example for rectification by events employing New Era Measures.

MARRIAGE

Glancing at the list of directions for the above events, it will be seen that there are two directions in which the ascendant is involved in B. A, only one involving M.C. in C. A, and two to M.C. and two to Asc in R. C. A; and that the minus element preponderates in the final result (Interplanetary aspects are of no value in New Era directions for rectification). It is also apparent that if M. C. is advanced by 8 minutes, the direction to M. C. in C. A. will pass beyond orbs allowed and the minus element in B. A. will be reduced though it will be increased in the R. C. A. group. With this amendment the total for B. A. group will come to only —71′ and the average —10$\frac{1}{7}$′ or 62 days before event. The total for C. A. will be —19′ and average —2$\frac{5}{7}$ or 33 days before event. For R. C. A. the total will come to — 139′ and average — $\frac{139}{13}$ or 32 days before event. Group average will be 42 days before event. True average will be 39 days before event. For an advance of 8 minutes to M.C. the R.A.M.C. will be 14 hrs. 1 min. 41 seconds, an advance of only 30 seconds in time.

Rectification by formulæ: Of these, there are a great many in Hindu Astrology. Almost all the methods are based on the interval between sunrise and time of birth expressed in Ghatikas and Vighatikas (A. table for conversion of hours and minutes into Ghatikas and Vighatikas is provided in the Appendix). From the many methods in vogue I shall select one that has been found satisfactory in a large majority of cases.

Formulæ

1. Ascertain the sunrise on the date of birth for the place of birth.
2. Convert the time into Ghatikas and Vighatikas
3. Multiply the above by two
4. Add 5, 9 or 7 to the product according as the ascendant falls in movable, fixed or common sign
5. Multiply the result by 4
6. Divide the product by 27 and ascertain the remainder in Ghatikas and Vighatikas (Reject quotient)
7. The whole number indicates the number of asterisms traversed before birth by Moon counting from Aswini or Chitrai.

8. The next number indicates the number of the asterisms occupied by Moon at birth or its trine asterism

9. The Vighatikas divided by 60 represent the portion of the asterism traversed already by Moon at birth (the arc for an asterism being 13 degrees and 20 minutes)

10. If the remainder does not correctly indicate either the asterism at birth or the portion elapsed before birth, adjust the birth time so as to make it conform. Though the above process when set out appears involved, it is really very simple as an example will show.

Rectification of birth time of King Edward VII

Data. Sunrise 7. 7 A. M. on date of birth in London.
Time of birth 10-48 A.M. Bulletin Time
Moon's Longitude Virgo 7° 49′

(1)	Interval between sunrise and birth		3 hrs. 41 mints.
		or	9 gh. 12½ vg.
(2)	Multiply by 2		18. 25
(3)	For common sign add		7. 0
		Total	25. 25
(4)	Multiply by 4		101. 40

(5) Divide by 27. Remainder 20 (gh) – 40 (vg) (Quotient 3 reject)

(6) 20 represents the number of the asterisms already traversed by Moon at birth

(7) 21 (next number) represents the number of the asterism occupied by Moon at birth i.e,, Uttarashada starting from Aswini, or, Punarvasu starting from Chitrai, or, their trine asterisms.

(8) Moon is in Uttaraphalguna (trine from Uttarashada) hence correct

(9) 40 divided by $60 = \frac{40}{60}$ is the fraction of that asterism traversed by Moon at the time recorded for the birth i.e., $\frac{40}{60} \times 13° 20' = 8° 53' 20''$

Therefore Moon's longitude should be Virgo 5° 33′ 20″
Actually it is ,, 7° 49′ 0″

Adjustment

Virgo 7° 49′ represents $7° 49' + 3° 20' = 11° 9'$ of Uttara Phalguna as that asterism begins from 26° 40′ of Leo.

Therefore $\frac{11° 9'}{13° 20'} \times 60$ should be the remainder in Vighatikas. Instead of 40 it should be 50

So, in column 4 the figure should be 101—50
3 25—27½
2 18—27½
1 9—13¾

or 3 h. 41 m. 30 seconds

Just the addition of 30 seconds in time was suggested in the rectification by New Era Measures.

———

CHAPTER XVII

CONCLUSION

Though there is nothing new in the materials placed before the reader hitherto, the combination of certain elements is new e.g., the system of aspects in Western Astrology is suggested for the Hindu Zodiac of constellations. If it is asked whether the term 'Aspects' in Hindu texts were meant to be interpreted in this fashion, the answer is "I do not know". But if the question is whether they are recommended to be so used in this work the answer is 'yes'. As has already been stated this system of aspects is not foreign to the Hindu system. The doctrine of change of nature by planets according to rulership of houses, though an axiom in Hindu Astrology is unknown in the West but is confidently incorporated here as part of New Era Astrology. Western Astrologers of repute, frankly confess they are not able to explain or account for so many things. Perhaps the adoption of this doctrine will explain some of them. An orderly collection of rules for determination of longevity, not found as such elsewhere, is given in the hope that it will be a great help to students of both schools of Astrology. This branch is not much in evidence in the treatises of the Western school if not deliberately avoided in the later books.

With this background, a new directional system is presented. It is the fixed increment system in which purely symbolical measures are used. One degree to one year measure has already gained much ground by its utility. To this, other measures are added derived from the natural divisions of the Zodiac to make the system a self-contained organic unit.

A distinction has been made between directions for judgment as to the nature of the event and directions for timing it. The whole life at the outset is easily mapped out with the help of planetary periods and sub-periods according to the Dasa system of directions. This will give an idea as to when the major events are to be expected. The directions are then worked out with the 'New Era Measures' as usual in all systems of directing, the measure itself furnishing here a clue as to the nature of the event and all directions within a reasonable range are to be taken into account in the judgment—how it will take effect, whether good or bad etc. For timing the event exactly, a selection is made of the above directions within a definite range (one year before and after) and these are averaged. **And no direction within orbs can be left out for this purpose.**

This is the plan that has been adopted throughout this work and it has yielded fairly good results. Those who are not familiar with the Hindu system of planetary periods and could not or would not use them may safely leave it out. The remaining is as good a system of direction as any that has been devised in the West with the added facility of the measure itself indicating the nature of the event to be expected, —a unique feature not found in other systems.

New Era Measures as applied to transits is in course of preparation and is expected to be ready shortly.

APPENDIX—A

S. No.	Name	Cusps of Houses			
		10	11	12	Ascen
1.	Gandhi	♋ 3·53	♌ 3·51	♍ 3·49	♎ 3·47
2.	Tagore	♐ 19·6	♑ 20·41	♒ 22·17	♓ 23·52
3.	J. C. Bose	♑ 18·2	♒ 22·24	♓ 26·46	♉ 1·8
4.	Edward VII	♎ 11·3	♎ 29·22	♏ 17·40	♐ 5·59
5.	George V	♐ 9.19	♑ 10·0	♒ 10·41	♓ 11·22
6.	George VI	♋ 14·30	♌ 11·16	♍ 8·1	♎ 4·47
7.	S. D. M. A. No. 2	♒ 19·53	♈ 1·9	♉ 12·26	♊ 23·42
8.	do No. 3	♌ 25·15	♍ 20·8	♎ 15·0	♏ 9·53
9.	do No. 4	♌ 0·39	♌ 27·3	♍ 23·27	♎ 19·51
10.	P. H. D. No. 4	♏ 13·4	♐ 5·16	♐ 27·29	♑ 19·41
11.	S. Freud	♓ 13·42	♈ 21·29	♉ 29·17	♋ 7·4
12.	S. D. M. A. No. 1	♈ 13·31	♉ 18·20	♊ 23·9	♋ 27·58
13.	A. A. No. 2	♌ 8·1	♍ 4·35	♎ 1·8	♎ 27·42
14.	do No. 19	♐ 14·11	♑ 17·49	♒ 21.26	♓ 25·4
15.	Q. Victoria	♑ 10·47	♒ 21·58	♈ 3·10	♉ 14·21
16.	Q. Mary	♏ 14·29	♐ 4·48	♐ 25·8	♑ 15·27
17.	J. Smith	♋ 11·13	♌ 8·24	♍ 5·36	♎ 2.47
18.	Q. Elizabeth II	♏ 2·56	♏ 21·31	♐ 10·5	♐ 28·40
19.	P. Eisenhower	♐ 17·41	♑ 19·50	♒ 21·59	♓ 24·8
20.	S.D. M.A. No. 8	♍ 11·6	♎ 0·30	♎ 19‘53	♏ 9·17
21.	J. Ruskin	♏ 20·9	♐ 11·49	♑ 3·9	♑ 25·9
22.	I. Kreuger	♏ 11·50	♏ 28·18	♐ 14.45	♑ 1·13
23.	P. H. D. No. 5	♌ 26·5	♍ 18·30	♎ 10·55	♏ 3·20
24.	do No. 8	♑ 6·21	♒ 17·31	♓ 28·4	♉ 9·51
25.	S. D. M.A. No. 6	♎ 14·37	♏ 4·49	♏ 25·1	♐ 15·12
26.	A. A. Ex 3	♍ 9·32	♍ 29·52	♎ 20·12	♏ 10·32
27.	do Ex 7	♌ 17·21	♍ 10·41	♎ 4·1	♎ 27·21

N B:—Cusps of 4,5,6, & 7th houses are opposite to those of 10,11,12 & Asc; cusp of 2nd is sextile to 12th. Cusp of 23rd is trine to 11th

APPENDIX—A

S. No.	Planets					
	Sun	Moon	Mercury	Venus	Mars	Jupiter
1.	♎ 16·55	♋ 27·57	♎ 11·44	♎ 24·26	♎ 26·23	♈ 28·9 ℞
2.	♈ 24·30	♓ 21·3	♈ 8·6	♈ 23·6	♊ 0·16	♋ 25·29
3.	♏ 16·9	♍ 19·0	♐ 2·56	♐ 6·46	♑ 21·0	♉ 25·47
4.	♎ 25·16	♍ 7·49	♏ 10·4	♍ 27·36	♐ 23·36	♏ 29·50
5.	♉ 20·29	♍ 9·7	♈ 21·32	♈ 17·50	♋ 13·38	♐ 3·43 ℞
6.	♏ 29·32	♏ 2·27	♏ 25·52	♎ 13·23	♏ 8·59	♋ 16.13 ℞
7.	♒ 5·10	♍ 25·23	♑ 13·28	♒ 24·55	♐ 19·28	♎ 21·44
8.	♈ 27·44	♏ 4·21	♉ 18·59	♊ 5·43	♍ 5·0	♒ 25·2
9.	♋ 8·9	♊ 24·16	♋ 28·35	♌ 22.20	♈ 13·24	♎ 12·46
10.	♎ 1·45	♉ 24·36	♎ 21·49	♎ 7·29	♎ 22·50	♒ 5·45 ℞
11.	♈ 24·7	♉ 17·22	♉ 5·10	♈ 4·2	♍ 11·35 ℞	♓ 7·40
12.	♊ 11·7	♑ 22 29	♉ 27·25	♉ 18·14	♊ 21·54	♒ 25·27
13.	♌ 9·1	♊ 3·9	♋ 21·11	♌ 0·25	♍ 16.40	♒ 10·48 ℞
14.	♓ 6·40	♍ 13·31	♒ 15·7	♈ 19·16	♋ 17·40 ℞	♓ 15·54
15.	♉ 10·48	♉ 12·22	♈ 17·37	♈ 5·16	♓ 26·19	♑ 25·38
16.	♉ 13·14	♒ 16·28	♉ 7·22	♈ 11·26	♋ 23·28	♒ 14·3
17.	♊ 7·7	♒ 7·1	♉ 21·18	♊ 22·9	♒ 6·3	♏ 20·19 ℞
18.	♈ 7·24	♋ 19·19	♃ 11·52	♒ 21·10	♑ 28·5	♑ 29·43
19.	♍ 29·16	♎ 11·20	♍ 11·13	♍ 13·48	♐ 21·47	♈ 10·28
20.	♓ 27·12	♌ 1·32	♓ 4·18	♉ 11·40	♓ 8·57	♏ 18·9 ℞
21.	♑ 27·27	♋ 5·49	♑ 3·27	♐ 14·30	♍ 5·16	♑ 9·1
22.	♒ 19·50	♎ 26·25	♓ 3·50	♑ 15·54	♉ 15·57	♓ 0·11
23.	♐ 27·16	♉ 22·45	♑ 14·12	♑ 7·37	♍ 16·21	♑ 28·4
24.	♎ 9·47	♒ 20·53	♎ 22·12	♍ 2.26	♉ 4·2	♒ 10·43
25.	♓ 8·7	♓ 10·51	♒ 20·52	♓ 15·43	♏ 15·6	♑ 12·48
26.	♌ 16·53	♈ 7·4	♌ 22·12	♍ 19·39	♎ 8·43	♐ 10·46
27.	♓ 28·15	♒ 28·53	♓ 9·10	♒ 19·24	♓ 3·29	♒ 23·6

APPENDIX—A

Planets					S. No.
Saturn	Uranus	Neptune	Pluto	Rahu	
♏ 20·20	♊ 29·45	♈ 26·25℞	♈ 25·30℞	♋ 12·10	1
♌ 10·47	♉ 18·43	♓ 8·51	♈ 17·6	♐ 24·51	2
♋ 20·25	♉ 9·22	♓ 0·15℞	♈ 14·4	♒ 11·57	3
♐ 8·31	♒ 28·59	♑ 22·41	♓ 27·48℞	♑ 12·29	4
♎ 2·9℞	♊ 6·40	♓ 18·13	♈ 21·22	♎ 6·1	5
♎ 22·23	♎ 29·45	♉ 24·7℞	♉ 19·5℞	♒ 15·5	6
♈ 9·1	♑ 4·31	♊ 26·37℞	♊ 3·22℞	♈ 21·19	7
♑ 16·47	♐ 2·28	♊ 9·23	♉ 25·57	♍ 21·46	8
♈ 26·15	♑ 4·38	♊ 29·3	♊ 5·34	♈ 13·0	9
♏ 0·55	♊ 20·57	♓ 21·26℞	♈ 23·24℞	♌ 20·6	10
♊ 5·40	♈ 28·46	♒ 28·0	♈ 12·29	♈ [illegible]1·38	11
♌ 19·35	♎ 5.2℞	♉ 15·13	♉ 15·34	♉ 11·37	12
♎ 26·21	♊ 19·39	♓ 22·45℞	♈ 23·59℞	♌ 22·56	13
♊ 16·56	♑ 25·23	♋ 7·19	♊ 8·35	♑ 12·52	14
♓ 7·27	♐ 2·1℞	♐ 7·13℞	♓ 6·11	♓ 26.49	15
♎ 27·42	♊ 14·38	♓ 22·22	♈ 22·59	♌ 27·40	16
♎ 2·53	♒ 28·43	♋ 25·34	♊ 18·47	♒ 3·6	17
♏ 1·38℞	♓ 4·34	♋ 29·14℞	♊ 19·56	♐ 27·39	18
♌ 20·25	♎ 4·26	♉ 14·11	♉ 15·15	♉ 25·3	19
♐ 12·34	♏ 19·49℞	♊ 2·6	♉ 22·40	♏ 21·28	20
♒ 25·46	♐ 2·6	♐ 7·3	♓ 4.0	♈ 2·26	21
♓ 22·2	♌ 14·33	♈ 17·36	♉ 3·15	♐ 20·35	22
♑ 6·30	♐ 0·40	♊ 9·21℞	♉ 25·29	♍ 28·9	23
♓ 18·41℞	♌ 15·44	♈ 18·46	♉ 4·36	♐ 27·23	24
♌ 5·59	♎ 3·23	♉ 9·53	♉ 12·47	♊ 6·2	25
♐ 17·26	♏ 20·28	♊ 8·44	♉ 26·4	♎ 24·25	26
♊ 4·30	♊ 22·22	♋ 5·0	♊ 7·36	♒ 1.5	27

N. B. For Ketu add 180° to Rahu.

APPENDIX—B

AYANAMSA

The Vernal Equinox is subject to a retrograde motion, the rate of which is generally agreed upon among astronomers as just over 50″ per year. There are a few who say that it is 58″.8 per year. But there is a great divergence of opinion as to the actual length of arc that separates the two Zodiacs at the present time—the Zodiac with V. E. as the starting point (Tropical Zodiac) and the Zodiac of the Constellations (Fixed Zodiac). The two Zodiacs must have coincided at one time and it is this Epoch that is in dispute. The subjoined table gives an idea of the Existing differences.

AYANAMSA FOR JAN. 1, 1946*

Graha Laghav	23° 43′ 35″
Revati (Leta Piscium)	19° 7′ 5″
Chitra	23° 5′ 7″
Madras	21° 39′ 0″

According to Lahiri's Ephemeris which is having an increasing circulation it is 23° 12′ 14″. In this state of affairs Mr. L. Narain Rao published an article in the Astrological Magazine (January issue 1947) fixing it at 23° 5′ 39″ on 1-1-1947 with the annual rate as 50.″ 2286.

* Astronomical Ephemeris for 1946 published by Shree Jewaji Observatory Ujjain.

Therefore the Ayanamsa for 1-1-1946 is 23° 4′ 49″ and differs from Chitra Ayanamsa by a few seconds. It is this that is adopted throughout this work and the tables have been calculated accordingly.

A common mistake made by students of astrology and sometimes by others also is to take a fixed Ayanamsa for the entire year. This is obviously an oversight. Retrogression is a continuous process and the correction for the date of the year in question has to be added to Ayanamsa on 1st January ; otherwise a serious error of several seconds may arise with regard to cusps of houses and longitudes of planets. Therefore, a table giving correction values for each date of the year has been added.

Ayanamsa on 1st January from—1850

Year	Ayanamsa			Year	Ayanamsa		
1850	21°	44′	27″	1886	22°	14′	36″
51	21	45	17	87	22	15	26
52	21	46	7	88	22	16	16
53	21	46	58	89	22	17	6
54	21	47	48	90	22	17	56
55	21	48	39	91	22	18	47
56	21	49	29	92	22	19	37
57	21	50	10	93	22	20	28
58	21	51	9	94	22	21	18
59	21	51	59	95	22	22	8
60	21	52	49	96	22	22	58
61	21	53	40	97	22	23	48
62	21	54	30	98	22	24	39
63	21	55	21	99	22	25	29
64	21	56	11	1900	22	26	19
65	21	57	1	01	22	27	9
66	21	57	51	02	22	27	59
67	21	58	41	03	22	28	50
68	21	59	32	04	22	29	40
69	22	0	22	05	22	30	29
70	22	1	12	06	22	31	20
71	22	2	2	07	22	32	11
72	22	2	52	08	22	33	0
73	22	3	43	09	22	33	50
74	22	4	33	10	22	34	41
75	22	5	22	11	22	35	31
76	22	6	14	12	22	36	21
77	22	7	5	13	22	37	12
78	22	7	55	14	22	38	2
79	22	8	45	15	22	38	53
80	22	9	35	16	22	39	42
81	22	10	26	17	22	40	33
82	22	11	16	18	22	41	23
83	22	12	6	19	22	42	13
84	22	12	56	20	22	43	3
85	22	13	46	21	22	43	54

Year	Ayanamsa		
1922	22°	44′	44″
23	22	45	34
24	22	46	24
25	22	47	14
26	22	48	4
27	22	48	55
28	22	49	45
29	22	50	35
30	22	51	26
31	22	52	15
32	22	53	6
33	22	53	56
34	22	54	46
35	22	55	37
36	22	56	27
37	22	57	17
38	22	58	8
39	22	58	58
40	22	59	48
41	23	0	38
42	23	1	28
43	23	2	19
44	23	3	9
45	22	3	59
46	23	4	49
47	23	5	39
48	23	6	30
49	23	7	20
50	23	8	11
51	23	9	1
52	23	9	51
53	23	10	41
54	23	11	31
55	23	12	21
56	23	13	11
57	23	14	2
58	23	14	52
59	23	15	42

Year	Ayanamsa		
1960	23°	16′	33″
61	23	17	22
62	23	18	13
63	23	19	3
64	23	19	53
65	23	20	44
66	23	21	34
67	23	22	24
68	23	23	15
69	23	24	5
70	23	24	55
71	23	25	45
72	23	26	35
73	23	27	26
74	23	28	16
75	23	29	6
76	23	29	56
77	23	30	46
78	23	31	37
79	23	32	27
80	23	33	17
81	22	34	8
82	23	34	58
83	23	35	48
84	23	36	38
85	23	37	28
86	23	38	18
87	23	39	9
88	23	39	59
89	23	40	49
90	23	41	40
91	23	42	29
92	23	43	20
93	23	44	10
94	23	45	0
95	23	45	51
96	23	46	41
97	23	47	31

Year	Ayanamsa			Year	Ayanamsa		
1998	23°	48′	22″	2015	24°	2′	35″
99	23	49	12	16	24	3	25
2000	23	50	2	17	24	4	16
01	23	50	52	18	24	5	6
02	23	51	42	19	24	5	56
03	23	52	33	20	24	6	47
04	23	53	23	21	24	7	36
05	23	54	13	22	24	8	27
06	23	55	3	23	24	9	17
07	23	55	53	24	24	10	7
08	23	56	43	25	24	10	58
09	23	57	33	26	24	11	48
10	23	58	24	27	24	12	38
11	23	59	15	28	24	13	29
12	24	0	5	29	24	14	19
13	24	0	55	30	24	15	9
14	24	1	45	31	24	15	59

Correction of Ayanamsa for each day of the year

Day	Jan. Sec.	Feb. Sec.	Mar. Sec.	Apr. Sec.	May. Sec.	June. Sec.	July. Sec.	Aug. Sec.	Sep. Sec.	Oct. Sec.	Nov. Sec.	Dec. See.
1	0	4	8	13	17	21	25	29	34	38	42	46
2	0	5	8	13	17	21	25	29	34	38	42	46
3	0	5	9	13	17	21	25	30	34	38	42	46
4	1	5	9	13	17	21	25	30	34	38	42	47
5	1	5	9	13	17	21	26	30	34	38	43	47
6	1	5	9	13	17	22	26	30	34	38	43	47
7	1	5	9	13	17	22	26	30	34	39	43	47
8	1	5	9	13	18	22	26	30	35	39	43	47
9	1	6	9	14	18	22	26	30	35	39	43	47
10	1	6	10	14	18	22	26	31	35	39	43	47
11	2	6	10	14	18	22	26	31	35	39	43	48
12	2	6	10	14	18	22	27	31	35	39	44	48
13	2	6	10	14	18	23	27	31	35	39	44	48
14	2	6	10	14	18	23	27	31	35	40	44	48
15	2	6	10	14	19	23	27	31	36	40	44	48
16	2	6	10	15	19	23	27	31	36	40	44	48
17	2	7	10	15	19	23	27	32	36	40	44	48
18	2	7	11	15	19	23	27	32	36	40	44	48
19	3	7	11	15	19	23	28	32	36	40	44	49
20	3	7	11	15	19	24	28	32	36	40	45	49
21	3	7	11	15	19	24	28	32	36	40	45	49
22	3	7	11	15	20	24	28	32	36	41	45	49
23	3	7	11	16	20	24	28	32	37	41	45	49
24	3	8	11	16	20	24	28	33	37	41	45	49
25	3	8	12	16	20	24	28	33	37	41	45	49
26	4	8	12	16	20	24	29	33	37	41	45	50
27	4	8	12	16	20	25	29	33	37	41	46	50
28	4	8	12	16	20	25	29	33	37	41	46	50
29	4	8	12	16	21	25	29	33	37	42	46	50
30	4		12	17	21	25	29	33	38	42	46	50
31	4		12		21		29	33		42		50

APPENDIX—C

HOW TO FIND THE BASIC ARC

Convert the interval between the birth date and the event or any date for which the arc is desired into years and days. Multiply the days by twelve and divide the product by 73. This will give the minutes of arc, to be added to the years which are degrees.

Example

King Edward VII was born on	9-11-1841	Interval 21 years and 121 days
His marriage took place on	10-3-1863	

$$\frac{121 \times 12}{73} = 19\frac{65}{73} = 20'$$

Basic Arc for marriage 21° 20′

———

APPENDIX—D

NEW ERA MEASURES

These can be worked mentally in nearly all cases. But as C. A. 5/12 (Accidents) and C. A. 7/12 (death) are not so easy, these alone are provided with their corresponding R. C. A.

New Era Measures : C. A. 5/12 = One Year

B.A.	C.A. 5/12°			R.C.A. 12/5°			B.A.	C.A. 5/12°			R.C.A. 12/5°		
1°	0°	25′	"	2°	24′	0″	26°	10°	50′	"	62°	24′	0″
2	0	50		4	48		27	11	15		64	48	
3	1	15		7	12		28	11	40		67	12	
4	1	40		9	36		29	12	5		69	36	
5	2	5		12	00		30	12	30		72	00	
6	2	30		14	24		31	12	55		74	24	
7	2	55		16	48		32	13	20		76	48	
8	3	20		19	12		33	13	45		79	12	
9	3	45		21	26		34	14	10		81	36	
10	4	10		24	00		35	14	35		84	00	
11	4	35		26	24		36	15	00		86	24	
12	5	00		28	48		37	15	25		88	48	
13	5	25		31	12		38	15	50		91	12	
14	5	50		33	36		39	16	15		93	36	
15	6	15		36	00		40	16	40		96	00	
16	6	40		38	24		41	17	5		98	24	
17	7	5		40	48		42	17	30		100	48	
18	7	30		43	12		43	17	55		103	12	
19	7	55		45	36		44	18	20		105	36	
20	8	20		48	00		45	18	45		108	00	
21	8	45		50	24		46	19	10		110	24	
22	9	10		52	48		47	19	35		112	48	
23	9	35		55	12		48	20	00		115	12	
24	10	00		57	36		49	20	25		117	36	
25	10	25		60	00		50	20	50		120	00	

Appendix—D (Contd.)

B.A.	C.A.	5/12°		R.C.A.	12/5°		B.A.	C.A.	5/12°		R.C.A.	12/5°	
51°	21°	15′	″	122°	24′	0″	64°	26°	40′	″	153°	36′	0″
52	21	40		124	48		65	27	05		156	00	
53	22	05		127	12		66	27	30		158	24	
54	22	30		129	36		67	27	55		160	48	
55	22	55		132	00		68	28	20		163	12	
56	23	20		134	24		69	28	45		165	36	
57	23	45		136	48		70	29	10		168	00	
58	24	10		139	12		71	29	35		170	24	
59	24	35		141	36		72	30	00		172	48	
60	25	00		144	00		73	30	25		175	12	
61	25	25		146	24		74	30	50		177	36	
62	25	50		148	48		75	31	15		180	00	
63	26	15		151	12								

New Era Measures : C. A. 7/12 = One Year :

B.A.	C A.		7/12°	R.C.A.	12/7°		B.A.	C.A.		7/12°	R.C.A.	12/7°	
1°	0°	35′	″	1°	42′	51″	39°	22°	45′	″	66°	51′	26″
2	1	10		3	25	43	40	23	20		58	34	17
3	1	45		5	08	34	41	23	55		70	17	09
4	2	20		6	51	26	42	24	30		72	00	00
5	2	55		8	34	17	43	25	05		73	42	51
6	3	30		10	17	09	44	25	40		75	25	43
7	4	05		12	00	00	45	26	15		77	08	34
8	4	40		13	42	51	46	26	50		78	51	26
9	5	15		15	25	43	47	27	25		80	34	17
10	5	50		17	08	34	48	28	00		82	17	09
11	6	25		18	51	26	49	28	35		84	00	00
12	7	00		20	34	17	50	29	10		85	42	51
13	7	35		22	17	09	51	29	45		87	25	43
14	8	10		24	00	00	52	30	20		89	08	34
15	8	45		25	42	51	53	30	55		90	51	26
16	9	20		27	25	43	54	31	30		92	34	17
17	9	55		29	08	34	55	32	05		94	17	09
18	10	30		30	51	26	56	32	40		96	00	00
19	11	05		32	34	17	57	33	15		97	42	51
20	11	40		34	17	09	58	33	50		99	25	43
21	12	15		36	00	00	59	34	25		101	08	34
22	12	50		37	42	51	60	35	00		102	51	26
23	13	25		39	25	43	61	35	35		104	34	17
24	14	00		41	08	34	62	36	10		106	17	09
25	14	35		42	51	26	63	36	45		108	00	00
26	15	10		44	34	17	64	37	20		109	42	51
27	15	45		46	17	09	65	37	55		111	25	43
28	16	20		48	00	00	66	38	30		113	08	34
29	16	55		49	42	51	67	39	05		114	51	26
30	17	30		51	25	43	68	39	40		116	34	17
31	18	05		53	08	34	69	40	15		118	17	09
32	18	40		54	51	26	70	40	50		120	00	00
33	19	15		56	34	17	71	41	25		121	42	51
34	19	50		68	17	09	72	42	00		123	25	43
35	20	25		60	00	00	73	42	35		125	08	34
36	21	00		61	42	51	74	43	10		126	51	26
37	21	35		63	25	43	75	43	45		128	34	17
38	22	10		65	08	34							

PROPORTIONAL PARTS FOR DASA OF PLANETS

(To be deducted from the balance of Dasa for increase by Minutes of Longitude of Moon

Min	Kethu	Venus	Sun	Moon	Mars	Rahu	Jupiter	Saturn	Mercury	Min
	m d	m d	m d	m d	m d	m d	m d	m d	m d	
1	0 3	0 9	0 3	0 5	0 3	0 8	0 7	0 9	0 8	1
2	0 6	0 18	0 5	0 9	0 6	0 16	0 14	0 17	0 15	2
3	0 9	0 27	0 8	0 14	0 9	0 24	0 22	0 26	0 23	3
4	0 13	1 6	0 11	0 18	0 13	1 2	0 29	1 4	1 1	4
5	0 16	1 15	0 14	0 23	0 16	1 11	1 6	1 13	1 8	5
6	0 19	1 24	0 16	0 27	0 19	1 19	1 13	1 21	1 16	6
7	0 22	2 3	1 19	1 2	0 22	1 27	1 20	2 0	1 24	7
8	0 25	2 12	0 22	1 6	0 25	2 5	1 28	2 8	2 1	8
9	0 28	2 21	0 24	1 11	0 28	2 13	2 5	2 17	2 9	9
10	1 1	3 0	0 27	1 15	1 1	2 21	2 12	2 26	2 17	10
15	1 17	4 15	1 11	2 8	1 17	4 2	3 18	4 8	3 25	15
20	2 3	6 0	1 24	3 0	2 3	5 12	4 24	5 21	5 3	20

APPENDIX—E

No. of Star from Aswini	Name of Star	Longitude	Planet ruling the star	Symbol	Period of Years	No. of star from Chitra
1.	Aswini	0° ♈ 13°20′ ♈	Kethu	☋	7	15
2.	Bharani	13 20 ♈ 26 40 ♈	Venus	♀	20	16
3.	Krithigai	26 40 ♈ 10 0 ♉	Sun	☉	6	17
4.	Rohini	10 0 ♉ 23 20 ♉	Moon	☽	10	18
5.	Mrigasira	23 20 ♉ 6 40 ♊	Mars	♂	7	19
6.	Ardra	6 40 ♊ 20 0 ♊	Rahu	☊	18	20
7.	Punarvasu	20 0 ♊ 3 20 ♋	Jupiter	♃	16	21
8.	Pushya	3 20 ♋ 16 40 ♋	Saturn	♄	19	22
9.	Aslesha	16 40 ♋ 30 0 ♋	Mercury	☿	17	23
10.	Makha	0 0 ♌ 13 20 ♌	Kethu	☋	7	24
11.	Poorva Phalguna	13 20 ♌ 26 40 ♌	Venus	♀	20	25
12.	Uthra Phalguna	26 40 ♌ 10 0 ♍	Sun	☉	6	26
13.	Hastha	10 0 ♍ 23 20 ♍	Moon	☽	10	27
14.	Chitra	23 20 ♍ 6 40 ♎	Mars	♂	7	1
15.	Swati	6 40 ♎ 20 0 ♎	Rahu	☊	18	2
16.	Visakha	20 0 ♎ 3 20 ♏	Jupiter	♃	16	3
17.	Anurada	3 20 ♏ 16 40 ♏	Saturn	♄	19	4
18.	Jyeshta	16 40 ♏ 30 0 ♏	Mercury	☿	17	5
19.	Moola	0 0 ♐ 13 20 ♐	Kethu	☋	7	6
20.	Poorvashada	13 20 ♐ 26 40 ♐	Venus	♀	20	7
21.	Uttarashada	26 40 ♐ 10 0 ♑	Sun	☉	6	8
22.	Sravana	10 0 ♑ 23 20 ♑	Moon	☽	10	9
23.	Dhanishta	23 20 ♑ 6 40 ♒	Mars	♂	7	10
24.	Sathabishak	6 40 ♒ 20 0 ♒	Rahu	☊	18	11
25.	Purva Bhadrapada	20 0 ♒ 3 20 ♓	Jupiter	♃	16	12
26.	Uttara Bhadrapada	3 20 ♓ 16 40 ♓	Saturn	♄	19	13
27.	Revati	16 40 ♓ 30 0 ♓	Mercury	☿	17	14

NB:—Stars having the same planetary ruler are in trine to each other.

APPENDIX—F

Pl	☉ 's Sub-periods 6 years	Pl	☽ 's Sub-periods 10 years	Pl	♂ 's Sub-periods 7 years	Pl	☊ 's Sub-periods 18 years	Pl	♃ 's Sub-periods 17 years
	y m d		y m d		y m d		y m d		y m d
☉	0 3 18	☽	0 10 0	♂	0 4 27	☊	2 8 12	♃	2 1 18
☽	0 6 0	♂	0 7 0	☊	1 0 18	♃	2 4 24	♄	2 6 12
♂	0 4 6	☊	1 6 0	♃	0 11 6	♄	2 10 6	☿	2 3 6
☊	0 10 24	♃	1 4 0	♄	1 1 9	☿	2 6 18	☋	0 11 6
♃	0 9 18	♄	1 7 0	☿	0 11 27	☋	1 0 18	♀	2 8 0
♄	0 11 12	☿	1 5 0	☋	0 4 27	♀	3 0 0	☉	0 9 18
☿	0 10 6	☋	0 7 0	♀	1 2 0	☉	0 10 24	☽	1 4 0
☋	0 4 6	♀	1 8 0	☉	0 4 6	☽	1 6 0	♂	0 11 6
♀	1 0 0	☉	0 6 0	☽	0 7 0	♂	1 0 18	☊	2 4 24
Total	6 0 0		10 0 0		7 0 0		18 0 0		16 0 0

Pl	♄ 's Sub-periods 19 years	Pl	☿ 's Sub-periods 17 years	Pl	☋ 's Sub-periods 7 years	Pl	♀ 's Sub-periods 20 years
	y m d		y m d		y m d		y m d
♄	3 0 3	☿	2 4 27	☋	0 4 27	♀	3 4 0
☿	2 8 9	☋	0 11 27	♀	1 2 0	☉	1 0 0
☋	1 1 9	♀	2 10 0	☉	0 4 6	☽	1 8 0
♀	3 2 0	☉	0 10 6	☽	0 7 0	♂	1 2 0
☉	0 11 12	☽	1 5 0	♂	0 4 27	☊	3 0 0
☽	1 7 0	♂	0 11 27	☊	1 0 18	♃	2 8 0
♂	1 1 9	☊	2 6 18	♃	0 11 6	♄	3 0 0
☊	2 10 6	♃	2 3 6	♄	1 1 9	☿	2 12 0
♃	2 6 12	♄	2 8 9	☿	0 11 27	☋	1 2 0
Total	19 0 0		17 0 0		7 0 0		20 0 0

APPENDIX—G

Balance of Dasa According to Moon's Longitude :—

Long. of Moon	Moon in Aries Leo, Sagittarius — Balance of Dasa				Moon in Taurus Virgo and capricorns — Balance of Dasa				Libra and Aquarius Moon in Gemini — Balance of Dasa				Moon in Cancer. Scorpio, Pisces. — Balance of Dasa			
		y	m	d		y	m	d		y	m	d		y	m	d
0° 0′	Kethu	7	0	0	Sun	4	6	0	Mars	3	6	0	Jupr.	4	0	0
0 20		6	9	27		4	4	6		3	3	27		3	7	6
0 40		6	7	24		4	2	12		3	1	24		3	2	12
1 00		6	52	1		4	0	18		2	11	21		2	8	19
1 20		6	3	18		3	10	24		2	9	18		2	4	24
1 40		6	1	15		3	9	0		2	7	15		2	0	0
2 00		5	11	12		3	7	6		2	5	12		1	7	6
2 20		5	9	9		3	5	12		2	3	9		1	2	12
2 40		5	7	6		3	3	18		2	1	6		0	9	18
3 00		5	5	3		3	1	24		1	11	3		0	4	24
3 20		5	3	0		3	0	0		1	9	0	Saturn	19	0	0
3 40		5	0	27		2	10	6		1	6	27		18	6	9
4 00		4	10	24		2	8	12		1	4	24		18	0	18
4 20		4	8	21		2	6	18		1	2	21		17	6	27
4 40		4	6	18		2	4	24		1	0	18		17	1	6
5 00		4	4	15		2	3	0		0	10	15		16	7	15
5 20		4	2	12		2	1	6		0	8	12		16	1	24
5 40		4	0	9		1	11	12		0	6	9		15	8	3
6 00		3	10	6		1	9	18		0	4	6		15	2	12
6 20		3	8	3		1	7	24		0	2	3		14	8	21
6 40		3	6	0		1	6	0	Rahu	18	0	0		14	3	0
7 00		3	3	27		1	4	6		17	6	18		13	9	9
7 20		3	1	24		1	2	12		17	1	6		13	3	18
7 40		2	11	21		1	0	18		16	7	24		12	9	27

Appendix—G (Contd.)

Balance of Dasa According to Moon's Longitude :—

Long. of Moon	Moon in Aries Leo, Sagittarius			Moon in Taurus Virgo and capricorns			Libra and Aquarius Moon in Gemini			Moon in Cancer. Scorpio, Pisces.		
	Balance of Dasa			Balance of Dasa			Balance of Dasa			Balance of Dasa		
	y	m	d	y	m	d	y	m	d	y	m	d
8°00′	2	9	18	0	10	24	16	2	12	12	4	6
8 20	2	7	15	0	9	0	15	9	0	11	10	15
8 40	2	5	12	0	7	6	15	3	18	11	4	24
9 00	2	3	9	0	5	12	14	10	6	10	11	3
9 20	2	1	6	0	3	18	14	4	24	10	5	12
9 40	1	11	3	0	1	24	13	11	12	9	11	21
10 00	1	9	0	Moon 10	0	0	13	6	0	9	6	0
10 20	1	6	27	9	9	0	13	0	18	9	0	9
10 40	1	4	24	9	6	0	12	7	6	8	6	18
11 00	1	2	21	9	3	0	12	1	24	8	0	27
11 20	1	0	18	9	0	0	11	8	12	7	7	6
11 40	0	10	15	8	9	0	11	3	0	7	1	15
12 00	0	8	12	8	6	0	10	9	18	6	7	24
12 20	0	6	9	8	3	0	10	4	6	6	2	3
12 40	0	4	6	8	0	0	9	10	24	5	8	12
13 00	0	2	3	7	9	0	9	5	12	5	2	21
13 20	Venus 20	0	0	7	6	0	9	0	0	4	9	0
13 40	19	6	0	7	3	0	8	6	18	4	3	9
14 00	19	0	0	7	0	0	8	1	6	3	9	18
14 20	18	6	0	6	9	0	7	7	24	3	3	27
14 40	18	0	0	6	6	0	7	2	12	2	10	6
15 00	17	6	0	6	3	0	6	9	0	2	4	15
15 20	17	0	0	6	0	0	6	3	18	1	10	24
15 40	16	6	0	5	9	0	5	10	6	1	5	3

Appendix—G (Contd.)

Balance of Dasa According to Moon's Longitude :—

Long. of Moon	Moon in Aries Leo, Sagittarius Balance of Dasa			Moon in Taurus Virgo and capricorns Balance of Dasa			Libra and Aquarius Moon in Gemini Balance of Dasa			Moon in Cancer, Scorpio, Pisces. Balance of Dasa		
	y	m	d	y	m	d	y	m	d	y	m	d
16°00′	16	0	0	5	6	0	5	4	24	0	11	12
16 20	15	6	0	5	3	0	4	11	12	0	5	21
16 40	15	0	0	5	0	0	4	6	0	Mercury 17	0	0
17 00	14	6	0	4	9	0	4	0	18	16	6	27
17 20	14	0	0	4	6	0	3	7	6	16	1	24
17 40	13	6	0	4	3	0	3	1	24	15	8	21
18 00	13	0	0	4	0	0	2	8	12	15	3	18
18 20	12	6	0	3	9	0	2	3	0	14	10	15
18 40	12	0	0	3	6	0	1	9	18	14	5	12
19 00	11	6	0	3	3	0	1	4	6	14	0	9
19 20	11	0	0	3	0	0	0	10	24	13	7	6
19 40	10	6	0	2	9	0	0	5	12	13	2	3
20 00	10	0	0	2	6	0	Jupiter 16	0	0	12	9	0
20 20	9	6	0	2	3	0	15	7	6	12	3	27
20 40	9	0	0	2	0	0	15	2	12	11	10	24
21 00	8	6	0	1	9	0	14	9	18	11	5	21
21 20	8	0	0	1	6	0	14	4	24	11	0	18
21 40	7	6	0	1	3	0	14	0	0	10	7	15
22 00	7	0	0	1	0	0	13	7	5	10	2	12
22 20	6	6	0	0	9	0	13	2	12	9	9	9
22 40	6	0	0	0	6	0	12	9	18	9	4	6
23 00	5	6	0	0	3	0	12	4	24	8	11	3
23 20	5	0	0	Mars 7	0	0	12	0	0	8	6	0
23 40	4	6	0	6	9	27	11	7	6	8	0	27

Appendix—G (Contd.)

Balance of Dasa According to Moon's Longitude :—

Long. of	Moon in Aries Leo, Sagittarius			Moon in Taurus Virgo and capricorns			Libra and Aquarius Moon in Gemini			Moon in Cancer. Scorpio, Pisces.		
Moon	Balance of Dasa			Balance of Dasa			Balance of Dasa			Balance of Dasa		
	y	m	d	y	m	d	y	m	d	y	m	d
24°00′	4	0	0	6	7	24	11	2	12	7	7	24
24 20	3	6	0	6	5	21	10	9	18	7	2	21
24 40	3	0	0	6	3	18	10	4	24	6	9	18
25 00	2	6	0	6	1	15	10	0	0	6	4	15
25 20	2	0	0	5	11	12	9	7	6	5	11	12
25 40	1	6	0	5	9	9	9	2	12	5	6	9
26 00	1	0	0	5	7	6	8	9	18	5	1	6
26 20	0	6	0	5	5	3	8	4	24	4	8	3
26 40	Sun 6	0	0	5	3	0	8	0	0	4	3	0
27 00	5	10	6	5	0	27	7	7	6	3	9	27
27 20	5	8	12	4	10	24	7	2	12	3	4	24
27 40	5	6	18	4	8	21	6	9	18	2	11	21
28 00	5	4	24	4	6	18	6	4	24	2	6	18
28 20	5	3	0	4	4	15	6	0	0	2	1	15
28 40	5	1	6	4	2	12	5	7	6	1	8	12
29 00	4	11	12	4	0	9	5	2	12	1	3	9
29 20	4	9	18	3	10	6	4	9	18	0	10	6
29 40	4	7	24	3	8	3	4	4	24	0	5	3
30 00	4	6	0	3	6	0	4	0	0	0	0	0

APPENDIX—H

HORA LAGNA

1. Take the interval between sunrise and time of birth in hours and minutes.
2. Convert into minutes and divide by 2.
3. This represents the distance in degrees of arc of Hora Lagna.

   (a) from the longitude of ascendant if even sign rises.

   (b) from the longitude of sun if odd sign rises.

Example

Mahatma Gandhi was born on 2-10-1869 at Lat 21°38′ N

Sunrise on 2-10-1869 at above Lat. is 5-51 A. M.

Time of birth			7-09 A. M.
Difference	1 h.	18 m. or 78	minutes.
Divide by 2	—	— 39	do.

ODD SIGN LIBRA RISES AT BIRTH

∴ H. L. = Long of Sun **Virgo** 16° 55′ + **39°**

Hora Lagna Libra 25° 55′

APPENDIX—K

Conversion Table for Hrs. and Minutes to Ghatikas and Vighatikas :

Hours	Min.	Gha.	Vigha.	Hr.	Min.	Gha.	Vigha.	Hr.	Min.	Gha.	Vigha.
0	1	0	2·5	0	22	0	55·0	4	30	11	15·0
0	2	0	5·0	0	23	0	57·5	5	00	12	30·0
0	3	0	7·5	0	24	1	0·0	5	30	13	45·0
0	4	0	10·0	0	25	1	2·5	6	00	15	0·0
0	5	0	12·5	0	26	1	5·0	6	30	16	15·0
0	6	0	15·0	0	27	1	7·5	7	00	17	30·0
0	7	0	17·5	0	28	1	10·0	7	30	18	45·0
0	8	0	20·0	0	29	1	12·5	8	00	20	0·0
0	9	0	22·5	0	30	1	15·0	8	30	21	15·0
0	10	0	25·0	0	35	1	27·5	9	00	22	30·0
0	11	0	27·5	0	40	1	40·0	9	30	23	45·0
0	12	0	30·0	0	45	1	52·5	10	00	25	0·0
0	13	0	32·5	0	50	2	5·0	10	30	26	15·0
0	14	0	35·0	0	55	2	17·5	11	00	27	30·0
0	15	0	37·5	1	00	2	30·0	11	30	28	45·0
0	16	0	40·0	1	30	3	45·0	12	00	30	0·0
0	17	0	42·5	2	00	5	0·0	15	00	37	30·0
0	18	0	45·0	2	30	6	15·0	18	00	45	0·0
0	19	0	47·5	3	00	7	30·0	21	00	52	30·0
0	20	0	50·0	3	30	8	45·0	24	00	60	0·0
0	21	0	52·5	4	00	10	0·0				

Appendix—K (Contd.)

Conversion Table for Ghatikas and Vighatikas to Houses and Minutes :

Gha.	Vigha	Hr.	Min.	Sec.	Gha.	Vigha	Hr.	Min.	Sec.	Gha.	Vigha	Hr.	Min.	Sec
0	1	0	0	24	0	25	0	10	00	14	00	5	36	00
0	2	0	0	48	0	26	0	10	24	15	00	6	00	00
0	3	0	1	12	0	27	0	10	48	16	00	6	24	00
0	4	0	1	36	0	28	0	11	12	17	00	6	48	00
0	5	0	2	00	0	29	0	11	36	18	00	7	12	00
0	6	0	2	24	0	30	0	12	00	19	00	7	36	00
0	7	0	2	48	0	35	0	14	00	20	00	8	00	00
0	8	0	3	12	0	40	0	16	00	21	00	8	24	00
0	9	0	3	36	0	45	0	18	00	22	00	8	48	00
0	10	0	4	00	0	50	0	20	00	23	00	9	12	00
0	11	0	4	24	0	55	0	22	00	24	00	9	36	00
0	12	0	4	48	1	00	0	24	00	25	00	10	00	00
0	13	0	5	12	2	00	0	48	00	26	00	10	24	00
0	14	0	5	36	3	00	1	12	00	27	00	10	48	00
0	15	0	6	00	4	00	1	36	00	28	00	11	12	00
0	16	0	6	24	5	00	2	00	00	29	00	11	36	00
0	17	0	6	48	6	00	2	24	00	30	00	12	00	00
0	18	0	7	12	7	00	2	48	00	35	00	14	00	00
0	19	0	7	36	8	00	3	12	00	40	00	16	00	00
0	20	0	8	00	9	00	3	36	00	45	00	18	00	00
0	21	0	8	24	10	00	4	00	00	50	00	20	00	00
0	22	0	8	48	11	00	4	24	00	55	00	22	00	00
0	23	0	9	12	12	00	4	48	00	60	00	24	00	00
0	24	0	9	36	13	00	5	12	00					

BIBILOGRAPHY

A. INDIAN AUTHORS

Dutt. F. C. —Predictive Astrology

Jupiter —What the Stars Foretell

Raman B. V. —Hindu Predictive Astrology
Manual of Astrology
How to Judge a horoscope
Studies in Jaimini Astrology

Rele —Directional Astrology of the Hindus

G. Sriramalu —The Span of Life

Sanskrit works —Bhavartha Ratnakara
Brihat Jataka
Hora Sara
Phala Deepika
Jataka Chandrika
Jataka Parijatha
Jataka Desa Marga
Jataka Tattwa
Sanketa Nidhi
Saravartha Chintamani
Saravali
Sripati Paddhathi
Uttara Kalamruta

Vijayaraghavalu —Judgment of Horoscope

B. WESTERN AUTHORS

Alan Leo —Art of Synthesis
Astrology for All
Casting the Horoscope
How to Judge a Nativity
Practical Astrology
Progressed Horoscope

Alan Leo —Astrological Manual Series:—
Directions and Directing
Medical Astrology
1001 Notable Nativities

Benjamin Elbert —Influence of Planet Pluto

Bailey —Prenatal Epoch

Bradley —Solar and Lunar returns

Carter C. E. O. —Astrological Aspects
Astrology of Accidents
Essays in Foundations of Astrology
Introduction to Political Astrology
Some Principles of Horoscopic Delineation
Symbolic Directions in Modern Astrology
Zodiac and the Soul

Fagan Cyril —Zodiacs Old and New

Frankland —Astrological Investigations
Key to Symbolic Directions

Harwood —Easy Lessons in Astrology
Primary Directions by the Polar Angle Method

Hone, Margaret E–Modern Text Book of Astrology

Lassen Leo —Practical Astronomy of the Fixed Stars

Lyndoe —Practical Astrology

Owen (O.H.W.) —Primary Progressed Horoscope

Ptolemy —Tetrabiblos

Raphael —Guide to Astrology

Robson —The Radix System
Student's Text Book of Astrology

Sepharial —Directional Astrology
New Manual of Astrology

Simmonite —Arcana of Astrology

Weymiss —Wheel of Life

Whitman —Aspects
Pluto, Transformer and Annihilator

Wohl —Secret Service of the Sky

GLOSSARY OF TECHNICAL TERMS

Adhana	—Epoch or moment of conception
Alpayu	—Short life; technically up to 33 years
Amsa	—Degree of planetary longitude
Anuradha	—Name of the 17th star (♏ 3° 20′ – 16° 40′)
Arooda	—A sensitive point as far removed from the lord of a house as the lord is from the ascending degree
Ardra	—Name of the 6th star (♊ 6° 40′ – 20° 6′)
Aslesha	—Name of the 9th star (♋ 16°40′–30° 0′)
Asterism	—Star, a division of the Zodiac into 27 equal parts
Aswini	—Name of the first of 27 divisions, (♈ 0° 0′ – 13° 20′)
Ayanamsa	—The arc that represents the difference between the Fixed Zodiac of Hindu Astrology and the Tropical Zodiac of the West
Ayurdaya	—Determination of longevity
Ayushkaraka	—Saturn, the planet holding the portfolio for longevity
Balarishta	—Death while young (technically before 12 years of age)

Bhava	—a house space
Bharani	—Name of the 2nd star (♈ 13° 20′ - 16° 40′)
Bhukti	—A subdivision of a planetory period
Brihat Jataka	—A compendium of Parashara astrology composed by Varaha Mihira
Charakanda	—Ascensional difference
Chitrai	—Name of 14th star (♍ 23° 20′ - ♎ 6° 40′)
Dasa	—Period of planet
Dhanishta	—Name of 23rd star (♑ 23° 20′ - ♒ 6° 40′)
Ghatika	—Unit of time representing 24 minutes
Graha	—A planet
Hastha	—Name of 13th star (♍ 10° 0′ - 23° 20′)
Hora	—Unit of time equal to one hour
Hora Lagna	—A sensitive point similar to Lagna (Vide Appendix. H)
Jaimini	—A great Indian sage who has expounded a distinct system of Astrology
Jataka	—Horoscope
Jyeshta	—Name of 18th star (♏ 16° 40′ - 30° 0′)
Jyotisha	—Astrology
Jyotish shastra	—Science of Astrology
Karaka	—Promoter

Kendra	—(1, 4, 7 and 10th houses)
Ketu	—Cauda, Moon's descending node
Krithigai	—Name of 3rd star (♈ 26° 40′ – ♉ 10° 0′)
Lagna	—Ascending degree, rising sign
Madhyayus	—Medium life, technically (34 – 70 years of age)
Makha	—Name of 10th star (♌ 0° 0′ – 13° 20′)
Maraka	—Death, a death inflicting planet or a planet who has powers for causing death
,, Dasa	—The period of a planet having such powers
,, Bhukti	—The sub-period of planet having such powers
Moola	—Name of 19th star (♐ 0° 0′ – 13° 20′)
Mrigasira	—Name of 5th star (♉ 23° 20′ – ♊ 6° 40′)
Navamsa	—ninth part of a sign = 3° 20′
Nakshatra	—Same as star, asterism, name for 27th part of the Zodiac
Nirayana	—Without precession (of Equinox)
Punarvasu	—Name of 7th star (II 20° 3′ to ♋ 3° 20′)
Poorvashada	—Name of 20th star (♐ 13°20′ – 26°40′)
Poorva bhadrapada	—Name of 25th star (♒ 20° 0′ – ♓ 3° 20′)

Poorva Phalguna —Name of 11th star (♌ 13° 20′ - 26° 40′)

Poornayus —Long-life (technically 70 years to 100 years of age)

Pushya —Name of 8th star (♋ 3° 20′ - 16° 40′)

Rahu —Caput—Moon's ascending node

Revati —Name of 27th star (♓ 16° 40′ - 30° 0′)

Rohini —Name of 4th star (♉ 10° - 23° 20′)

Satabhishak —Name of 24th star (♒ 6° 40′ - 20° 0′)

Sravana —Name of 22nd star (♑ 10° - 23′ 20°)

Trikona —Trine, same as Kona

Uttara Bhadrapada —Name of 26th star (♓ 3° 20′ - 16° 40′)

Uttarashada —Name of 21st star (♐ 26° 40′ - ♑ 10° 0′)

Vighatika —A unit of time equal to 24 seconds

Vimshottari —Name for system for directions in Hindu astrology in which the total period of 9 planets equals 120 years

Visakha —Name of 16th star (♎ 20° 40′ - ♏ 3° 20′)

Yoga —A sanskrit term signifying, power, wealth and prosperity for a native

Yoga Karaka —A planet capable of causing Yoga for nativity.

ERRATA

Page	Line	Error	Correction
Fore-word XI	7	?	(Full Stop)
,,	18	a	the
13	8	delete "feel that"	Insert "do much good and"
do.	22	more	move
23	14	table	tables
92	23	be speaks	bespeaks
98	Chapter heading	"New Era directions"	"New Era Measures"
107	16	Still	"Still retain"
112	7th from bottom	Quincunox	Quincunx
114	14	"less"	delete
	19	change	charge
117	20	"and the"	delete
131	13	bring about of	bring about the death of
,,	14	his	the
137	(3)a.	Arc	Asc
139	14	May	may
140	10	if	is

143	fig.1	3♍51 3♓51	3♍49 3♓49
151	5th bottom	☋⊼8 (Zod)	☋⊼8 (Zod)—50
,,	Total	—99	—49
,,	Average	—$14\frac{1}{7}$	—$6\frac{1}{8}$
,,	Time Equivalent	143 days	39 days
157	fig. 2	♃, 25·29	♃, 25·59
186		☽ □8th+47	— ☽ □8th+41
	Total	+ 98	+ 85
191	3rd from bottom	arc	arc
195	uniform average	$\frac{51}{31}$ 10 days	$\frac{51}{32}$ 13 days
197	2	within	beyond.
197	11	arc	are
198	C-A	8th ✶ ☿	8thC ✶ ☿
	R C A	♃ □ ☿ +13	♃ □ ☿ +18
203	C A total	+26	+25
	Average	+$3\frac{1}{4}$	+$3\frac{1}{8}$
204	Group Average	20 20 days before event	+20 20 days after event
204	True Average	—$\frac{19}{25}$	Delete
220	4th from bottom	Zod ✶ ♀	Zod ✶ ♀ —14
	Total	—14	—25

224	2nd from bottom	$\times_{12}$	$\times^{5}_{12}$
226	C A	6thC ☌ ♅	6thC ☌ ♆
232	10th from bottom	☉	omit
237	last line	is	are
239	Procedure 1.	'for'	'from'
250	♓	☿ ⚹ ♀	☿ ⚹ ♂
259	8th from bottom	☽ ☊ Zdo	☽ ☊ Zod.
260	True Average	$\times_{2}$	$\times^{8}_{2}$
273	6th from bottom	"for that is"	"for C. A. that is"
280	line 7	"M.C reduced"	"M. C is reduced"
281	8th from bottom	♃	♄
286	9th from bottom	♅	♅
288	9th from bottom	MC ⚹ MCZ	MC ⚹ MC(Zod)
313	Example No. 50	"♆ ☌ ♂ 10′ ☌"	"♆ ☌ ♂ + 10′;"
332	Formulae 2	"Convert the time"	"Convert the interval between Sunrise and birthtime"
329.	APPENDIX A. 24 cusps of Houses 12	♓ 28·4	♓ 28·41
"	Appendix A. last line	23rd	3rd
330	Planets line- (S. No. 3) Jupiter	♋ 25·29	♋ 25·59

331	Planets-Uranus		
	Last line	♊ 22·22	♑ 22·22
332	Appendix B		
	12th line	Existing ascending	existing Cusp of that
332	14th line	Leta	Zeta.
342	Whole page		Put at the end of App. G & before App. H.
357	Punarvasu	(♊ 20° 3′ to	(♊ 20° 0′ to
358	6th line from bottom	(♎ 20° 40′—♏	♎ 20° 0′—
358	4th line	3° 20′)	3° 20′) ♏
	from bottom	sanskrit	Sanskrit
393	Page No.	393	351